THE UNIVERSITY OF MICHIGAN
CENTER FOR SOUTH AND SOUTHEAST ASIAN STUDIES

MICHIGAN PAPERS ON SOUTH AND SOUTHEAST ASIA

Ann Arbor, Michigan

COMPADRES: Aurora (Mrs. Manuel) Quezon and Frank L. Murphy
stand as godparents to Mary Aurora Teahan, adopted daughter of
Marguerite Murphy Teahan (far right), sister and former "First
Lady" of ex-Governor-General Murphy, as President Quezon looks
on. Detroit, April 25, 1937. (Photograph from the Murphy Papers,
by courtesy of the Michigan Historical Collections, The University
of Michigan.)

COMPADRE COLONIALISM
STUDIES ON THE PHILIPPINES UNDER AMERICAN RULE

edited by

Norman G. Owen

Michigan Papers on South and Southeast Asia

Number 3

1971

Open access edition funded by the National Endowment for the Humanities/ Andrew W. Mellon Foundation Humanities Open Book Program.

Library of Congress Catalog Card Number 75-175623

Printed and bound by CPI Group (UK) Ltd, Croydon, CR0 4YY

ISBN 978-0-89148-003-7 (paper)
ISBN 978-0-472-12827-3 (ebook)
ISBN 978-0-472-90227-9 (open access)

ACKNOWLEDGMENTS

Grateful acknowledgment is made to the following for permission to quote materials:

Alice Worcester Day (Mrs. Kenneth B. Day)
    The Worcester Papers and the Worcester Philippine
        Collection.
Elizabeth O. Hayden (Mrs. Joseph R. Hayden)
    The Hayden Papers.
Houghton Mifflin Company
    W. Cameron Forbes, The Philippine Islands.
        Copyright 1928, by W. Cameron Forbes.
The Macmillan Company
    Dean C. Worcester, The Philippines, Past and
        Present. Revised edition, Copyright 1914, 1930,
        by The Macmillan Company.
    Joseph Ralston Hayden, The Philippines: A Study
        in National Development. Copyright 1942, by
        The Macmillan Company.
Michigan Historical Collections, The University of Michigan
    Manuscripts from the Hayden Papers.
The National Library of the Philippines
    The Quezon Papers.
Pacific Affairs, The University of British Columbia
    Frank Golay, "Economic Consequences of the
        Philippine Trade Act" (Vol. XXVIII, No. 1, 1955).
The University Library, The University of Michigan
    Manuscripts from the Worcester Philippine Collection.

The authors also wish to thank publicly, for their assistance in the preparation of this volume:

Mrs. Elizabeth O. Hayden, Miss Marjory Drake, Miss
Harriett Jameson, Miss Mary Jo Pugh, Miss Debbie
de Schweinitz, Mrs. Arline Olvitt, Mrs. Roberta Owen,
Dr. Robert Warner, Dr. Sidney Fine, and, of course,
Dr. David Joel Steinberg, whose idea it was.

PREFACE

For generations scholars at the University of Michigan have
been fascinated by the Philippines. This tradition, dating back
to the nineteenth century work of Dean Worcester and extending
through the career of Joseph R. Hayden, continues unabated. As
a result of this scholarly contact and of the work of a great number
of Michigan graduates in the Philippines, the University has a
rich lode of Filipiniana. Among the many collections housed
either at the University Library or at the Michigan Historical
Collections are those of Dean Worcester, Justice George Malcolm,
Frank Murphy, Joseph Hayden and G. Mennen Williams.[1] The
University has also been enriched by the countless pensionados,
Fulbright exchange scholars, and Barber Exchange scholars who
have come from the Philippines and studied in Ann Arbor.

Over the past decade as a result of support from the Ford
Foundation and the federal government, there has been a new
surge of interest in the Philippines, and especially in the complex
interaction of Filipino and American institutions during the
American colonial interregnum. Under the successive leadership of Professors L.A. Peter Gosling, Gayl Ness and John
Broomfield the Center for South and Southeast Asian Studies has
developed an active Philippine studies community within the
University. In conjunction with Dr. Robert Warner of the Michigan
Historical Collections, the University has collaborated with Dr.
Serafin Quiason of the National Library in Manila to sort, catalog
and microfilm the papers of Manuel Luis Quezon. One copy of
that film is now at Michigan; in exchange, a copy of the Malcolm
papers has been given to the National Library.

This volume is a manifestation of that continuing interest
in Philippine studies. Written by a generation of post-colonial
scholars, it attempts to unravel some of the historical problems
of the colonial era. Again and again the authors focus on the
relationship of the ilustrados and the Americans, on the problems of continuity and discontinuity, and on the meaning of
"modernization" in the Philippine context. As part of the
Vietnam generation, these authors have looked at American
imperialism with a new perspective, and yet their analysis is
tempered, not strident, and reflective, not dogmatic. Perhaps

the most central theme to emerge is the depth of the contradiction inherent in the American colonial experiment.

Although a number of these papers were first written for a seminar I gave on modern Philippine history in the autumn of 1970, this is not a collection of those papers. Since that time, the group has been engaged in revision. The project has been entirely student-directed. The sensitive and skillful editorship of Norman Owen has brought the project to fruition. Others in the seminar contributed much though their papers do not appear here. Similarly, the staffs at the Michigan Historical Collections, the Center for South and Southeast Asian Studies, and the University Library gave generously to assist at every stage. However, the credit properly rests with these dedicated students, who lingered in Ann Arbor during the summer of 1971 to finish the job, even while their professor was thousands of miles away in Europe enjoying the first glories of a sabbatical year. The University of Michigan can take pride in them; scholars of the Philippines can take pleasure at the promise of things to come.

David Joel Steinberg

---

[1] See Thomas Powers, Balita mula Maynila (News from Manila) (Ann Arbor, 1971), for a brief description of these holdings.

Contents

ABOUT THE AUTHORS

NORMAN G. OWEN graduated from Occidental College (Los
Angeles), then took a B.A. Honours in History of South-East
Asia at the University of London, School of Oriental and African
Studies. He obtained his M.A. from the University of Michigan
in 1971, and is currently doing dissertation research, under a
Foreign Area Fellowship, in Spain and the Philippines on "The
Impact of the Abaca Industry on Bicol Society in the Nineteenth
Century." Previous publication: "The Rice Trade of Mainland
Southeast Asia: 1850-1914," Journal of the Siam Society, July
1971.

MICHAEL CULLINANE, after graduation from the University of
California, Santa Barbara, with a double major in History and
Asian Studies, went as a Peace Corps Volunteer to the Philippines,
where he taught math and social studies at the Normal College in
Cebu City. On returning to the United States, he went to Ohio
University for his M.A. in Foreign Affairs: Southeast Asian
Studies, then taught in high school for a year. He is currently
working for his doctorate at the University of Michigan, with a
proposed dissertation topic on the history of the Visayas in the
19th and 20th century, emphasizing local politics in Cebu.

FRANK JENISTA, JR., went to Brent School, Baguio, then for
undergraduate work to Cedarville College, Ohio, then studied
for his M.A. in Southeast Asian History at the University of
Dayton. He has returned to Brent to become Director of the
newly established Asian Studies Program there, while continuing
research for his doctoral dissertation (University of Michigan)
on "The White Apos: Traditional Leadership Patterns and the
Spread of American Influence in Upland Luzon, 1900-1913."

HARRY LUTON did his undergraduate work at the University
of Michigan, left for an M.A. in American Civilization at the
University of Pennsylvania, and returned to enroll in the Ph.D.
program in American Studies at Michigan. His special interest
is American imperialism, with an eye toward eventual research
comparing the cases of the Philippines and the Caribbean area.

JOSEPH F. HUTCHINSON, JR. wrote this paper (in an earlier version) as his Senior Honors Thesis at the University of Michigan; he is now attending Law School at Ohio State University.

RONALD K. EDGERTON went into the Peace Corps after graduation from DePauw University; he taught English at the Normal College in Malaybalay, Bukidnon. On his return to the United States, he obtained his M.A. in American History from the University of Massachusetts, then came to the University of Michigan for doctoral work on Southeast Asia. He has already spent a year in the Philippines reading the Roxas Papers and doing research on the reintegration of Philippine society after World War II. He was largely responsible for compiling the 80 pages of glossary, bibliography, and maps in David Joel Steinberg, et al., In Search of Southeast Asia (New York, 1971).

CHRONOLOGY

Of Selected Events related to the Philippines under American Rule

1896		Katipunan Revolt. Rizal executed.
1897	December	Pact of Biyak-na-Bato.
1898	May	UNITED STATES INTERVENES. Battle of Manila Bay. Aguinaldo returns to the Philippines.
	June	Aguinaldo proclaims Philippine Independence.
	August	Fall of Manila.
	December	Treaty of Paris; Spain cedes Philippines to U.S.
1899	January	Malolos Constitution.
	February	Beginning of hostilities: "Insurrection"/Philippine-American War. U.S. Senate ratifies Treaty of Paris.
	March	[Schurman] Philippine Commission arrives.
	April	Proclamation "To the people of the Philippine Islands."
	May	First municipal governments under American rule organized. Supreme Court of Philippines reorganized, Arellano named Chief Justice.
1900	January	Military Governor organizes committee on local government. Publication of Schurman Report, Volume I.
	June	William H. Taft arrives as President of Philippine Commission.
	December	Partido Federal formed.
1901	January	Municipal Code.
	February	Provincial Government Act. First province (Pampanga) formally organized for civil government.
	March	Spooner Amendment gives U.S. President power to establish civil government for Philippines.
	May	Aguinaldo captured. First of "Insular Cases" (U.S. Supreme Court).
	July	Formal creation of civil government; Taft becomes first Civil Governor.

(1901)	September	Full civil government created; Worcester named Secretary of Interior; three Filipinos (Pardo de Tavera, Legarda, Luzuriaga) join Commission.
	November	New tariff, enacted by Commission, takes effect.
	December	"Fourteen Diamond Rings" case (U.S. Supreme Court) definitely places Philippines outside U.S. tariff wall.
1902	February	First provincial elections held.
	March	U.S. Congress passes Philippine Tariff Act.
	April	General Malvar surrenders; end of major Filipino resistance.
	July	Organic Act (Philippine Act) by U.S. Congress establishes structure of insular government. Official termination of hostilities proclaimed.
1903	March	First Census of Philippines under American rule.
1904	January	Taft resigns as Governor to become Secretary of War.
	April	Hearings begin on internal revenue structure.
	July	Internal Revenue Law of 1904.
1905	October	Reorganization Act.
1906		De facto restriction on nationalist parties lifted.
	March	Opium Law enacted.
1907	March	Partido Nacionalista formed by fusion of other parties.
	July	Elections for first Philippine Assembly; Quezon elected representative from Tayabas.
	October	Taft presides over Inaugural Session of Philippine Assembly; Osmeña elected Speaker, with Quezon support.
	November	First popular election of provincial governors and "Third Members" of provincial boards.

1908	January	Taft issues <u>Special Report</u> on his 1907 mission.
	November	Taft elected U.S. President.
1909	May	Quezon goes to U.S. as Resident Commissioner.
	September	Payne-Aldrich Tariff institutes nearly unrestricted trade between U.S. and Philippines.
	November	W. Cameron Forbes becomes Governor-General.
1910	March	Extraordinary Session, Philippine Legislature.
	October	Second Legislature convenes.
1912	March	First Jones Bill introduced in U.S. Congress, never reaches floor.
	October	Third Legislature convenes.
	November	Woodrow Wilson elected U.S. President, first Democrat since intervention.
1913	October	Francis B. Harrison arrives as Governor-General (to 1921); end of "Taft Era." Underwood Tariff, virtual free trade.
1916	August	Organic Act of 1916 (Jones Act/Philippine Autonomy Act) passes U.S. Congress; Clarke Amendment fails.
	October	Quezon elected President of first Philippine Senate.
1918	October	Harrison, pushed by Osmeña, forms Council of State.
	December	Quezon leaves for Washington as head of first Philippine Independence Mission; marries enroute.
1919	February	Rest of Independence Mission leaves for Washington.

1920	November	Harding (Republican) elected U.S. President.
1921		Special [Wood-Forbes] Investigating Mission; report issued October. Quezon breaks with Osmeña, forms new party (1922).
	October	Leonard Wood becomes Governor-General.
1922	May	Hayden comes to Philippines as Exchange Professor, U.P. (to 1923).
	June	Quezon's Colectivistas defeat Osmeña's Nacionalistas and the Democratas. Quezon assumes leadership of post-election coalition.
	September	Fordney-McCumber Tariff, U.S., not applicable to Philippines.
1923	July	"Cabinet Crisis," Filipino politicians vs. Gov. Wood.
1926		Carmi Thompson Mission, Hayden advises; report, Conditions in the Philippine Islands, issued December.
1927	August	Wood dies in office.
1928	March	Stimson arrives as Wood's successor.
1929	October	Bills in U.S. Congress propose import quotas.
1930	January	Senator King proposes Philippine Independence Bill. First OsRox Mission to Washington.
	February	Philippine Independence Congress.
	March	Hawes-Cutting Bill introduced, U.S. Senate.
	May	Hayden's revised edition of Worcester, Philippines, Past and Present, published.
	June	Hawes-Cutting Bill favorably reported by committee, then set aside for 18 months.
	July	Smoot-Hawley Tariff, peak of U.S. protectionism, not applied to Philippines.

(1930)	October	Hayden comes to Philippines as Visiting Professor, U. P. (to 1931).
1931	July	Quezon re-elected with "dominion" plan.
	September	Japan invades Manchuria.
	December	Second OsRox Mission.
1932	November	Franklin Roosevelt, heavily Democratic Congress, elected.
	December	Hare-Hawes-Cutting Bill passes Congress.
1933	January	"Lame Duck" President Hoover vetoes H-H-C Bill; Congress passes it over his veto.
	February	Beginning of open "Pro-Anti" fight.
	April	Frank Murphy appointed Governor-General (arrives June).
	June	Osmeña, Roxas lose high positions in Legislature.
	October	Philippine Legislature rejects H-H-C Act.
	November	Hayden appointed Vice-Governor (and Secretary of Public Instruction). Quezon leaves for Washington to seek new independence bill.
1934	March	Tydings-McDuffie Act passes, signed by Roosevelt.
	May	Philippine Legislature approves Tydings-McDuffie Act. Jones-Costigan Amendment makes Philippine sugar quota retroactive to January; Revenue Act of 1934 (U. S.) places processing tax on coconut oil.
	June	Quezon faction wins decisively in elections.
1935	May	Sakdalista revolt.
	June	New coalition of Quezon, Osmeña factions. Cordage Act (U. S.) revises Philippine quota.
	November	Philippine Commonwealth formed; Quezon becomes first President, Osmeña Vice-President. Hayden leaves Philippines.

1937	April	Joint Preparatory Committee for Philippine Affairs created; report issued May 1938.
	July	Marco Polo Bridge incident; Japan attacks China.
1939		Tydings-Kocialkowski (Trade) Act revises economic provisions of transition to independence.
1941	November	Hayden finishes writing <u>The Philippines</u> (published 1942).
	December	Japan attacks Philippines, Pearl Harbor.
1942		Quezon, Osmeña evacuated from Philippines.
	May	Corregidor falls, end of major formal resistance.
1944	August	Quezon dies in U.S.
	October	American troops land in Leyte; Hayden accompanies McArthur.
1945	February	Osmeña, Commonwealth Government, officially restored.
	March	Manila liberated.
	April	Hayden leaves Philippines for last time.
	May	Hayden dies.
	August	Japan surrenders.
1946	April	Philippine Trade Act of 1946 (Bell Trade Act) passes.
	July	PHILIPPINE INDEPENDENCE granted by U.S.
1947	March	Parity Amendment passed, fulfills condition for implementing Bell Trade Act, aid.

ABBREVIATIONS

CSM   Christian Science Monitor

FES   Far Eastern Survey

HP   Hayden Papers, Michigan Historical Collections, The University of Michigan

JAS   Journal of Asian Studies

JPC   Journal of the Philippine Commission

JSEAH   Journal of Southeast Asian History

PA   Pacific Affairs

PS   Philippine Studies

PSS[H]R   Philippine Social Science [and Humanities] Review

QP   Quezon Papers, National Library of the Philippines, microfilm at Michigan Historical Collections, The University of Michigan

RCIR   Report of the Collector of Internal Revenue, Philippines

RPC   Report of the Philippine Commission . . .

UMJEAS University of Manila Journal of East Asiatic Studies

WPC   Worcester Philippine Collection, Department of Rare Books and Special Collections, Harlan Hatcher Library, The University of Michigan

Introduction: Philippine Society and American Colonialism

by

Norman G. Owen

When these papers were first assembled for possible publication, recurrent themes and mutual presuppositions began to
appear. These reflect in part the similarities in the academic
experience of the authors, in part our interaction with each other.
None of our conclusions are unanimous, of course; these ideas
are hypotheses, not axioms; they lead not to final answers, but
to further questions. Nevertheless, there did seem to be an
underlying consensus -- above all, an appreciation of the ambiva-
lences within the two societies that confronted each other, and
their consequent tendency to seek compromises. The Filipino
elite demonstrated both a genuine desire for national independence
and a natural predilection for individual and class preservation;
the American administrators were torn between their reforming
zeal and the need to cooperate with existing Filipino leadership.
What follows is one man's elaboration of the "sense of the
meeting," how we came to see Philippine society and American
colonialism. [1]

By the time of American intervention in 1898, there was in
the Philippines a wealthy, politically astute, consciously
"Filipino" elite. It is difficult, perhaps futile, to define the
precise origins or boundaries of this group. It may have included
direct linear descendents of pre-Spanish datus as well as Chinese
mestizos who had risen along with the rising export economy in

1

the nineteenth century. Clearly it included such Manila-based
ilustrados as Rizal and Pardo de Tavera, but it shaded off into
hacenderos, caciques, and principalía with only local followings.[2]
In the late Spanish period, this Filipino elite had increasingly
begun to agitate for colonial reform, as it saw its political
ambitions thwarted by Spanish civil, military,[3] and religious
bureaucracies. The ilustrados themselves did not lead the early
revolutionary movement; while they were urging reform, the
active revolt was begun by urban clerks and provincial gentry.[4]
Not until after Admiral Dewey and General Aguinaldo had effectively destroyed Spanish power did most ilustrados align themselves with the emerging Philippine Republic; yet by the time of
the Malolos Constitution (January, 1899) they were clearly on
their way to dominating it.[5] At the same time, some ilustrados
were already collaborating with the Americans, an arrangement
which culminated in the appointment of three Filipinos to the
Philippine Commission in 1901.

The career of the brilliant jurist Cayetano Arellano illustrates
this natural gravitation of the ilustrados toward the sources of
power, or vice-versa. He had served in the Spanish bureaucracy
since 1887 and did not join Aguinaldo until after the battle of
Manila Bay; on September 26, 1898, he was named Secretario
de Negocios Extranjeros for the Philippine Republic; on May 29,
1899, he was appointed the first Chief Justice of the Supreme
Court of the Philippines by President McKinley. Similar examples
could be drawn from the careers of such men as Pedro Paterno
and Pardo de Tavera at the national level and a host of provincial
and municipal officials at the local level.[6] Whether their motives
were patriotic or opportunistic is not germane to this study; the
fact remains that wherever there was potential influence in the
Philippines, there were the ilustrados.

There were three basic interlocking components of ilustrado
power -- education, a personal clientele, and wealth. Education,
in Manila or Europe, was the overt sign of ilustrado status; it
led to the professions, to contact with other members of the elite,
to political sophistication, and ultimately to ideological leadership of Philippine nationalism, based upon the ability to articulate
national aspirations and to command respect. A constituency of
followers and friends bound by ties of personal loyalty gave the
elite a local base of power which Manila -- whether Spanish,
American, or Filipino -- has never been able to challenge effectively. The dyadic patron-client relationship was given a

particularly Filipino flavor and intensity through such concepts as <u>utang</u> <u>na</u> <u>loob</u> (debt of gratitude) and such institutions as <u>compadrazgo</u> (ritual co-parenthood). Wealth, usually landed, sometimes commerical, was nearly indispensible to the elite -- it provided both the funds for their education and the means to reward their followers and to play the role of patron properly. [7]

The indigenous Philippine polity can best be understood as a pyramid of personal relationships, reinforced by economic dependence and socio-intellectual respect. In the nineteenth century this was a truncated pyramid; the <u>ilustrados</u> had risen as high as the Spanish would allow them to, and now found their upward path blocked. They were unable to obtain the high positions which could have helped them reward their clients (in the old Spanish bureaucratic tradition, which fit so well with Filipino values), protect their wealth, and enhance their prestige. The educated rhetoric of a Rizal or del Pilar led not to a senatorship but to exile. Although they had too much at stake to risk direct, violent confrontation with the Spanish, when the events of 1898 cleared the way, the <u>ilustrados</u> were ready; they stepped forward as the rightful leaders of the country, successfully claiming (though not without initial challenge from the Bonifacios, Aguinaldos, and Aglipays) the right to speak for the Philippines.

If the <u>ilustrados</u> had not existed, however, it would have been necessary for the Americans to invent them. From the beginning, the colonialism of the United States was undercut by a strong current of anti-imperialism, and American policy was characterized by a "vacillation in motives and aims . . . almost to the very end of the colonial regime."[8] By the narrowest of margins the Senate had decided in 1899 to proceed with the annexation of the Philippines, but the nation lacked the will to pay the full cost of complete subjugation of the islands. The possibility of a long, brutal campaign to suppress insurgency, or of extensive commitment of funds and personnel for direct district-by-district American rule of a faraway land did not agree with either the democratic conscience or the budget. So the Schurman Commission was informed: "The President earnestly desires the cessation of bloodshed, and that the people of the Philippine Islands at an early date shall have the largest measure of self-government consistent with peace and good order."[9] By 1899, the United States was already looking for Filipino leaders with whom a modus vivendi could be arranged, a means of saving not only the costs of repression and local administration, but also what was left of her ideals and self-image.

This approach is reflected in Colonel Charles Denby's articulation of the object of the Schurman Commission, ". . . to find out the views of all the respectable and influential people whom we can get to tell them to us, and when we go over them we will come to some conclusion."[10] The witnesses who testified before the Commission in the summer of 1899 exemplified the class Denby had in mind. Fourteen Philippine-born witnesses were identified by profession; all were (or had been) lawyers, doctors, notaries, merchants, or planters. In their testimony they repeatedly referred to the "rich and intelligent," and to the "most enlightened people," in contrast to "low people, vulgar."[11] The Commission responded in kind by repeated references to "eminent Filipinos," "men of property and education," "leading and prominent men," "people of wealth and intelligence," or simply "the better classes."[12] The witnesses were, of course, those who lived in or could get to Manila; by definition they did not include those who would have nothing to do with Americans; they were hardly representative of the whole nation. Nevertheless, the Commission was happy to draw from their testimony the conclusion that "the masses of the Filipino people, including practically all who are educated or who possess property, have no desire for an independent and sovereign Philippine state."[13] In short, the Americans and the ilustrados had discovered each other, and found in each other familiar values; by mid-1899 a symbiotic relationship had begun that was to continue throughout the American period and beyond.

The United States had a practical political motive for dealing with the ilustrados, that of implementing the first of the "regulative principles" by which the Philippines was to be governed—enforcing "the supremacy of the United States . . . throughout every part of the Archipelago."[14] It was clearly realized that "educated Filipinos" would play a crucial role in this, and it was anticipated that their "support and services [would] be of incalculable value in inaugurating the new government."[15] Before the end of 1901, civilian municipal and provincial governments had been organized in most of the country, Aguinaldo had been captured, and the Taft Commission was praising the newly formed Partido Federal, whose "members were most active and effective in inducing insurgent leaders to surrender."[16]

But cooperation with the ilustrados was not only a matter of sound tactics for the Commission, it was also a matter of principle. One consistent theme runs through the pronouncements of McKinley, Root, Schurman, and Taft--that the United States ruled the Philippines not only for the ostensible benefit of the Filipinos,[17] but in accordance with their autonomous desires and cultural values. This was implied in the second of the "regulative principles" of the Schurman Commission, which promised, "The most ample liberty of self-government will be granted to the Philippine people" reconcilable with good government and American rights.[18] It was made more explicit in a famous passage from the instructions to the Taft Commission, which reminded the members that:

> . . . the government which they are establishing is designed, not for our satisfaction or for the expression of our theoretical views, but for the happiness, peace, and prosperity of the people of the Philippine Islands, and the measures adopted should be made to conform to their customs, their habits, and even their prejudices, to the fullest extent consistent with the accomplishment of the indispensable requisite of just and effective government.[19]

It is clear that a colonial power which proposes to respect even the "prejudices" of the subject people is already thoroughly committed to compromise.

Yet the Americans were equally committed to "just and effective government," and it was not long before they began to suspect that the two purposes might be in conflict. In theory there were "certain great principles of government . . . liberty and law . . . [which] must be . . . maintained . . . however much they may conflict with the customs or laws of procedure" familiar to the Filipinos.[20] But it was never easy to define, much less enforce, these principles in a Philippine context; it was always easier to enlist the support of the "enlightened classes" than to attempt to institute sweeping reforms without them, or to implement rigorously the full panoply of programs the United States envisaged for the islands.

As a result, the Americans found from an early date that they were never in complete command of events; by 1902, Taft was already describing the obstacles created by "caciqueism" and "feudal relations of dependence."[21] Bonifacio S. Salamanca,

in his excellent revisionist history of the Taft era, after emphasizing the "limited role played by Filipinos in the provincial
government" in this period, and the "almost exclusive power
of lawmaking exercised with patent arbitrariness by Americans"
up to 1907, still concludes that "if the Filipino elite did not in
fact determine American actions, they nevertheless made it
impossible for the United States to have a free hand with any
important undertaking which did not have their endorsement or,
at the very least, their tacit approval."[22] It seems as if the
United States, in the process of obtaining *ilustrado* support, may
have unwittingly sacrificed the efficient implementation of certain
other aspects of her policy--education, civil service reform,
public health, economic development, and, above all, the genuine
democratization of the Philippine polity. However mixed the
motives of the Americans in annexing the Philippines, however
unjust the attempt to impose on an alien culture their own institutions and values, it would at least have been logically consistent
for the United States, having intervened, to retain the ability to
carry through her dream of making the Philippines a "Showcase
of Democracy." Instead, through a combination of political
tactics and republican principles, the American administrators,
by granting to Filipino leaders as much influence as they did,
renounced the necessary means to enforce their own conception
of what the Philippines should become. The result was an odd
mixture of theory and expediency, a perpetual compromise, a
modern variant of indirect rule.

This tension between the American conception of policy and
the Filipino execution of it continued throughout the period of
American rule. When Francis B. Harrison arrived in 1913 as
the first Governor-General appointed by the Democrats, many
Republicans objected that he would grant effective self-government
too soon, and that the irretrievable Filipinization of American
rule by Harrison would bring an untimely end to the laudable
ambitions of the United States to prepare the Philippines for the
modern world. Leonard Wood arrived as Harrison's successor
in 1921 and attempted to slow down or reverse this process; the
frustrations he encountered in this effort plagued his entire
administration.[23] The balance shifted slightly during the time
of the later Governors-General and the Commonwealth, but the
tension remained; Filipinos were more active in creating policy,
but only within the limits established by the Congress and
President of the United States. Each Filipino politician, each

American administrator had to discover for himself the fine balance between what was desirable and what was possible; the process was a continuous one.

Historians have usually tended to concur with both Democratic claims and Republican accusations in calling 1913 the turning point, for better or worse, within the American period. But a closer look at the Taft era suggests that the crucial decisions may have been made much earlier. In the fall of 1907 Taft, once President of the Philippine Commission, now Secretary of War, visited the Philippines once more. In his report of January 23, 1908,[24] he states that "Thus far the policy in the Philippines has worked"--an assertion which is not surprising, inasmuch as Taft himself was largely the creator of that policy. But between the lines of the report there are hints that the American dream was not being realized with the swiftness and efficacy he had once hoped for. Taft notes "the desire of the upper class to maintain the relation of the ruling class to the serving and obedient class," and imputes to this both the "languid sympathy" given by _ilustrados_ to the education program and the urgency of Filipino demands for independence. He finds it necessary to warn that the purpose of the United States was not "merely to await the organization of a Philippine oligarchy or aristocracy competent to administer government and then turn the islands over to it." And he concludes that "it will take longer than a generation to complete the . . . education of the common people. Until that is done we ought not to lift our guiding hand from the helm of the ship of state of the Philippine Islands." Implicit in this report is the awareness that the United States had not really succeeded in altering Philippine society in the short run; from this perspective, the "Filipinization" under Harrison seems less a radical departure from the past than a public recognition of continuing sociopolitical realities.

The implications of this _modus_ _vivendi_, this early tacit agreement between _ilustrados_ and Commissioners, are not yet entirely clear. It is somewhat simplistic to conclude that either party to the deal was deliberately betraying principles in favor of expediency. The _ilustrados_ were not solely collaborators who abandoned the revolution to seek selfish ends. Once McKinley had made the decision to annex the Philippines, resistance was probably futile, and it is doubtful that the Philippine Republic could have survived long in that era of hungry imperialism even if Dewey had turned around and sailed away. Nor is it wholly fair to blame the ilustrados for failing to carry out a radical social revolution; they were clearly sincere (if self-centered) in their belief that what was good for them was good for the country. Perhaps the only valid charge against the ilustrados is that they assumed that they were leaders by right and acted on that assumption; this should not qualify them as national heroes, but it hardly makes them traitors.

For that matter, neither had the American administrators betrayed any deeply held radical principles. They were committed to protect property rights not just by the Treaty of Paris, but by American tradition and personal inclination. The members of the Commission had much in common with the ilustrados who testified before them, and the two groups seemed to compete with each other in proposals for limiting the franchise and prolonging American "tutelage and protection" of the Philippines, under which the educated Filipinos would join the Commissioners in guiding and instructing the unenlightened masses.[25] The United States had, in the long run, only one basic proposal for reshaping Philippine society--education, over generations[26]--and to this the ilustrados, themselves the product of modern education, had no objection. It may be that what occurred in the Philippines was less a "Co-Optation"[27] of the ilustrados than a genuine meeting of minds between the "rich and intelligent" of both nations.

Indeed, it is difficult to assess just what difference full American control, a firmer hand at "the helm of the ship of state," would have made to the Philippines. If there was a difference between direct American administration and Filipino semi-autonomy it was probably in the area of implementation of policy rather than in policy itself. American officials repeatedly complained of the decline in efficiency and honesty which seemed to occur along with Filipinization. More recently, historians and social scientists have tended to emphasize the difference in social values between the two societies, pointing out that what would be considered "corruption" by the high-minded Commissioners might well appear to the Filipinos a proper fulfillment of personal obligations. Yet even in terms of simple honesty, the difference, if it existed, was only one of degree; by 1903 Taft had to admit, "Americans responsible for the government of these islands have suffered a most humiliating experience during the past year in the numerous defalcations of Americans charged with the official duty of collecting and disbursing money."[28] Further research into the actual day-to-day administration of the Philippines may shed more light on the difference, if any, between American and Filipino rule -- or between rhetoric and reality under any government.

If, finally, the United States never did assume full power in Philippine life, it may imply a need to reassess our periodization of Philippine history, perhaps even to discard the "American period" as a useful frame of reference. Instead of stressing the new institutions brought by the Americans, we might look more closely at the amalgam of Hispanic and Filipino values held by those who worked within these institutions. Do patterns of local government in the Philippines derive primarily from the American town meeting, from the Maura Law, or even from the original barangay? We realize that the political maneuvers of the 1970's have much in common with the Quezon-Osmeña rivalry of the 1920's and 30's; we are beginning to see that both owe much to a political style well developed by 1907, a style which must have evolved in the nineteenth century. In economic history, we may yet conclude that 1898 is less significant than 1869, when the Suez Canal was opened. If these papers reach any common conclusion, it may be this emphasis on continuity in Philippine history, this awareness that a change in flags need not imply a change in culture, that there is always a gap between sovereignty and society.

Notes

1. It will be obvious to most readers that this consensus derives
in large part from the works of such scholars as Carl F.
Landé, Bonifacio S. Salamanca, and David Joel Steinberg,
among others; see the bibliography for a more complete
listing. The introduction is chiefly intended to provide background for readers who are not familiar with these works,
and to refresh the memories of those who are.

2. The terms applied to the upper class(es) in the Philippines are
ill-defined and frequently overlapping. An ilustrado was an
educated person, which in that society usually implied high
social and economic status as well. A hacendero (hacendado)
was the owner of a large estate; thus presumably wealthy.
Principalía (principales) was a term used to describe the
leaders within a particular community, e.g., the notable
residents of a municipality. Cacique is a term imported by
the Spanish from the West Indies; originally meaning native
chief, by this time it referred to a political boss, and generally carried a derogatory connotation.

3. The tension among peninsular, criollo, and native elements in
the military is documented in the research in progress of
Theodore Grossman, University of Michigan, on "The Spanish
Colonial Army in Philippine Society."

4. Cf. the statement of ilustrado-landowner Felipe González
Calderón to the Schurman Commission in 1899, imputing
(correctly?) the continuation of hostilities to "clerks and
writers, who have a habit of stirring up the town," distin-
guishing this group from both the "rich and intelligent" and
the "poorer element." Report of the [Schurman] Philippine
Commission to the President (Washington, 1900), II
[April-May, 1900], 68. (Hereinafter referred to as Schurman
Report.)

5. Teodoro A. Agoncillo, Malolos: The Crisis of the Republic
(Quezon City, 1960); Bonifacio S. Salamanca, The Filipino
Reaction to American Rule: 1901-1913 ([Hamden, Conn.],

1968), pp. 14-19; David Joel Steinberg, et. al., In Search of Southeast Asia (New York, c. 1971), pp. 260-63.

6. Gregorio F. Zaide, Great Filipinos in History (Manila, 1970); John A. Larkin, "The Place of Local History in Philippine Historiography," JSEAH, VIII-2 (1967), 309-16.

7. On the nature of Philippine political values and social relations, see the works by George M. Guthrie, Mary Hollnsteiner, Carl F. Landé, and Frank Lynch, S.J., cited in the bibliography.

8. Salvador P. Lopez, "The Colonial Relationship," in The Unites States and the Philippines, ed. by Frank H. Golay (Englewood Cliffs, N.J., c. 1966), p. 10.

9. Hay to Schurman, May 5, 1899, Schurman Report, I [January, 1900], 9.

10. Ibid., II, 66. Italics mine.

11. Ibid., II, 68, 94, 118, 138, et passim. Not all the witnesses are identified by national origin or occupation; there appear to be 23 Filipinos and 25 foreigners (including two Chinese merchants long resident in Manila).

12. Ibid., I, 83, 121, 169, 176; II, 54.

13. Ibid., I, 93.

14. Proclamation "To the people of the Philippine Islands," April 4, 1899, Ibid., I, 5.

15. The Preliminary Report of the Commission [November, 1899], Ibid., I, 183.

16. Report of the United States Philippine Commission to the Secretary of War for the period from December 1, 1900 to October 15, 1901 (Washington, 1901), I, 7. (Hereinafter these Reports, except for the Schurman Report, will be referred to as RPC).

17. "The United States does not desire to make one cent of money out of the Philippine Islands." Jacob Gould Schurman, President of the Philippine Commission, Schurman Report, II, 231. (But contrast Henry Cabot Lodge at the 1900 Republican Convention: "We make no hypocritical pretence of being interested in the Philippines solely on account of others. We believe in Trade Expansion.")

18. Proclamation, "To the people . . . ," Schurman Report, I, 5.

19. Annual Reports of the War Department . . . 1900, Vol. I, Part 1, "Report of the Secretary of War," (Appendix B), p. 74. Italics mine. The instructions, or extended excerpts, are also quoted in other government sources, such as Affairs in the Philippines, Sen. Doc. 331, 57th Cong., 1st sess., 1902, I, 105-11, and Reports of various Missions and Commissions, as well as in the works of Dean C. Worcester, W. Cameron Forbes, and Bonifacio S. Salamanca (see bibliography), who also provide background and commentary.

20. Ibid., pp. 74-75.

21. RPC 1902, I, 4.

22. Salamanca, pp. 56, 61, 184.

23. See Michael [P.] Onorato, A Brief Review of American Interest in Philippine Development and Other Essays (Berkeley, c. 1968.)

24. Special Report of Wm. H. Taft, Secretary of War, to the President on the Philippines. Sen. Doc. No. 200, 60th Cong., 1st sess., 1908, pp. 7, 24-26, 75.

25. Schurman Report, II, 22-27, 51-73, 138-143; see also Salamanca, pp. 55-56, 65-66.

26. See especially Special Report of . . . Taft, pp. 24-31, 74-75.

27. Onofre D. Corpuz, The Philippines (Englewood Cliffs, N. J., c. 1965), p. 66; see also Onorato, pp. 1-11.

28. RPC 1903, I, 64. Sixteen Americans were so convicted in 1902/03. Taft points out that he had warned of this possibility in an earlier Report.

Implementing the "New Order": The Structure and
Supervision of Local Government During the Taft Era

by

Michael Cullinane

The elimination of Spanish authority in the Philippines in
1898 provided the United States with the option of becoming a
colonial power in Asia. The decision to remain in the Islands
was not an easy one for a country that professed anti-colonialism.
The situation was further complicated by the emergence of the
Philippine Republic; the newly organized Filipino government
would surely oppose any claim of sovereignty on the part of the
United States. All too quickly, however, the Americans decided
in favor of colonization and rapidly convinced themselves that
the Malolos government, with its "oligarchic" leadership, would
be devastating for the future of the Archipelago.[1] The Filipino
leaders, many of whom were reluctant to fight but were even
more reluctant to permit the Americans to pre-empt their newly
acquired political authority, chose to resist; and thus the Filipino-
American War ensued.[2]

At the outset most Americans anticipated an early victory
over the "insurgent" regime of Emilio Aguinaldo. Increasingly,
however, many Americans realized that subduing the militant
Philippine Republic would be neither swift nor complete without
first enticing its leaders, the Filipino elite,[3] to transfer their
allegiance from the nationalist movement to the United States.[4]
Furthermore, military conquest, though pursued with vigor, was
certainly not a basis on which to build the "benevolent" colonial
government intended by the early planners; nor was it an effective
way to bring about the collaboration of the ilustrados. It therefore

became the immediate task of the Americans "to convince the Filipinos that their aspirations would be realized within the framework of American sovereignty."[5] "Conciliation" soon emerged as the "guiding spirit" of the American policy toward the Filipinos, particularly toward the literate upper classes.[6]

The earliest commissioners carefully studied the "aspirations and ideals" of the Filipino nationalist leaders[7] and designed their policy suggestions accordingly. Most of these policies (e.g., the separation of state and church, the introduction of an education system, the guarantee of individual rights and liberties, the implementation of local self-government, etc.) would naturally have been part of any American program; but by stressing those goals which were shared with the ilustrados and making them appear as concessions, many of the doubts held by the Filipino elite concerning United States intentions could be overcome, thereby encouraging the necessary collaboration. These and other conciliatory efforts, combined with military force, proved to be fruitful. As it became clear that the United States planned to respect property rights and to refrain from substantial interference in local affairs, large numbers of the landed and educated Filipinos abandoned the revolutionary cause to join with the Americans.[8]

Having turned the tide against the Philippine nationalist struggle, it remained for the Americans to devise an appropriate colonial government for the Islands. The early civil authorities, led by William Howard Taft and expressing a high degree of altruism, pursued their task with confidence. They rapidly familiarized themselves with the basic realities of Philippine life, at least as these could be perceived through late nineteenth century American minds. From the beginning their dilemma lay in striking a balance between their commitment to implant an efficient Anglo-Saxon style democratic government throughout the Archipelago and the necessity to continue to satisfy the political aspirations of the Filipino elite.

The contradictions of these two aims were not immediately evident, yet they gave rise to an increasing American ambivalence toward the Filipino elite. It was only natural that the American colonial officials would form their closest associations with the educated Filipinos, with whom they could more easily communicate in every sense. A number of "educated mestizos" were incorporated into the American ruling circle at the very start; it has also become clear that a great deal of the Commission's information and opinions about the Filipino people and the Malolos government was derived from the testimony of these early "collaborators."[9] The cooperation of this steadily growing group of Filipinos was felt to be essential in order to bring about a lasting peace and to carry out the multiplicity of functions intended by the insular government; furthermore, as Taft noted, it was only this "small percentage" of the people who were "able to exercise the suffrage."[10]

On the other hand, the educated Filipinos and their landed colleagues were from the beginning considered a major hindrance to the functioning of a truly democratic society, especially in the light of the predominantly illiterate mass of people who fell under their sway. As Taft wrote to Elihu Root in 1900,

> While they [the ilustrádos] deal in high sounding phrases concerning liberty and free government they have very little conception of what that means. They can not resist the temptation to venality, and every office is likely to be used for the personal aggrandizement of the holder thereof in disregard of public interest.[11]

The Filipino elite, Taft observed later, "needed as much education in practical civil liberty as their more ignorant fellow-countrymen in reading, writing, and arithmetic."[12] For these reasons he frequently held that one of the main roles of the United States was to be the protector of the Filipino masses from the menacing upper classes.

Quite often the Americans found themselves elaborating the evils of elite rule in the Philippines while at the same time allowing such rule to become firmly implanted through their association with and their dependence on the ilustrados and the local principalía. This ambivalence towards the Filipino elite continued throughout the entire colonial period and certainly must be viewed as a major factor in mitigating the full impact of the American "democratization" effort and its implied reordering of the society.

The expressed desire of the American administrators was to establish an efficient and progressive colonial government which would at the same time allow for the participation and education of the Filipinos in Anglo-Saxon democracy. The United States was

clearly not prepared, nor inclined, to commit thousands of American bureaucrats to serve in the Philippines; it was much less
expensive and less disturbing to the ilustrados to utilize Filipino
personnel and local officials. [13] Thus the prevailing view was
that by the insertion of an American-style and American controlled civil service, coupled with an extensive system of public
education, the Filipinos could learn in time the techniques and
responsibilities of democratic self-government. [14] In simple
terms it was believed that the public schools would educate the
"ignorant, superstitious people" as to their rights under a democratic government, while the American colonial administrators
would restrain the "ambitious" Filipino leaders by supervising
their activities and would in turn educate them through direct
participation in the government. [15] Presumably this system was
to continue for at least two or more generations. [16] As it progressed William Cameron Forbes ideally envisioned that "gradually the natives would come surging up from beneath, working
their way little by little throughout the service," eventually
replacing the Americans as the Philippines made their journey
toward self-government. [17]

Implicit in the colonial scheme, therefore, was the intention
to remake Filipino society along American lines. The extent to
which it is possible for a colonial (or neo-colonial) power to
induce significant societal change in an alien environment remains debatable. This paper will discuss some of the dynamics
of the American effort to instigate change in the Philippines; the
primary focus will be on local government[18] during the so-called
Taft period (1900-1913), the years that exhibited "a continuity of
policy unmatched in the whole era of American control."[19]

The Taft period has generally been regarded as a time of
positive accomplishment. It was during this era of Republican
dominance that all the basic American democratic institutions
were introduced into the Philippines. Some of the more important of these were an electoral process, a civil service based
on merit, an extensive judicial mechanism, a bill of rights, a
functioning system of municipal, provincial and national governments, a Filipino legislature, and a political party system. By
the close of the period in 1913 large numbers of Filipinos had
already been brought into the government; Taft had stressed that
Filipinization must be "slow work," yet in little more than a
decade Filipinos filled seventy-one percent of the public service

positions, ninety-nine percent of all municipal government offices, and over ninety percent of all provincial posts.[20]

Regardless of these accomplishments, by 1913 most of the colonial officials of the Taft era were convinced of the necessity of maintaining strict American rule over the Filipinos for a long time to come. Most of them described Philippine society in much the same way that the Schurman and Taft Commissions had in 1900. They warned that rigid supervision must continue and that the important positions in the government must remain in American hands. Some among them, particularly Dean C. Worcester, even suggested that the United States assert its ultimate authority and initiate a sterner policy towards what was viewed as recalcitrant Filipino leadership.[21] Few of the early colonialists, though sympathetic with the methods, were overly satisfied with the results of the past years; the political behavior of the local and national politicians remained more Filipino (or even Spanish) than Anglo-Saxon, and clearly the education of the masses had barely gotten under way. On looking back on the experience, most of them emphasized that the real answer lay in the passing of years, or more realistically generations, in order to allow for the seeds of change to mature.

In 1924, during one of the frequent discussions over the readiness of the Filipinos to conduct their own government, one observer reminded the Americans that "the greatest act of Filipinization was in 1901, when Governor-General Taft completely Filipinized the municipal governments."[22] In actual fact local governments had been organized even earlier under the military authorities. Out of the necessity to consolidate captured territory and to gain the support of the local leaders, municipal governments were organized in some towns as early as May, 1899.[23] These first town governments were patterned after the pueblo system of the late Spanish period.[24] They consisted of a presidente and a town council, all elected under American direction. In January, 1900, the Military Governor, General Elwell Otis, established a committee of Americans and "distinguished" Filipinos to devise a more permanent plan for municipal governments. By March its plan was promulgated as General Order Number 40, and not long afterwards this same

plan became the basis for the Municipal Code (Act Number 82)
passed by the Philippine Commission under Taft in January,
1901.[25]

In the spirit of the Anglo-Saxon tradition of local self-rule,
and the desire "to secure the confidence and affection of the
Filipinos," the Schurman Commission had recommended that
"in all local affairs" they be allowed to "govern themselves in
their own way."[26] The same spirit pervaded President
McKinley's instructions to the Taft Commission, where the
intention to implement substantial local autonomy in the Philippines was clearly set forth. Considerable antipathy had been
expressed by Filipinos and Americans alike for what they
described as the strict centralism of the later Spanish colonial
government. McKinley's instructions, therefore, stressed that
"in the distribution of power" under the Americans "the pre-
sumption is always to be in favor of the smaller subdivision."[27]

Operating on these basic premises the Taft Commission set
out to build democracy "from the bottom up." A number of
problems, however, were anticipated in the implementation of
substantial local autonomy. Could efficient government be conducted if local Filipino leaders were given a free hand? This
was thought to be doubtful, for relatively few local leaders had
the training and experience in the "proper" administration of
municipal governments; those that did were accustomed to the
centralized Spanish system and allegedly lacked the initiative
to instigate and carry out their own projects, except where their
own self-interest was involved. Summarizing the experiences of
Filipinos under Spanish rule, Taft wrote,

> No responsibility for government, however local or
> unimportant, was thrust upon Filipinos in such a way
> to give them political experience, nor were the
> examples of fidelity to public interest sufficiently
> numerous in the officeholders to create a proper
> standard of public duty.[28]

Furthermore, the centralization of authority, which had been
continued under the American military government in its effort
to subdue the insurrectos, seemed essential in the establishment
of permanent peace and order. As a result, by 1901 it was
already evident to the commissioners that complete local autonomy, as envisioned theoretically in the McKinley Instructions,

could not be institutionalized with effectiveness in the Philippines at this early stage.

With these and other doubts in mind, the Commission proceeded tentatively to put the Municipal Code into effect. The pueblo boundaries derived from the Spanish period were adopted at first, but by 1905 the original number of towns had been drastically cut by integrating many smaller municipalities into larger, wealthier ones.[29] Each municipality was given a corporate status and classified according to its population. The Municipal Code provided that the qualified voters of each town elect (by secret ballot) a president, a vice-president, and a council (the number of councilors depended on the class of the municipality).[30] The president in turn was to appoint (with the council's approval) a municipal secretary, who functioned as a recorder for the council, and a municipal treasurer, who handled the town finances and was responsible for collecting "all moneys paid to the municipality."[31] Municipal councils were permitted to devise their own projects and vote on the distribution of the public funds at their disposal. Town governments, therefore, enjoyed a considerable degree of independence from the higher levels of government; but as will be seen this situation was short-lived.

Six days after issuing the Municipal Code, the Commission passed the Provincial Government Act (Act Number 83). In most cases the Spanish provincial divisions were adopted, but they were reorganized along different lines. Each province was to be governed by a three-member board. At first the only elected member was the provincial governor; he was chosen indirectly by the municipal councilors of his province in a special election held at the provincial capital.[32] The other two provincial board members, the supervisor and the treasurer, were appointed by the Philippine Commission, and later by the governor-general with the consent of the Commission. By appointing Americans to these two offices, the commissioners felt that firm control over the provincial governments could be maintained. The implication was that the American majority on the board would at least guarantee the honesty and efficiency of the provincial governments, and would serve as a positive model for the Filipino local officials.[33] In theory each board member was to have a particular function. The governor was to administer the province by supervising the activities of municipal officers, the

supervisor, usually an engineer, was to concern himself with
the physical improvement of the province, and the treasurer
was to work with the municipal treasurers to collect the taxes
and supervise the distribution of public funds. The overall
role of the provincial governments was outlined by the Commission as follows,

> The first function . . . is to collect, through the
> provincial treasurer, all the taxes, with few ex-
> ceptions, belonging to the towns or the provinces.
> Its second and most important function is the con-
> struction of highways and bridges and public build-
> ings. Its third function is the supervision, through
> the governor and the provincial treasurer, of the
> municipal officers in the discharge of their duty. [34]

The entire local government system, particularly the provincial boards, was placed under the supervision and direction
of the Executive Bureau, that is, the office of the Civil Governor
(later the Governor-General). Headed by the Executive Secretary,
a high-ranking American bureaucrat, the Bureau was established
in 1901 to assist the Governor in carrying out the many requirements of his position. It is not surprising, then, that the responsibilities and personnel of the Executive Bureau grew rapidly.
Throughout the Taft period it was the most important government
agency dealing with local institutions; Arthur W. Fergusson,
Executive Secretary from 1901 to 1908, once stated that the
control over provincial governments "brings the Bureau into
closer contact with the nearly 7,000,000 inhabitants of the Archipelago than any department or other office of the Central Government."[35] Specifically the Bureau was responsible for advising
the chief executive on local appointments, all correspondence with
local officials, and investigating all the charges brought against
local officers and recommending the action to be taken. The
ultimate authority over all officials and employees in the government service was held by the Governor-General, who generally
acted on the advice of the Executive Bureau.

Even before the first official elections in 1902, reports of
irregularities and "undemocratic" activities flowed into the
Executive Bureau from the provinces. Soon after the election
it was obvious to the commissioners that centralization and a
stricter form of supervision of local government were needed.
What concerned them the most was not so much the "abnormal"

political behavior of the Filipinos, but rather their mishandling of public funds, which prevented them from carrying out many important functions; in short, local governments were accomplishing nothing. Among the "crying evils" described by the American administrators was the disturbing inefficiency of most municipal treasurers, and

> the disposition of municipal councils to vote all of the available funds for the payment of their own salaries and leave nothing for the improvement or repair of roads, the construction of buildings, or the payment of schoolteachers.[36]

"The truth is," wrote Governor Taft in 1903, "that municipal governments have not been as satisfactory in their operation as could be wished."[37]

To remedy this state of affairs the Commission initiated a series of changes in 1903. To begin with, municipal treasurers were made members of the civil service, to be appointed by, and act as deputies of, the provincial treasurers. In this way the American provincial treasurer ("an honest and efficient man") would control the financial system and a "much-needed lesson" would be taught to the municipal officials, especially to the town council, which lost its direct authority over its own treasurers, as well as the greater part of the money collected within its jurisdiction.[38] Provincial boards were also given the power to review and annul all municipal ordinances, and the provincial governor was required to make periodic visits of inspection to the town and was empowered to suspend unruly officials on the spot. In essence, 1903 marked the end of American efforts to institute municipal autonomy. The emphasis was thereafter on putting more teeth into the provincial governments (which were still controlled by Americans) by increasing their supervisory authority over the towns.

The emphasis on provincial supervision soon caused tensions to mount within the local governments. It frequently became necessary for the two American provincial board members to apply pressure in order to induce the provincial governor to take action against municipal officials suspected of misconduct or any number of other charges. Quite understandably this placed the Filipino governor in an uncomfortable position. The restructuring of provincial government had, therefore, been a major concern of Filipino politicians "almost from the beginning," and was one of the main topics at the first national convention of provincial governors in Manila in 1905.[39] The Commission's desire to eliminate the inherent frictions on the provincial boards and to appease the Filipino politicians, combined with a genuine concern to initiate constructive public works projects, led to the reorganization of the system of local government and to a readjustment and clarification of the entire central-local relationship.

In late 1905 a law was passed removing the supervisor from the provincial board, and replacing him with another appointed American, the superintendent of schools.[40] The expressed purpose for this action, which withdrew from the board its "most important function," was to release the supervisor, who became the district engineer, from the less professional duties of provincial government so that he could concentrate more time and effort on public works.[41] A little over a year later, in 1906, another change was made by the Commission, which was "doubtless the most radical step" taken thus far with respect to provincial government. At this time the superintendents of schools were similarly removed from the boards and replaced with a third member who was to be popularly elected within the province, thus guaranteeing that two of the three board members from then on would be Filipinos.[42] The Commission emphasized that this new arrangement was designed to test Filipino "capacity for local self-government" and that it should not be taken as an indication of a slackening of supervision; Manila would be keeping a careful eye on the provincial officers to be sure that they performed properly.[43] Nevertheless, this amendment of the Provincial Government Act was viewed as a concession and "was hailed with a great deal of satisfaction by the Filipino press and the Philippine public generally."[44]

During the same period of reorganization, the authority of the provincial treasurer over municipal finances was increased. Along with his direct control over the town treasurer, he was empowered to review all municipal budgets and to rule on the legality of proposed expenditures.[45] In a similar fashion the power of provincial governments was extended more directly over the municipal councils, and the disciplinary authority of the provincial governor was re-emphasized. "The most important political work" of the provincial governments henceforth became "the supervision of the governments of the municipalities."[46]

The jurisdiction of the Executive Bureau was also more clearly defined and its functions considerably expanded. All local government activities and officials were concentrated under the supervision of the Executive Secretary, even the administrative control over provincial treasurers, which had formerly been under the Insular Treasurer.[47] All provincial ordinances, executive orders and budgets were to be closely examined by the Bureau; and in many cases municipal acts were even passed on by the provincial boards for inspection and ratification by the Bureau.[48] By 1908 the Executive Secretary stated that, although the Bureau was in charge of "the dispatch of many matters concerning the insular government," its involvement in local government affairs "has become perhaps its most important function."[49] Within the Bureau itself, most of the functions with respect to local government were performed by the office of the Law Clerk (later known as the Chief of the Law Division). Almost all of the legal and administrative responsibilities concerning the local level were centered in the Law Division, the most critical of these being the handling of "the voluminous records in cases of charges against provincial and municipal officials and justices and auxiliary justices of the peace."[50] At the apex of the entire system remained the Governor-General, whose authority could reach, if necessary, into the smallest town; thus in 1909, Governor-General Forbes declared,

> I have the power to remove any officer and disqualify him from holding any office, and every day I either suspend or remove and often disqualify several.[51]

Two significant patterns emerged out of the above institutional changes, a distinct centralizing tendency of the colonial government, and an increased Filipinization of local governments. By 1907 local governments had been stripped of most of their legitimate, independent authority to affect their own local communities or provinces. Almost all of the important governmental functions, such as taxation, public works, public health, constabulary, and exploitation of lands, forests and mines, were either placed directly under the insular government or one of its regional agents.[52] Contrary to American tradition, even education, through a system of district superintendents, became highly centralized in its Philippine setting.[53] The extent of municipal autonomy was limited to the election of the town president and council, which could enact local ordinances and initiate some minor programs of its own, all of which were subject to the scrutiny of the higher levels of government. Provincial governments were also dependent on Manila in order to obtain the funds and permission necessary to conduct local projects, and the Commission increasingly defined their main function as that of watchdogs over the municipalities. [54]

Although limited in their functional capacities, local governments themselves became rapidly Filipinized. The municipalities had been run by Filipinos since 1901, and by 1907 the majority control of the provincial boards had been relinquished by the Americans. The major beneficiaries of this Filipinization were naturally the socio-economic elite. It is unlikely that many of the early ilustrados and principalía had anticipated such substantial concessions so soon after the American takeover; even Taft recalled that,

> The Filipino people did not expect the liberal and popular provisions of the municipal and provincial codes, and their enactment created the revulsion of feeling that enabled the Federal party to bring peace. The part that the people were given in governing both towns and provinces stimulated them to efforts in behalf of order that became greatly more sympathetic and effective. [55]

The Filipino elite quickly found cooperation with the United States more advantageous than their original expectations. By preserving the peace and order, they were also preserving the traditional system which gave them support. Aided in part by the high suffrage qualifications, the elite easily monopolized the elective offices. American emphasis on political education had been interpreted by most Filipinos to be the main criterion for self-government, and it was in this area that they most readily excelled; the major focus, however, was on politics rather than efficient government as the Americans would have had it. In anticipation of the municipal and provincial elections in 1902, the Filipino politicians immediately set out to build up their local power bases, conveniently associating themselves with one or another of the emerging political groups. [56] In 1907, with the inauguration of the Philippine Assembly, the Filipinos began to consolidate a system of national alliances; and as many of the smaller local factions coalesced into the Partido Nacionalista, the national political stage was constructed. During these early years many Filipino politicians and officials mastered the rhetoric of American democracy, as well as many of the subtle workings of the institutions that had been superimposed upon them. What resulted was the political entrenchment of the Filipino socio-economic elite, or as Taft put it in 1908, "They [the Filipino politicians] are now a real part of the government of the Islands."[57]

It can be argued, however, that the Filipino elite became "a real part of the government" as early as 1901, when it first began to consolidate its political position at the municipal level; for it was this position within the local power structure that was never effectively challenged by the American colonial officials with all their efforts at supervision, intervention, and manipulation of institutional structures.

Assuming that the Americans were legitimately concerned with redirecting the attitude of local Filipino leaders towards "honest and efficient" government, the means of achieving this were hardly obvious. Certainly the long term results of education were to play an important part, but what of the intervening years? Was the democratization of Filipino society to wait for two or more generations before the stigma of elite rule, with all its negative implications, would disappear? Although many Americans on the ground may have held this view, the rhetoric and policies of the Taft era definitely indicated that no effort would be spared to keep the local officials on the path to "good" government. For the most part this was to be accomplished through strict supervision and direction of local government officials by the American dominated central government. [58] Consequently when supervision was intentionally relaxed under the administration of Governor-General Francis Burton Harrison (1913-1921), the older colonial officials stressed that the quality of local government declined significantly. [59] While the validity of this contention is beyond the scope of this paper, it remains to be asked how the system operated during the earlier years of the American administration. Was it really possible to maintain a system of strict supervision while also pursuing a policy of Filipinization?

There is no doubt that the Executive Bureau dedicated con-

siderable time and effort to the many forms of supervision.
Each year, for instance, the Bureau reviewed between 20,000
and 30,000 provincial ordinances, plus a hundred or so municipal enactments. This in itself was a major task; yet its overall effect was negligible. Relatively few of these local enactments were disallowed, and it seems that the main criteria for
reviewing them was to "check deliberate abuse of authority."[60]
Furthermore, reviewing local ordinances does not go far toward
effecting their implementation, nor, more importantly, does it
do much to alter the official behavior of the officers involved.
Nonetheless, this activity was felt to be a critical part of the
supervision process.[61]

The most important mechanism of control over local officials
and their activities was the heavy arm of the Governor-General,
whose ultimate authority empowered him to suspend, discipline,
remove or disqualify any officer in the government service. It
was primarily for the purpose of advising the Governor-General
when to exercise this power that the Law Division was established
within the Executive Bureau. The procedure that emerged for
investigating illegal acts and irregularities at the local level
seemed rather clear-cut, but in actual practice it exhibited many
weak points. By necessity and design almost all complaints and
charges against municipal officials originated at the local level,
where they were theoretically to be channelled to Manila through
the provincial boards. Since the provincial governor was responsible for supervision over the municipalities, he was instructed
to inquire into the nature and severity of the charges, and, if
warranted, to suspend the official, notify the Executive Bureau
immediately, and conduct an investigation. The particulars of
each case were then forwarded to the Law Division, which would
review the charges and if necessary conduct a further investigation before transferring the report and the recommended action
to the Governor-General, who would take the final steps. Many
variations of this procedure existed; for example, charges were
frequently preferred directly to the Governor-General by individuals (both Filipinos and Americans) from the towns, and quite
often it became necessary for the Law Division to conduct investigations without first suspending the official in question.

Many cases were assembled in this manner, and disciplinary
action was both swift and thorough; but for the most part the
process was very complicated and time-consuming, requiring

"a very thorough examination of the facts, and, often, the law."[62] Steeped in a long legalistic tradition, the American "supervisors" were not inclined to take action against an official without first obtaining sufficient reasons for doing so. Many hours were spent on building cases; Dean C. Worcester noted that,

> Practically all the time of three lawyers in the executive bureau is taken up in examining evidence and reports of administrative investigations of charges against municipal officials. [63]

To make matters worse the Law Division was heavily burdened with numerous unofficial reports and charges stemming from a wide variety of sources. The great majority of these kinds of cases were probably explained by what Forbes referred to as the habit of accused Filipinos "to build a 'backfire' for their own protection by bringing counter charges against the officials concerned in their exposure."[64] Another explanation was offered by the Law Clerk in 1903, who contended that,

> The natives of these Islands, especially those of half-blood, are by nature contentious and fond of litigation; and a preliminary inquiry usually shows the charges to be groundless. [65]

Most of these charges were dismissed without being formally recorded.

Above all, official investigations required reliable testimony; without it little could be done against a wrongdoer, and conversely, with intentionally slanted evidence great evils could be perpetrated against a truly honest official. Determining the reliability of witnesses proved to be a formidable task. Too often it was discovered that the key witnesses against an official were relatives or compadres of the official's political enemy. To act effectively, therefore, it was necessary for the Bureau, or its local representatives, usually the provincial treasurers, to be familiar at any given time with the nature of each local power structure. [66] Without knowing the important relationships between local officials and their followings, their friends and kin, and their political opponents, serious injustices would, and surely did, result from the intervention of the central government.

Without first suspending an accused official, it was believed that collecting enough valid evidence against him would be extremely difficult; few Filipinos would testify against an officer who still held his position of authority. Thus from the very beginning the suspension of suspected wrongdoers became a problem. The Governor-General of course was empowered to take this step, but the Executive Bureau was generally reluctant to intervene directly into municipal governments and preferred that such action initiate at the provincial level; for this reason the Law Clerk in 1903 reported that this crucial act was "almost entirely in the hands of the provincial governor."[67] Understandably this policy, which persisted throughout the Taft era, facilitated many objectionable practices. For instance, if a municipal officer was allied with the governor's political rival, the possibility of a suspension was quite likely; but for a governor to suspend and pursue action against one of his own local supporters was not as likely. In practice the power of suspension in the hands of a shrewd governor could easily become a tool for punishing his enemies. In 1905 the Executive Secretary complained,

> There is a tendency on the part of some provincial governors to work an injustice upon suspended municipal officials by failing to report the fact of the suspension to this Bureau as required by law. Instances have come to my notice where officials have been suspended for many months to the utter disregard of their rights, without informing the Bureau of the fact. [68]

Even if the charges were properly filed with the Bureau, it was still possible for the provincial governor, or the board, to delay the investigation of an official long enough for his term of office to expire;

> Provincial boards have been universally slow in conducting investigations of charges, and there have been more than a few cases where officials have been suspended for two years before final determination of the charges against them. [69]

The American officials in Manila were not unaware of the mutual dependence between provincial and municipal politicians, and must have known that the governor's ability to stay in office depended a great deal on his relationships with the same officials he was obliged to supervise. No real attempt, however, was made by the Americans to alter this situation, and occasionally the colonial administrators even took advantage of these relationships to encourage material progress. [70]

Even when guilt was determined, however, difficulty arose
over how to punish the official. The type of penalty depended to
a considerable degree on the personality of the Governor-General
and the circumstances involved. In the early years removal from
office was the most frequently applied punishment. In the later
years, however, there seems to have been an increasing reluctance among the chief executives to administer harsh penalties,
and reprimands (written or verbal) were preferred. [71] A
revealing expression of the reluctance to remove local officers
was made by Governor-General James Smith in 1908. Great
difficulty existed in stimulating interest in road building and
maintenance throughout the local governments. The negligence
of local officials was cited as one major cause for this, where-
upon the Governor-General was reminded that he could remove
any official who failed to perform his prescribed duties. Smith's
reply was,

> But that is a very severe measure. I always have a
> a good deal of reserve about removing officials
> who have been named by the people of the province. [72]

Regardless of the difficulties involved, many cases were
decided against municipal officials; Forbes calculated that
between 1903 and 1913 there were 2,315 cases involving municipal officers and of these 1,499 received penalties of one variety
or another. [73] Less than half of the officials found guilty suffered
removal. Since these figures represent a ten year period involving more than 6,000 municipal officers each year, they are not
particularly alarming, especially when it is realized that punish-
ments were frequently given to groups of officials, such as a
whole municipal council. Furthermore, the mere presentation
of such figures tends to conceal or ignore more important questions and considerations. For instance, did the punishment of
individuals in office decrease their local authority of influence,
or make any significant contribution to their "practical political
education"? Did it tend to make the next official more dedicated
to the public good or merely more subtle in his activities and
more wary of the supervisory authorities? It would be far more
instructive to determine how many officials receiving punish-
ments were later re-elected to similar positions at the local level,
whether the conduct of those re-elected was noticeably altered,
and how many officials who succeeded a removed predecessor
were subsequently reprimanded for like causes. Needless to say,
finding the answers to these sorts of questions was beyond the

scope of the already overburdened Executive Bureau. Nonetheless, in 1908, Taft touched on some of these sore points when
he noted,

> The chief sense of restraint felt by municipal
> officials . . comes from a fear of inspection
> by the central government and its prosecution.
> The fear of condemnation by the public opinion
> of the local community has a much less deter-
> rent force, even if the official is to seek re-
> election. [74]

It was becoming painfully clear that the selection or rejection of
most local political leaders was not determined by American
standards; loyalty to candidates and officials was not always
based on "honest and efficient" government, but more on the
social and economic relationships between the leaders and their
followers; and a different set of circumstances existed for each
local community and province. One particularly good example
of this was the results of the first election for the Philippine
Assembly in 1907. Following the election it was found that a
substantial number of the newly elected deputies to this exalted
body had been accused of a wide range of charges while holding
previous government positions, usually at the local level. [75]
In spite of their very questionable backgrounds and records, few
of these politicians were hampered in their pursuit of national
office. It was also not uncommon for provincial boards or
municipal councils to offer open support to officials charged
with wrongdoing. Chastisements by the American executive, or
by Filipinos at the higher levels, may well have made their
impact at the time, but in general it appears that these "lessons"
seemed short-lived and without enduring consequence.

Implicit in the supervisory scheme of the early planners was
the extended use of qualified American personnel at the critical
levels of control. In the beginning these controlling institutions
were the Executive Bureau and the provincial boards, and it was
stressed that the key positions within them should remain in
American hands for as long as necessary. In 1906, when Filipinos were given the majority control of the provincial boards,
the commissioners continued to emphasize the important role
of the American provincial treasurer and the overall restraining
power of the American dominated Executive Bureau. In other
words, after six years of civil government, "strict" American

supervision over local officials was being conducted for the most part by the Governor-General, several high ranking officials in the Bureau, and thirty-two provincial treasurers. By 1910 all provincial governors and third members of the provincial boards were Filipino, and ten out of the thirty-two provinces by this time had Filipino treasurers; out of a total of 1,069 "regular officials and employees" at the province level, only thirty-six were American, or barely one per province.[76] During the previous year a Filipino had been appointed Second Assistant Executive Secretary, the third ranking official in the service of the Bureau.[77] Furthermore, as early as 1904, a great deal of the administrative work of the Law Division was "under the immediate charge of" a Filipino bureaucrat, "who is assisted by four Filipino clerks."[78]

The point to be made here is not that Filipino officials and employees were more corruptible or less efficient, but that the Americans experienced considerable difficulty in trying to sustain the degree of control that they felt was necessary. Referring to the provincial treasury service, the Executive Secretary informed the Governor-General in 1906 that "much difficulty has been experienced in the past in securing competent men" from the United States "to be trained for these positions."[79] For this reason the service was steadily Filipinized.[80] Related to the difficulty of obtaining Americans was the problem of keeping them in the service long enough to maintain consistent operation. The Executive Secretary frequently complained of the "instability of the service";

> . . . few Americans care to remain in this climate for more than three years . . .

> Indeed there are now [1906] in the service of the Bureau only 7 employees altogether who were connected with it at its organization in 1901.[81]

The three most common causes for investigation and intervention by the Executive Bureau were neglect of duty and abuse of authority, protested elections and violations of the election laws, and the misuse of public funds.[82] The latter problem had been the main reason for readjusting the roles of the provincial and municipal treasurers in early 1903 and the advent of the district auditor system in late 1905. Nevertheless, the misuse of funds and difficulties in the collection of taxes continued throughout the Taft period and after. Since the bulk of the taxes collected within the municipalities was channelled out of the town to the provincial capital, and from there to Manila, many officials found it necessary to devise other means of acquiring money, both for legitimate community projects or for their own pocket. Illegal collections of many varieties were not uncommon. [83] A problem related to this, which constantly harassed the Executive Bureau, was that of "voluntary contributions." Many local leaders, according to the Law Division, developed the habit of eliciting voluntary funds ("by compulsion and threats") from the people for any number of purposes, few of which were considered justifiable. [84] These "contributions" were often collected with more zeal than were the insular taxes, the amount of taxes to be collected was ₱ 2,135, yet the municipal treasurer reported that only ₱ 534 could be raised. Upon investigation it was discovered that during the ten month period prior to the collection of taxes the municipal officials had succeeded in raising ₱3,000 through contributions. In an effort to attack this problem directly the Law Division, in 1907, submitted an act to the Philippine Commission designed to prohibit officials from accepting contributions without the Governor-General's approval. A month later the Law Division was informed that voluntary contributions were not illegal, and that their collection under threat or compulsion was already outlawed by the Penal Code; therefore, no special legislation was necessary. [85] The only recourse of the Law Division was to send circulars around to all the provincial fiscals, making them aware of the law in this regard; but this certainly did not stop "voluntary contributions." In the later years it appears that the central government's attitude toward such activities mellowed somewhat; in 1913, the Governor-General reported,

> The financial resources of many municipalities have
> not been sufficient to permit them to undertake
> necessary public works or even in some cases
> satisfactorily to operate their schools. The people
> have shown a commendable willingness to contri-
> bute money, material, and labor for these purposes.

He quickly added, however, that "this method . . . despite all safeguards" was "open to abuse," and that legislation should probably be enacted to allow municipal councils to increase their own tax money "for limited periods of time."[86]

The direct control of provincial treasurers over their municipal counterparts appeared to curtail many of the financial infractions that were so prevalent during the first few years of local administration. From 1904 on, the number of municipal treasurers found guilty of illicit acts decreased sharply and remained far below the number of infractions committed by municipal presidents and councilors. [87] It also seems that success was achieved in the attempt to separate the municipal treasurers from the control and influence of the town council. In fact, the council's loss of control over the financial duties of the town treasurer may well have been an important cause for the increase in illegal collections and "voluntary" contributions instigated by municipal officials. Another questionable outcome of all this was that the municipal treasurer was rapidly excluded from the local power structure; he was occasionally even from another town. Consequently, the municipal treasurer, regardless of his important function in the town, exerted little influence over local officials and probably enjoyed only minimal political authority in the community. [88]

Supervision over local elections became another early source of frustration and time-consuming effort on the part of the Executive Bureau. As the electorate gradually grew in size and political competition became more and more involved, the number of election protests and violations of the election laws increased accordingly. Many of these infractions focused on the restrictive nature of the suffrage qualifications. From the very beginning voter turnout had been heavy and the franchise "highly esteemed," for frequently "a man's vote possessed a distinct material value." [89] Vote buying occurred in some municipalities in the earliest elections, and increased with time; but apparently voter intimidation and the use of threat or force did not emerge until later when the electorate became much larger and more unwieldy. Considerable effort was made by Filipinos to qualify as many voters as possible. Property values were enlarged on paper and extensive holdings were subdivided (in name only) among relatives and close friends in order to enfranchise sure supporters. By underestimating property values it was also possible to deprive unfavorable or uncommitted individuals of their franchise. [90] The participation of unqualified candidates, as well as voters, was quite common; one Filipino governor informed the Executive Secretary in 1906 that "one-half the councilors of my province can not write, and 15 percent of them do not know their rights or duties." [91] Another similar case, and "one of the best illustrations," said the Executive Secretary, "of how things are done in the municipalities," took place in Oriental Negros in the election of 1906. Following the election and confirmation of the municipal officials of this province, it was disclosed that nearly fifty-nine percent of them were unqualified even to vote, "a truly deplorable condition of affairs" and one which the Executive Secretary speculated was not unique to that province.[92] This situation becomes even more distorted when it is realized that the provincial governor was still chosen at that time by the municipal councilors. Since these officials had already been confirmed, the Bureau could do little except pursue charges against each individual official in the courts.

The large number of illiterate voters (i.e., those who qualified through the property ownership, but could not read or write Spanish or English) also posed a significant problem. In such instances the election inspectors were designated to assist them in filling out their ballots. This naturally subjected the inspectors to the possibilities of bribery, a situation that persistently led to anomalies. Late in the Taft period (June, 1912), for example, a constabulary officer in Bulakan reported that the officials in that province "were not elected by popular suffrage but by the suffrage of the election inspectors."[93] Another such case occurred in Laguna in 1910. Immediately after the election, the incumbent governor, who had been unseated, charged the governor-elect with bribing the election inspectors. The case was taken to the court of first instance in Laguna and amid further charges of intimidating witnesses, the newly elected governor was found guilty. The Filipino judge, however, decided that since the number of votes involved was not enough to reverse the election results, the guilty candidate should be allowed to take office. The Governor-General was forced to intervene and finally denied confirmation to the convicted candidate; at the same time he sent in an American investigator who soon unearthed "a system of corruption that staggers one."[94]

To further complicate the investigations of the Executive Bureau it was reported that Filipino politicians "were disinclined to accept the results of the official returns of defeat," which continually resulted in an almost ritual-like contesting of elections, whether or not any infraction had actually been committed.[95] Gathering evidence and establishing a clear cut case was not easy, especially since much of the preliminary work of investigations was conducted by the provincial boards. By 1904 the

Executive Secretary noted that contested elections could not be justly handled by provincial boards;[96] and it was always necessary to weigh all the evidence carefully. Commenting on the frequency of election disorders, Forbes warned that they indicate "the dangers of letting these people go too far in election matters . . ."[97] It is unclear what he meant by "too far", but Filipinos continued to be given a free hand in the election of their local officials and the system established in 1901 remained basically unchanged. By the end of the Taft era elections were still peaceful for the most part, but each one brought with it more allegations and more investigations; in 1913 alone there were 206 cases, involving 794 persons accused of violating the election law, and by the end of that fiscal year, 340 of those individuals were still under investigation.[98]

Probably the most disturbing problem for the Bureau was the large number of cases involving neglect of duty and abuse of authority by municipal officials.[99] In 1908 Taft wrote,

> The greatest difficulty we have had to contend with in vesting Filipinos with official power in municipalities is to instill in them the idea that an office is not solely for private emolument.[100]

Not only did this problem persist, but the number of these kinds of infractions increased with the years. Quite often the Executive Secretary tried to rationalize this increase as a positive trend. In 1905, for example, Arthur Fergusson explained the situation with,

> This does not necessarily imply a decline in the morale of the service, but is due, I think, rather to the fact that the public is learning the standard required of officials and that all complaints received impartial attention, whereby a less number of delinquencies escape punishment than formerly.[101]

Six years later, as the case load continued to swell, Frank Carpenter, the second Executive Secretary, reported that,

> This increase can not decisively be taken as evidence of greater wrongdoing on the part of municipal officials. It is rather due to the fact that the ignorant people are losing the fear, formerly entertained by them, of officials as

officials and are no longer silently suffering
under real or imaginary acts of oppression. [102]

Although these statements may in fact hold some truth in particular municipalities, they seem to have been based more on
wish than on reality. This becomes especially evident when they
are compared with other explanations emanating from the
Philippine government. In his discussion of "caciquism" in
1908, for instance, Taft revealed that,

> Too often the presidente and other town officers
> use their offices to subject the ignorant resi-
> dents of their respective towns to their business
> control in the sale of farm products . . . The
> evil is hard to reach because the same power
> which compelled the sale can usually compel
> silence and no complaint is heard from the
> victims. [103]

In general it seems more likely that a great many violations by
town officials were never filed with the Executive Bureau.

With provincial governments, however, the general disciplinary situation was very different. The number of cases
brought against provincial officers was exceedingly low; as far
as can be determined only four provincial governors were
removed from office during the entire Taft era. [104] Concerning
the officials at this level Taft wrote,

> When we come to the provincial governments,
> we naturally have to deal with a higher order
> of public servants, and although we here and
> there find . . . defects . . . they are less glaring
> and less discouraging. [105]

The small number of cases pursued against these officers is
partially due to the fact that from the outset the Americans
depended on provincial governors, and on provincial boards
in general, to supervise the towns. A more important reason,
as Taft observed, was that provincial officials were of "a
higher order," that is, they were able to control a larger political following. The Americans were fully aware that the elected
officers at the province level were invariably highly influential
figures; and tampering with their authority required judicious
care. [106] Consequently, it appears that the Bureau dealt gently

with these leaders, limiting their disciplinary action to acts of an obvious criminal nature.

One final but important factor affecting American supervision and direction at the local level resulted from the strict central-ization of the government. This had been viewed by many of the early colonial administrators as necessary to guarantee that most of the important functions of the government would be properly performed. Men like Dean C. Worcester, Luke M. Wright, W. Cameron Forbes and others, all of whom exerted considerable influence on policy in the early years, stressed that the tasks to be accomplished first were those of a material nature, such as health programs and public works projects. Such activities, they contended, would provide a substantial base for the future growth of the Archipelago. These men de-emphasized politics and were convinced that self-government could not be realized until the Islands were economically stable. The neces-sary social changes would not occur, they believed, until the education of the masses was complete, for only then would the people begin to challenge the entrenched elite.[107] In the interim certain positive contributions could be made. This emphasis on "getting things done" was one of the main forces that led to the centralizing of most of the governmental services during the first five or six years of the Taft period. Furthermore, this attitude may also have been responsible for a decrease in the genuine interest of many high officials in promoting better local government. In other words, as long as practical goals could be accomplished, and local governments either helped or did not interfere, the eccentric behavior of local officials and their enthusiasm for politicking could be tolerated.

Throughout the Taft era the American administrators ex-perienced many frustrations in their efforts to control the direc-tion of political and social change in the Philippines. Although the colonial officials spoke of instilling "the American spirit of service" within the system, they just as often brooded over the the fact that "wherever supervision was relaxed, the old order of things [would] immediately crop up again."[108] Under the circumstances described herein, it is not particularly surprising that this was the case. The Americans, Forbes contended, "set themselves to uproot or modify all impediments to democratic institutions."[109] In reality, however, nothing as dynamic as this was ever attempted by the United States. Lacking a "philosophy of radical improvement,"[110] as well as the inclination to devise one, the American planners preferred to operate within the realm of their own experience.

The most striking inconsistency of the early years, and of the entire American period for that matter, was the ambivalence displayed toward the Filipino elite. This group was invariably depicted as a major obstruction to the realization of a truly democratic society and the establishment of social justice; yet no significant effort was made to "uproot" the social and economic conditions that lay at the heart of cacique rule. What is more, the problem of "caciquism" was generally discussed separately from local politics and government, almost as though the two were unrelated; the implication was that local officials could be instructed in the operation of honest and efficient government even while the endemic "evils of caciquism" existed around them. By ignoring the sensitive agrarian problems, the United States allowed the traditional elite to maintain its long established social and economic dominance.[111] Furthermore, the Americans legitimized the elite's de facto power at the local level by supplying it with a strong political identity through the holding of public office. By 1901 local governments were controlled by the principalía, and six years later a Filipino legislative assembly was organized, thus furnishing the elite with an important institution on which to consolidate its national authority. In seven short years of American presence the so-called "greedy politicians" were well on their way to establishing a nearly unchallengeable position within the governmental structure. Having acquired this position, there was little the Americans could do within the framework of their own commitments to impede the continued entrenchment of these politically articulate Filipinos.

Many of the early American administrators realized what had happened; Taft himself indicated this when he remarked,

> If we are to be criticized at all for what has been done in the islands down to 1913, it is that we went a little too rapidly in extending the political power of the native Filipino.[112]

Some officials emphasized the long term effects that would derive
from the education system, while others concentrated on public
works projects and larger economic questions. Nearly all,
however, placed a rather naive faith in the capacity of a few
Americans "on the ground" to regulate the activities of thousands
of Filipino government officers.

In the area of local government the Americans focused on
certain key institutions of control (i.e., the provincial boards
and the Executive Bureau) in order to exert the necessary
restraint on Filipino politicians and to direct them toward "good"
government. Supervision through this system proved to be quite
difficult and, in the final analysis, ineffective. The whole spirit
of supervision was undermined by the increasing dependence on
Filipino officials and personnel at all levels of the government;
as Filipinization of the service progressed, the process of
supervision of local government became as much a Filipino
phenomenon as an American one. Consequently, in 1906, the
Executive Secretary admitted that "for obvious reasons the
Government has acted on the theory that Filipino officials ought
not to be as yet and they have not been held up to the standards
required of Americans."[113] Equally detrimental to the
American scheme was the growing necessity for accommodation
and cooperation with the Filipino politicians. Complaining of
this, Worcester recalled that,

> In the past the clamor of politicians has not
> infrequently resulted in concessions granted
> in the vain hope of arousing their gratitude,
> and bringing about a state of friendliness the
> advantages of which would far outweigh certain
> clearly foreseen resulting difficulties. [114]

Seen from the bottom up, it can be said that the American
colonial officials exerted little influence over the daily affairs
of Filipino life at the barrio, municipal and even the provincial
levels. The "democratization" of the Philippines was carried
out more by the Filipino leaders, operating within their own
cultural values and their own conceptions of American democracy,
than by the colonial "supervisors." Without fully intending to,
the Americans permitted the political process to conform more
to "the customs, the habits, and even the prejudices" of the
Filipinos, or more specifically those of the elite, than they
initially realized. Over thirty years later, Joseph Ralston Hayden

concluded that, "Despite Manila supervision, to a considerable degree the quality of Philippine local government has been determined locally," and political behavior remained "genuinely representative of the ideas and other forces which dominate Filipino life."[115]

While Filipino leaders were left relatively free to develop their own political character and seek their own self-interests, the institutions that emerged under American rule left the Philippines with a highly centralized government structure. Almost all meaningful authority was concentrated at the higher levels, especially in Manila. Although the expressed desire of the United States had been to build democracy "from the bottom up," the type of government that developed focused on supervision from the top down. Considering the commitments of the Taft years, such a trend was unavoidable. The Americans, pledged to bringing material progress (although at no expense to American taxpayers), were convinced that such a goal could not be realized through Filipino-controlled local governments, and in a rather short time all pretense of local autonomy was abandoned. By retaining "dedicated" Americans in certain public service positions outside local governments, it was felt that the necessary accomplishments could be achieved; and it must be admitted that many important improvements were initiated during the Taft period.[116] Most of the American officials of the Taft years did not intend centralism to become a permanent part of the Philippine government; it was their assumption that as the municipal and provincial leaders became more efficient and more familiar with the proper uses of their offices, and as more and more trained Filipinos entered the government service, decentralization and increased local autonomy would be gradually implemented. What occurred, however, was the opposite; as Filipinization progressed so did centralization.[117] Most of the centralization that took place after the Taft era was instigated by the Filipinos themselves.[118]

Whereas the supervisory mechanism established by the Americans interfered only slightly with the political activities of the local Filipino leaders, the centralization of authority often shielded these same leaders from the responsibilities that went along with their office; this situation, among other things, greatly deterred the development of self-reliance within local government, particularly at the municipal level.[119] In most

cases the activities of the central government, both in general
supervision and in public services, came to be viewed by local
citizens as external phenomena, conducted mostly by officials
residing outside their local community.

The Taft era concluded with the administration of Governor-
General Forbes (1909-1913), who incessantly instructed the
Filipinos to pay more attention to business, and less to politics.[120]
He expressed a confidence in the political capabilities of the
Filipinos and assumed that they would eventually outgrow their
eccentric ways. He was, therefore, somewhat hesitant to incite
any political outbreaks that might interrupt his programs for
development. In 1911 Forbes denounced the illicit acts committed
by a certain group of municipal officials from Bohol, claiming
that these Filipinos "haven't wakened up to the fact that a new
order of things is in effect."[121] There is no doubt that a "new
order" was emerging, but it is clear that it was much more
complex than anything envisioned by Taft and McKinley in 1900.

APPENDIX I

The following are the summaries of two particularly revealing cases involving local officials dealt with by the Executive Bureau. They have been related here in order to provide at least two examples of the many variables that had to be considered by the Bureau in its investigations of municipal and provincial officers.

Case I

This case actually derives from two related cases filed with the Law Division. The first case, "Gives Results of Investigation of Joaquin Gil: Benito Lopez, Governor of Iloilo, and of political situation generally in Iloilo, particularly the testimony of Quintin Salas," was dated November 26, 1907, and was found in WPC, Documents, Vol. I, Item No. 27. The second case, "Report of the Chief, Law Division in the matter of charges against Quintin Salas, municipal councilor of Barotac Nuevo," was dated December 17, 1907, and was found in WPC, Documents, Vol. I, Item No. 40. For purposes of clarity the summary combines the two cases.

> The cases centered around the activities of the provincial governor of Iloilo, Benito López, and a municipal councilor of Barotac Nuevo (Iloilo Province), Quintin Salas. Governor López was charged with buying votes, misconduct in office, and misuse of public funds. Although the charges were made in 1907, most of them referred to events that took place as far back as 1905. The accusations were preferred by one Joaquin Gil of Iloilo, who produced three witnesses, the most important of which was Salas, a former henchman of López. It seems that through a debt of gratitude López, who planned to run for governor in February, 1906, was able to obtain the services of Salas, "the most influential man in the pueblo and . . . virtually the 'boss' of the local party." Having won the office, allegedly through substantial bribery and vote buying, López later failed to satisfy

the expectations of Salas, who turned his favors to the anti-López faction led by one Jalandoni. Friction developed between Salas and López soon after the latter announced that he would run again for governor in 1908. Shortly after charges were brought against López, Salas himself was formally accused of misconduct in office, larceny and estafa (swindling), based on his activities as municipal councilor. The provincial board, headed by López, unanimously recommended Salas' removal and permanent disqualification, and produced abundant evidence and witnesses to support the charges. The Law Division was convinced of the guilt of both men, but was also cognizant of the political implications involved. Joaquin Gil, Salas, and the other two witnesses against López were all allied with the Jalandoni faction. The case against Salas was also entangled in the same political trappings. It was certain that substantial abuses of authority had occurred, but executive action could not be taken immediately in either case. As for Salas, it was recommended that criminal action be pursued, but the Chief of the Law Division warned that "in view of the present condition in Iloilo it will . . . be necessary to send some capable American lawyer to do this successfully." With respect to López, it was clear that other witnesses would be necessary for a conviction. In this sense the Chief stressed that "it is doubtful, however, whether much testimony can be obtained without the suspension of the Governor." Governor López was never suspended, and no further action was taken against him up to the time of his death in late January, 1908.

Case II

The second case involves an attempt by the Executive Bureau to accumulate evidence against the Governor of Rizal Province, Lope K. Santos, in 1911, with the expressed purpose of removing him from office. The case, "Memorandum for the Governor-General in re: Lope K. Santos, Provincial Governor of Rizal," was submitted by the Assistant Executive Secretary on October 31, 1911, and was found in WPC, Documents, Vol. I, Item No. 41.

The central government was convinced that Lope K. Santos, the Governor of Rizal, was guilty of dishonesty, oppression, and misconduct in office, not to mention the fact that he had on occasion been discourteous and contemptuous toward certain Americans in high positions. Despite their knowledge of Santos' wrongdoing the Executive Bureau officials proceeded cautiously. They carefully prepared their precedents in all of the six specific cases involving the above charges. In one particular case Santos was accused of preventing the provincial board "from making an investigation" of charges against Pedro Santos, a municipal president, and later against a municipal councilor accused of beating a woman of his town. The necessity of first suspending him before collecting the final testimony was stressed, especially in the light of Santos' influence in the province (and in nearby Manila). It was warned that the government must be ready to act quickly and effectively, for "The case is almost sure to be given a political aspect-- by Santos and the politicians--and he will claim everything that can be claimed in the way of bias on the part of the prosecution and the witnesses." Due to the tenseness of the situation the chief executive was instructed to have the case handled by an efficient investigator outside the executive office, thereby emphasizing impartiality to the onlooking Filipino community. In general the report revealed a noticeable reluctance among the officials involved to act without first being assured of success. Quite possibly for this reason the Governor-General decided not to act and the case was dropped. The whole mood of the report suggests the vulnerability of the Executive Bureau in attempting to maintain strict supervision.

APPENDIX II

FILIPINIZATION OF LOCAL GOVERNMENTS AND THE EXECUTIVE BUREAU, TAFT ERA

Table I

Nationality of Municipal Officers, 1903-1913[a]

Year	Americans[b]	Filipinos	Percent Filipinos
1903	24	14,102	99.8
1904	44	11,289[c]	99.6
1905	58	10,725[c]	99.5
1906	68	10,774	99.4
1907	88	11,350	99.2
1908	82	11,760	99.3
1909	81	12,275	99.3
1910	102	12,417	99.2
1911	108	12,685	99.2
1912	132	12,183	98.9
1913	111	13,324	99.2

[a] The data for the above table were taken from the Report of the Executive Secretary in RPC 1913, p. 86. The figures include all municipal and township officials, justices of the peace and notaries public in both the regularly and the specially organized provinces.

[b] The increase in Americans over the years is explained by the increase of American personnel primarily in the specially organized provinces and in Manila. In 1911, for instance, the Executive Secretary explained, "Twenty-three hold appointive municipal offices in the Moro Province, 20 are justices of the peace or auxiliary justices in that Province and the Province of Mindoro or on military or naval reservations where they are appointed to deal with American soldiers and sailors, and 62 are notaries public, 44 in Manila and 18 in the Provinces being mostly lawyers

who obtained appointment for the convenience of their clients . . .
there are really but three American municipal officers in the
self-governing municipalities and two of these are elected by
popular votes. The same facts are applicable to the figures
given for former years and account for the apparent increase
in percentage of Americans." RPC 1911, pp. 39–40.

[c] The rather sudden fall in the number of Filipino municipal
officials during 1904 and 1905 is due to the overall reduction
of the number of municipalities, which were consolidated and
reorganized by the Philippine Commission under Governor-
General Luke M. Wright. As the number of towns increased
after 1906, the number of municipal officials increased
accordingly.

Table II

Nationality of Provincial Officers, 1903-1913[a]

Year	Americans[b]	Filipinos	Percent Filipinos
1903	86	238	73.5
1904	87	143	62.2
1905	80	246	75.4
1906	60	183	75.3
1907	50	96[c]	65.8
1908	49	101	67.3
1909	47	102	68.5
1910	39	101	72.1
1911	43	104	70.8
1912	44	97[d]	68.8[d]
1913	42	111	72.6

[a] The data for the above table were taken from the Report of Executive Secretary in RPC 1913, p. 86. These figures include governors, third members of the board, treasurers, supervisors, secretaries, fiscals, and other officials in both the regularly and the specially organized provinces, which ranged respectively from 31 to 34 and 6 to 7 in number.

[b] The number of Americans serving in the regularly organized provinces was considerably lower than indicated by these figures, since most of the American provincial officers, with the exception of the treasurers and the supervisors before 1906, were in the specially organized provinces. By 1910 the provincial government service within the self-governing provinces was 91.8% Filipino, by 1911 it was 92.6%, and by 1912 it was 93%. RPC 1911, p. 24, and RPC 1912, pp. 32-33.

[c] The large decrease in Filipino officers in 1907 is "mostly due to the abolition of the offices of provincial secretary and president of the provincial board of health and the expiration of the terms of office of the members of the board of tax appeals." RPC 1907, I, p. 163.

[d] The reason for the apparent decrease in Filipinos here was that eleven vacancies for third members of the board had not yet been filled by special elections. "Had these been filled by Filipinos, as they all will be, the percentage of Filipino officers would have been 71.05 per cent." RPC 1912, p. 55.

Table III

Nationality of Provincial Boards and Other Important Provincial Positions, 1906-1913[a]

	1906	1907	1908	1909	1910	1911	1912	1913
Governors[b]								
Americans	9	8	7	6	6	7	7	7
Filipinos	29	30	31	31	32	31	31	31
Treasurers[c]								
Americans	34	33	29	26	22	22[d]	22	20
Filipinos	0	1	5	7	10	11[d]	11	13
Supervisors[e]								
Americans	2	2	1	1	1		1	1
Filipinos	—	—	—	—	—		—	—
Third Members								
Americans	—	—	—	—	—		—	—
Filipinos	—	27	31	30	31		20[f]	30
Fiscals								
Americans	2	1	1	1	1		—	—
Filipinos	30	25	26	24	25		27	29
Secretaries								
Americans	1	—	1	1	1		1	1
Filipinos	31	2[g]	1	1	—		—	—
TOTALS								
Americans	48	44	39	35	31		31	29
Filipinos	90	85	94	93	98		89	103

[a] Except where noted, the above data were obtained from the Reports of the Executive Secretary in RPC (1906 to 1913). These figures include the provincial officials of both the regularly and the specially organized provinces. Prior to 1906 information of

this nature was not published in the reports of the Philippine Commission.

[b] From 1910 on there were no American governors in the regularly organized provinces.

[c] Prior to 1906 all the provincial treasurers were Americans. It should be pointed out, however, that by 1906, several Filipinos were being utilized in the capacity of deputy provincial treasurers due to the difficulty of obtaining qualified Americans.

[d] From the report of the Governor-General in RPC 1911, p. 24. No other figures for 1911 were available.

[e] Prior to 1906 the supervisor, an appointee, served as the third member of the board and was an American. For a brief period in 1906 the superintendent of public schools replaced the supervisors, thus accounting for the small number of supervisors during that year. After 1906 the third member became an elective official, invariably a Filipino.

[f] See Appendix II, Table II, note d.

[g] Although the position of provincial secretary was abolished as an official appointive office, the provincial governor continued to have Filipino secretaries whom they personally selected.

Table IV
Filipinization of the Executive Bureau, 1901-1913[a]

Year	Americans	Filipinos	Total	Percent Filipinos
1901	31	19	50	38.0
1902	32	29	61	47.5
1903	46	77	123	62.6
1904	52	76	128	59.4
1905	45	92	137	67.2
1906	52	114	156	73.1
1907	43	118	161	73.3
1908	37	102[b]	140[b]	72.9
1909[c]	35	117	152	76.9
1910	32	112	144	77.8
1911	30	122	152	80.3
1912[d]			195[d]	
1913	45	160	208[e]	76.9

[a] The data for this table were taken from <u>RPC</u> (1900-1913), mostly from the Reports of the Executive Secretary under the heading "Bureau Personnel." It should be pointed out here that since the Executive Bureau handled a vast number of administrative duties, its involvement at the local government level was primarily through the office of the Law Clerk (after 1906 known as the Law Division), thus limiting further the number of Americans (and Filipinos) directly responsible for supervision over provincial and municipal governments.

[b] The figures for 1908 seem to be the only ones to exclude "janitors" from the tally, presumably accounting for the decrease in Filipino employees, who made up the custodial staff of the Bureau. <u>RPC 1908</u>, I, 144.

[c] Up to 1909 the three top officials in the Bureau (i.e., the Executive Secretary, the Assistant Executive Secretary and

the Second Assistant Executive Secretary) remained Americans, although several of the divisions within the Bureau were headed by Filipinos. In 1909 a Filipino was appointed Second Assistant Executive Secretary. RPC 1909, pp. 92-93. Throughout the Taft Era the Executive Secretary, his Assistant and the Chief of the Law Division remained Americans.

[d] A nationality breakdown for the Bureau personnel was not provided in 1912, probably due to the reorganization of the Bureau.

[e] The total Bureau personnel in 1913 included three employees described as "Spanish". RPC 1913, p. 77.

APPENDIX III

CHARGES BROUGHT AGAINST LOCAL OFFICIALS, TAFT ERA

Table I

Cases Involving Charges against Municipal Officials and their Disposition, 1903-1913[a]

	1903	1904	1905	1906	1907[b]	1908[b]	1909	1910	1911	1912	1913	TOTALS
Cases Filed	144	186[c]	203[c]	212[c]	182	318	321[c]	338[c]	253	23[c]	152[c]	2,539[c]
Officer Suspended	135	164	198	198			206	173	174	178	102	
Officer Not Suspended	9[d]	22	5	14			104	165	79	52	50	
Found Guilty	88	116	142	69	127	196	223	262	220	197	80	1,720
Reprimanded	12	2	18	13			72	164	119	102	18	
Asked to Resign	—	6	11	5			13	12	10	5	7	
Removed	76	79	106	29	80	117[e]	46	53	56	73	26	741
Disqualified	—	—	2	17			92	24	28	16	16	
Found Not Guilty	47	66	54	51	55	f	87	57	33	30	27	629
Reinstated	47	32	53	41			60	40	23	21	22	
Other Disposition	—	34[g]	1[g]	10[g]			27[h]	17[h]	10[h]	9[h]	5[h]	

a These data were taken from the Reports of the Executive Secretary in RPC (1903-1913). The charges were made against municipal presidents, vice presidents, treasurers, councilors, secretaries, justices and auxilliary justices of the peace.

b The specific breakdowns for 1907 and 1908 were withheld by the Bureau of Insular Affairs.

c The cases unaccounted for were filed, but not acted on by the governor-general before the expiration of the official's term of office. In 1904 there were 4 such cases, in 1905, 7, in 1906, 92, in 1909, 11, in 1910, 19, in 1912, 3, and in 1913, 45.

d Presumably no action was taken against these nine officials who were not suspended.

e The other officials found guilty in 1908 "escaped punishment either by reason of the expiration of their term or for other causes." RPC 1908, I, p. 151.

f Presumably the remaining 122 officials accused in 1908 were either acquitted or no action was taken on their cases. This figure of 122 has, therefore, been included in the total at the end of the line.

g These officials had not been reinstated in office when their terms expired.

h The charges against these officials were dismissed.

Table II

Cases Against and Removals of
Specific Municipal Officers, 1904-1913[a]

	Presidents	Vice Presidents	Councilors	Treasurers	Secretaries	Justices of the Peace	Auxiliary Justices of the Peace	Others[b]
1904								
Cases	58	10	60	11	8	33	6	—
Removals[c]	22	4	23	6	5	23	2	—
1905								
Cases	51	15	70	—	3	50	13	1
Removals	23	8	43	—	2	33	10	—
1906								
Cases	55	13	84	—	2	47	11	—
Removals	10	2	24	—	—	10	5	—
1907[d]								
1908[d]								
1909								
Cases	64	18	133	4	4	41	18	28
Removals	20	9	52	3	1	33	14	19
1910								
Cases	67	14	166	7	4	40	14	26
Removals	12	4	18	5	—	27	11	12
1911								
Cases	54	14	100	1	7	29	13	35
Removals	9	5	23	1	4	25	11	16
1912								
Cases	51	15	111	2	2	24	10	15
Removals	19	8	30	1	—	21	9	7
1913								
Cases	50	14	53	—	4	16	7	8
Removals	13	3	10	—	2	12	6	3
TOTALS								
Cases	450	113	777	25	34	280	92	113
Removals	128	43	223	16	14	184	68	57

[a] These data were taken from the Reports of the Executive Secretary in RPC (1904-1913). Similar information was not published prior to 1904.

[b] The category "others" includes chiefs of police, various other policemen, health inspectors, barrio lieutenants, and municipal clerks.

[c] The term removal is used here and throughout this table to mean all officials who were removed from office and/or disqualified, as well as those who were forced to resign.

[d] The specific breakdown for the years 1907 and 1908 was withheld by the Bureau of Insular Affairs. Nevertheless the Executive Secretary reported that in line with previous years municipal presidents and councilors were the greatest offenders.

Table III

Nature of Charges against Municipal Officials, 1905-1913[a]

	Neglect of Duty	Abuse of Authority	Violation of Election Laws, etc.[b]	Malversation, etc.[c]	Extortion, etc.[d]	Bribery, etc.[e]	Crimes of Violence	Slander, etc.[f]	Bad Habits, etc.[g]	Forgery, etc.[h]	False Arrest	Ignorance, etc.[i]	Interference with Religious Affairs	Larceny, etc.[j]	Others[k]
1905															
Guilty	58	56	1	31	36	40	5	11	6	5	8	1	1	5	—
Not Guilty	39	58	—	22	17	11	1	5	11	4	3	6	6	4	1
No Action	—	—	—	—	—	—	—	—	—	—	—	—	—	—	—
1906															
Guilty	54	16	7	16	15	3	—	3	16	1	4	3	1	3	1
Not Guilty	31	5	4	1	5	1	—	4	4	1	2	2	2	2	—
No Action	39	18	19	19	21	10	—	11	2	7	6	9	8	12	6
1907[l]															
1908[l]															
1909															
Guilty	151	36	59	13	5	—	12	26	9	8	4	8	6	—	18
Not Guilty	103	28	11	12	5	3	17	1	1	2	1	1	3	1	14
No Action	4	—	—	—	—	—	4	1	—	1	—	—	—	—	—

1910															
Guilty	181	59	31	14	4	4	13	14	22	3	7	9	1	1	—
Not Guilty	29	44	21	8	5	—	9	9	2	23	6	2	1	1	—
No Action	4	6	15	1	—	—	2	5	1	2	2	—	1	2	—
1911															
Guilty	83	86	32	11	2	3	7	1	3	3	7	5	2	—	—
Not Guilty	33	49	28	7	2	13	8	2	10	2	1	2	2	1	—
No Action	7	—	—	—	—	—	—	—	—	—	—	—	—	—	—
1912															
Guilty	110	57	29	14	6	19	4	—	4	6	9	2	19	3	3
Not Guilty	22	14	9	9	3	1	5	1	2	1	6	—	2	—	—
No Action	—	2	2	—	—	—	1	—	1	—	—	—	—	—	—
1913															
Guilty	33	47	22	11	5	2	3	2	3	3	6	17	3	1	5
Not Guilty	10	12	6	7	—	—	7	1	—	1	2	4	4	1	—
No Action	13	23	21	10	3	—	—	1	1	2	1	3	6	1	3
Total Cases	922	616	317	206	130	110	98	98	77	75	75	74	68	37	51

a These data were taken from the Reports of the Executive Secretary in <u>RPC</u> (1905-1913). The same data were not published for the years 1901 to 1904.

b "Violations of laws, election, executive orders, and municipal ordinance."

c "Malversation and breaches of trust."

d "Extortion and illegal collections."

e "Bribery and kindred crimes."

f "Slander, disrespect, and use of bad language."

g "Bad habits and immorality."

h "Forgery and falsification."

i "Ignorance and incapacity."

j "Larceny and bandolerismo."

k The category "others" includes the charges "lunacy" (1), "perjury and kindred crimes" (18), and "gambling" (32).

l The specific breakdowns for 1907 and 1908 were withheld by the Bureau of Insular Affairs. For 1907 the Executive Secretary noted that the figures for that year showed "a great increase in charges of abuse of official position--a total of 100 as against 39 for 1906." RPC 1907, I, p. 162. For 1908 it was reported that "neglect of duty continues to be the most common failing, 47 officials having been removed for that cause. Abuse of authority follows with 37, and gambling is third with 29." RPC 1908, I, p. 151.

Table IV

Provincial Officials Removed or Forced
to Resign from Office, 1903-1911[a]

	1903[b]	1904	1905	1906	1907[c]	1908	1909	1910	1911
Governors	1	1	–	–		1	–	–	1
Treasurers	4[d]	3[d]	–	–		–	–	–	–
Supervisors	3[d]	–	–	–		–	–	–	–
Third Members	–	–	–	–		–	–	–	–
Fiscals	3	1	1	–		–	1	–	–
Secretaries	2	2	1	–		–	2	–	–
Others[e]	2	5	4	1		–	2	–	–
TOTALS	15	12	6	1	2[c]	1	3	0	1

[a] The above data were taken from various Reports of the Executive Secretary in RPC (1903-1911), and do not necessarily represent a complete listing. No information on removals at the provincial level was provided in the Executive Secretaries' Reports for 1912 and 1913.

[b] From July, 1902, to November, 1903, seventeen American officials, fifteen of whom were involved at the provincial level, were convicted of "defalcations" in "collecting and disbursing money." Five of these were in the provincial treasury service. All were later imprisoned. See RPC 1903, I, 64-71, and Jones, p. 289.

[c] The official positions of these two removals for 1907 were not given; however, it was reported that both were American. RPC 1907, I, 162.

[d] In 1903 and 1904 all provincial treasurers and supervisors were Americans.

[e] The "others" include 5 supervisor-treasurers, 2 secretary-treasurers, 2 presidents of provincial boards of health, 1 district health officer, 1 lieutenant governor, and 4 unidentified officials.

Notes

1. The following year (August, 1900), Taft wrote that "an
independent government of the Filipinos could produce a
condition worse than in Hades." Cited in Oscar Alfonso,
"Taft's Early Views on the Filipinos," Solidarity, IV-6
(1969), 56.

2. William Pomeroy convincingly argues that the American
resort to a military solution, which brought great loss of
life and property, could have been avoided with more
shrewdness on the part of the United States in dealing with
the Filipino elite. William Pomeroy, "'Pacification' in
the Philippines, 1898-1913," France-Asie, 21-189/190
(1967), 427-32.

3. See above, Owen, "Introduction . . .," note 2.

4. This view is clearly expressed by Dean C. Worcester, a
member of the first U.S. Philippine Commission, in a cable-
gram [July, 1899?]. Here he emphasized that the coming
over of the "influential leaders" would be the "beginning of
the end" (of hostilities) in the Philippines. Worcester
Philippine Collection [Harlan Hatcher Library, The University
of Michigan], Documents and Papers, 1834-1915, Vol. XVII,
p. 177. (Hereinafter referred to as WPC, Documents.)

5. Bonifacio S. Salamanca, The Filipino Reaction to American
Rule: 1901-1913 (Hamden, Conn.] , 1968), p. 51. A similar
view is expressed by Leopoldo Yabes, "The American
Administration in the Philippines," Solidarity, II-5 (1967), 22.

6. Salamanca, pp. 38-39. An earlier account of the period by
David Barrows also states that American policy was based
on "conciliation and generous concession." David Barrows,
A Decade of American Government in the Philippines (New
York, 1914), pp. 1-2. The phrase "policy of permissiveness"
is used by Theodore Friend, Between Two Empires: The
Ordeal of the Philippines, 1929-1946 (New Haven, 1965), p. 264.

See also Oscar Alfonso, "Expediency in Taft's Philippine Administration," Philippine Journal of Public Administration, XII-3 (1968). The spirit of conciliation was evident in the report of the Schurman Commission in 1900, where it was recommended that "to secure the confidence and affection of the Filipinos, it is necessary not only to study their interests but to consult their wishes, [and] to sympathize with their ideals and prejudices even . . . " Report of the [Schurman] Philippine Commission to the President (Washington, 1900), I [January 31, 1900], 90. (Hereinafter referred to as Schurman Report.)

7. Schurman Report, I, 82. The Schurman Commission devoted a full chapter to "Government Reforms Desired by Filipinos," Ibid., I, 84-97.

8. This point is made particularly clear in Yabes, p. 23, and in Romeo Cruz, "The Filipino Collaboration with the Americans, 1898-1902," Comment, No. 10 (1960). A slightly different view is expressed by Pomeroy, p. 445, who feels that the significant transfer of loyalty by the "revolutionary leaders" did not occur until after the inauguration of the Philippine Assembly in 1907. It should be noted that a wide variety of reasons existed to encourage the collaboration of most ilustrados, for not all was harmonious within the Philippine Republic, and some discontent with Aguinaldo and his policies was evident. See David Joel Steinberg, et al., In Search of Southeast Asia (New York, 1971), pp. 263-66, and Teodoro Agoncillo, A Short History of the Philippines (New York, 1969), pp. 138-41.

9. See Cruz, pp. 15-18, and Alfonso, "Taft's Early Views . . .", pp. 54-57.

10. From excerpts of Taft's letter to John Harlan (June 30, 1900) in Alfonso, "Taft's Early Views . . .", p. 52. Strict suffrage qualifications were also the desire of the Filipino elite, and in the same letter Taft showed his awareness of this when he wrote that the Filipino leaders "do not recommend universal suffrage, but a high qualification for it." See also Alfonso, "Expediency . . .", pp. 246-50.

11. Taft to Root (August 18, 1900), in Alfonso, "Taft's Early Views . . .", p. 56.

12. Special Report of the Secretary of War, Wm. H. Taft, to President Theodore Roosevelt, January 27, 1908, Sen. Doc. No. 200, 60th Cong., 1st sess., 1908, p. 24.

13. In 1908 Taft stated, "It is undoubtedly true that the municipalities would be much more efficient had the policy been pursued of appointing Americans to the important offices in the municipalities, but there would have been two great objections to this course, one that the municipal government would not have attracted the sympathetic attention of the people as the present municipalities have--and we would thus have lost a valuable element in making such government a success--and the other that the educational effect upon the people in training them for self-government would have been much less." Ibid., p. 33.

14. This view is reflected in a letter by Taft to Henry M. Hoyt (September 8, 1900), in Alfonso, "Taft's Early Views...", p. 51, and even more clearly later in a speech to the Brooklyn Institute of Arts and Sciences (November 19, 1913), as reproduced in William Cameron Forbes, The Philippine Islands (Boston and New York, 1928), Vol. II, appendix xxiv.

15. Taft was strongly committed to what he later called the policy of "practical political education" and he believed that one of the best ways to teach democracy was to have the Filipinos participate in it. See Special Report of... Taft, pp. 26, 31.

16. Taft once noted that the Filipinos "need a training of fifty or a hundred years before they shall even realize what Anglo-Saxon liberty is." Taft to Harlan (June 30, 1900), in Alfonso, "Taft's Early Views...", p. 52. Twenty-six years later Taft still saw Filipino readiness to be at least two generations away. See Taft's letter to J. T. Williams, Jr. (June 8, 1926), in Michael Onorato, "Leonard Wood as Governor-General: A Calendar of Correspondence," Philippine Studies, XIII-4 (1965), 846.

17. A speech by Forbes given at the Lake Mohonk Conference concerning the Philippines (October 14, 1914) as found in WPC, Documents, Vol. VI.

18. Throughout this paper the expression "local government" will be used to refer to the municipal and provincial governments in the "regularly organized" provinces (i.e., excluding the "specially organized" provinces of the non-Christian peoples). No specific attention is paid to the barrio, since the municipality was the lowest administrative unit to involve American supervision. The organization of "chartered cities" has also been omitted. Although non-elected officials at the local level (e.g., police, justices of the peace, judges of the first instance, etc.) are mentioned occasionally, the main emphasis here is on the elected officers at the town and province levels.

19. Garel Grunder and William Livezey, The Philippines and the United States (Norman, Oklahoma, 1951), p. 84.

20. See Forbes, II, 167, and Report of the United States Philippine Commission to the Secretary of War 1913, p. 86. (Hereinafter referred to as RPC.)

21. Conditions in the Philippines: A Speech Delivered by Dean C. Worcester, Manila, October 13, 1913, p. 18. (Hereinafter referred to as Worcester, Conditions in the Philippines.) Describing the Filipino politicians as "the horse-leech's daughter crying, Give! Give!," Worcester exclaimed, "they will not cease constantly to demand powers which they are as yet wholly unfit to exercise until something has been taken away from them. It may be a novel and instructive experience for them to discover that this could be done."

22. O. Garfield Jones, "Teaching Citizenship to Filipinos by Local Self-Government," American Political Science Review, XVIII-2 (1924), 295.

23. Among the key personalities in this endeavor were General H. W. Lawton and Dean C. Worcester, who re-established town governments in the secured areas adjacent to Manila.

24. The early American ideas were based to a great extent on the Maura reforms introduced by the Spanish in 1893. These reforms were mainly an effort to liberalize the older Spanish structure in order to allow for more local autonomy. Five-member town councils (with one member serving as capitán)

were to be elected by the 12 principalía of the pueblo. These councils were to handle local problems, administer public works projects, and collect revenues. Due to the Revolution, however, these reforms were never effectively implemented. See Jose P. Laurel, Local Government in the Philippines (Manila, 1926), chapter iv.

25. This code was the basis of municipal government during the Taft years and in 1916 it was incorporated in the Administrative Code and in that form it remained predominantly the same throughout the American period and after. See Joseph Ralston Hayden, The Philippines: A Study in National Development (New York, 1942), pp. 264-65.

26. Schurman Report, I, 90.

27. "The President's Instructions to the Commission," (April 7, 1900), as quoted in Forbes, II, appendix vii, 442.

28. Special Report of . . . Taft, p. 23. See also John H. Romani and M. Ladd Thomas, A Survey of Local Government in the Philippines (Manila, 1954), pp. 120-21, and Virgil B. Zimmerman, "Philippine Clues to the Future of Local Government in South-East Asia," Journal of African Administration, XII-1 (1960), 39-40. Often the great dependence on the Spanish friar for decision-making at the local level was viewed as the main cause for a lack of self-reliance among local officials.

29. The main reason for integrating towns was due to their meager populations and/or financial potential. By 1903 there were some 1,035 municipalities, and after reorganization (1905-1906) there were 597. The number of towns, however, grew rapidly, reaching 1,173 by 1927. Forbes, I, 157. See also the Reports of the Executive Secretary in RPC, 1904-1913. Oftentimes the ability of local leaders to gain the "independence" of their town through their contacts in Manila could greatly enhance their political popularity, and dealings in this matter were an important factor in early central-local politics. Cf. Mary Hollnsteiner, The Dynamics of Power in a Philippine Municipality (Manila, 1963), pp. 39-40.

30. [U.S. Philippine Commission], The Municipal Code, Act
    No. 82, (Manila, 1905), pp. 4-6. By 1905 the term of office
    for town officials was two years. The following people were
    eligible to vote: all legal residents, twenty-six years and
    over, who 1) were previous office holders; 2) paid at least
    30 pesos in taxes or had property valued at 500 pesos or
    more; or 3) could speak, read, and write English or Spanish.
    Ibid., p. 6. These high qualifications severely limited the
    suffrage. In 1903 an estimated 2.44% of the population, which
    consisted mostly of the principalía and ilustrado classes,
    was qualified to vote. The voting qualifications remained
    the same up to 1916, when the franchise was expanded to
    include those who could read and write a native dialect.
    See Hayden, p. 266.

31. Municipal Code, p. 19.

32. Prior to the first elections in 1902, provincial governors
    and town officials were appointed by the Commission. By
    1903 there were 34 "regularly organized" provinces operating
    among most of the Christian Filipino population.

33. See RPC 1901, I, 21. There were naturally other function-
    aries at the provincial level, e.g., the secretary (at first
    appointed by the Civil Governor, and after 1904 selected
    by the provincial governor), the fiscal (prosecuting attorney),
    the assessor, the justices of the peace and the judges of
    first instance (all appointed by the Civil Governor with the
    consent of the Commission). Except for the latter, almost
    all of these positions were filled by Filipinos from the
    beginning, thus greatly increasing the number of Filipinos
    at this level of the government. See Hayden, p. 266.

34. RPC 1901, I, 9.

35. RPC 1903, I, 687. It is important in this regard to note that
    the influence of American teachers at the local level (and to
    a lesser degree Constabulary officers) is not discussed in
    this paper. The impact of their work in local political
    education remains a neglected study.

36. Special Report of. . . Taft, p. 34. See also RPC 1903, I,
    83-84.

37. RPC 1903, I, 84. In 1908, after making a similar statement,
    Taft quickly reminded his American readers not to be too
    hasty in their judgment of Philippine local government,
    since municipal government in the United States "has not
    been such a shining success." Special Report of . . . Taft,
    p. 37. Since most of the irregularities and offenses dis-
    cussed throughout this paper are commonly referred to as
    "corruption," it is necessary here to say a few words about
    this subject. The main purpose of this paper is to illustrate
    some of the problems experienced by the Americans in
    attempting to establish democracy as they envisioned it at
    the local level; and for this reason it does not focus on
    "corruption" as such, with all of its contemporary impli-
    cations. In fact the word itself has been intentionally
    avoided. It should be noted that "corruption" has never
    been the exclusive possession of Filipinos. American
    history is replete with examples of "corrupt" public
    servants, even during a comparable time period. See
    for example, William L. Riordon (recorder), Plunkitt of
    Tammany Hall: A Series of Very Plain Talks on Very
    Practical Politics (New York, 1963), which was first
    published in 1905. Furthermore, a considerable number
    of Americans in the early years of colonial rule in the
    Philippines, especially at the provincial level, were heavily
    involved in embezzling government funds, a situation which
    brought great embarrassment to the early planners and
    high administrators. Many of the important problems of
    dealing with the phenomenon of corruption and some of the
    difficulties of applying it to cross-cultural studies are
    discussed in James C. Scott, "An Essay on the Political
    Functions of Corruption," Asian Studies (Quezon City),
    V-3 (1966).

38. Forbes, I, 154-55. One of the first things done by the
    Commission at this time was to fix the salaries of municipal
    officials to correspond to a certain percentage of their town's
    total tax intake. In 1905 a system of travelling district
    auditors under the Insular Auditor was added to this scheme
    to further guarantee a rigid check on the activities of the town
    treasurers as well as the provincial treasurers.

39. RPC 1907, I, 152.

40. This act was dated October 4, 1905. Ibid., I, 151.

41. RPC 1906, I, 101. Taft claims that the supervisors were removed primarily because the requirements of the position were a financial burden on the province. Special Report of. . . Taft, p. 32.

42. The date of this act was October 20, 1906. At the same time the election of provincial governors was changed to a popular vote. Provincial boards remained in this form throughout the Taft period. See RPC 1907, I, 151-52, and Forbes, I, 162.

43. RPC 1907, I, 44-45. Hayden, p. 270, suggested that one reason for these changes was that the Filipinos had "already gained much experience in administration." This seems highly unlikely after only six years.

44. Forbes, I, 162.

45. According to Hayden, p. 270, the Filipino majority on the provincial boards reduced the pressure on the provincial treasurers, who were able at this time to function with less difficulty. All of the activities of the provincial treasurers, and much of the financial control over local governments, were centralized in the Executive Bureau. See Hayden, p. 272.

46. Hayden, p. 266.

47. This change was made on November 1, 1905. RPC 1906, I, 101.

48. Jones, pp. 290-91. The Executive Bureau was normally required to inspect the titles of all municipal acts and if it so desired could request the full text to be sent for examination. Hayden, p. 272.

49. Report of the Executive Secretary, RPC 1908, I, 149.

50. For the specific duties see the Report of the Executive Secretary in RPC 1904, I, 341.

51. Quoted in Forbes, I, 155-56. The statement is, of course, an exaggeration.

52. Hayden, p. 276, and Barrows, p. 17.

53. "The peculiar conditions existing [in the Philippines] demand a centralized control of the public-school education. There should be careful State supervision of all public schools." RPC 1900, p. 108. See also Manuel Lacuesta, "Foundations of an American Education System in the Philippines," Philippine Social Science and Humanities Review, XXIII-2/4 (1958), 130-36. Local health boards were also abandoned at this time in favor of a District Health Officer directly responsible to Manila. See Barrows, p. 17.

54. Commenting on the whole process of centralization of services, Hayden, p. 276, noted that "this arrangement reduces enormously the sphere of local government." In 1908 Taft continued to claim that local governments were autonomous. He based this contention strictly on the fact that they elected their own officials. Special Report of . . . Taft, pp. 32-33.

55. Special Report of . . . Taft, pp. 16-17.

56. At the outset Filipino leaders placed heavy emphasis on expanding the powers of local governments, and much enthusiasm was exhibited for local politics and elections. Thus the provincial election in 1907 attracted fifty percent more voters than the election for the Philippine Assembly held the same year. See Dapen Liang, The Development of Philippine Political Parties (Hong Kong, 1939), pp. 89-90.

57. Special Report of . . . Taft, p. 46.

58. See Forbes, I, 156, and Dean C. Worcester [and J. R. Hayden], The Philippines, Past and Present (New York, 1930), pp. 682-84.

59. Worcester described the Harrison period as "a return to the conditions of the Spanish days," which to him was an era of poor government with almost no restraint on the activities of government officials. See Worcester's very

informative letter to the Wood-Forbes Mission (August 4, 1921), in the Worcester Papers (Michigan Historical Collections), Box 2. Hayden, p. 282, also put heavy blame on Harrison for a decline in the quality of local government.

60. Hayden, p. 272.

61. In fact, Hayden, p. 269, has contended that "local governments were given the widest powers consistent with the lowest allowable minimum of good government and the power of supervision was, in most instances, confined to the disallowance of acts which exceeded the legal authority of local officials."

62. RPC 1905, I, 101.

63. Worcester [and Hayden], p. 282.

64. Forbes, II, 83.

65. RPC 1903, I, 694. A similar view is given by a different Law Clerk in RPC 1904, I, 342.

66. See for example Appendix I, Case I.

67. RPC 1903, I, 694.

68. RPC 1905, I, 101.

69. "The number of this class of cases reaching this Bureau every year is very large." Ibid.

70. For a good example of how the central government utilized the political patronage wielded by the provincial governments in order to inspire more efforts in road building, see Forbes, I, 370-77.

71. See Appendix III, Table I. This tendency was particularly evident during the administration of Governor-General Forbes (1909-1913).

72. This statement appears as part of a debate on Assembly Bill No. 1 during a joint conference of the Philippine

Assembly committee leaders and the Philippine Commission
held on two different occasions, the first on March 13, 1908,
and the second on March 24, 1908. See Journal of the
Philippine Commission (Manila, 1910), pp. 423-53. Governor-
General Smith's quote appears on p. 443.

73. Forbes, I, 156. See also Appendix III, Table I, which shows
all cases, including those not acted on prior to the end of
each respective fiscal year.

74. Special Report of . . . Taft, pp. 33-34.

75. The basis for this statement derives from the "Personal and
Police History of Deputies to the First Filipino Assembly,"
WPC, Documents, Vol. XI, Item No. 18. Although the record
is incomplete, it shows that out of 54 deputies listed (from
the original 80), 32 had been accused of at least one illicit
act or irregularity in a lower government post before 1907;
many had multiple charges, and several had been convicted
in the courts, forced to resign, or were removed from office.
The most common charges were neglect of duty and abuse of
authority (17), election protests and/or violations of the
election laws (10), giving sympathy and/or aid to the
insurrectos (7), bribery (3), swindling (2), extortion,
violating an oath, brigandage, fraud, illegal land registration and attempted rape (1 each). One good example
was Juan Villamor (Ilocos Sur), who, according to an
American general, was responsible (along with his fellow
officials) for a reign of terror and assassination in 1901
while he was serving as provincial secretary; nonetheless,
in 1902, he was elected provincial governor, and by 1907
he was a deputy in the Assembly.

76. RPC 1910, p. 50. See also Appendix II, Table III. As early
as 1905 Filipinos had been filling the posts of deputy
provincial treasurers.

77. In 1909 Manuel Yriarte was promoted to this position.
RPC 1909, pp. 92-93.

78. RPC 1904, I, 341. The responsibilities of this branch of
the Law Division, which were "considerable," consisted
of general supervision over municipal officers and the

proceedings and complaints against them, and "generally the briefing of and preparation for action of all papers ." RPC 1905, I, 113. The rapid Filipinization of the Bureau in general can be seen in Appendix II, Table IV.

79. RPC 1906, I, 106. Much of this problem was due to the relatively low salaries offered by the Philippine service in comparison to similar stateside positions and because of the "hazardous" climate.

80. Referring to a later period, Hayden, p. 274, suggested that "in view of its power and central position it is perhaps inevitable that the Executive Bureau should have become a very important factor in Philippine party politics." He claims that it was unclear how well the "permanent personnel of the Bureau" kept themselves removed from partisan politics.

81. RPC 1905, I, 90; RPC 1906, I, 98.

82. See Appendix III, Table III, for the specific nature of all charges brought against municipal officials up to 1913.

83. One group of municipal officials was found charging people a fee in order to leave town for any reason. See Forbes, I, 154-55.

84. See "Memorandum of the Chief of the Law Division re: voluntary contribution, March 6, 1907," in WPC, Documents, Vol. I, No. 26.

85. Ibid.

86. RPC 1913, p. 40.

87. See Appendix III, Table III.

88. It is interesting to note here that after the establishment of the Philippine Assembly, the Filipinos frequently sought legislation that would amend the Municipal Code in order to return some of the authority over municipal treasurers back to the council. In 1908 the Assembly got the Commission to accept a law that required the municipal treasurers

to be appointed from a list of three eligibles selected by the
municipal council. Since the town treasurers were still
subject to the direct supervision of the provincial treasurers, this law did not contribute significantly to the council's effort to regain control; it did, however, show their
concern in this direction. Several other attempts were
made along this line by the Assembly, but most of these
were rejected by the Commission. See Journal of the
Philippine Commission, 1st Legis., 1st sess., 1908,
p. 193, and 2nd Legis., 1st sess., 1911, p. 447.

89. Hayden, pp. 903-04.

90. Many similar techniques used at the time are described in
Hollnsteiner, p. 40.

91. RPC 1906, I, 138.

92. Ibid., pp. 138-39. See also Jones, pp. 292-93.

93. Cited in Forbes, II, 165.

94. Ibid.

95. Ibid., II, 123.

96. RPC 1904, I, 315-16. See also Barrows, p. 32.

97. Forbes, II, 165.

98. RPC 1913, p. 85. See also Appendix III, Table III, and
Forbes, II, 123-24, where he gives the statistics on election
protests and violations.

99. See Appendix III, Table III.

100. Special Report of . . . Taft, p. 23.

101. RPC 1905, I, 114. For a breakdown of the number and
nature of these charges and others, see Appendix III,
Tables I, II, and III.

102. <u>RPC 1911</u>, p. 39. The same idea is also expressed in
     <u>RPC 1907</u>, I, 162.

103. <u>Special Report of . . . Taft</u>, pp. 35-36.

104. See Appendix III, Table IV. It is interesting to note that
     in 1906 the Executive Secretary suggested that the decrease
     in cases against provincial officials was partly due to
     "the elimination from the service of the class of adventur-
     ers or soldiers of fortune of the early days of American
     occupation." <u>RPC 1906</u>, I, 115.

105. <u>Special Report of . . . Taft</u>, pp. 37-38.

106. See, e.g., Appendix I, Case II.

107. For the attitude of Forbes see Robert Spector, "W. Cameron
     Forbes in the Philippines: A Study in Proconsular Power,"
     <u>JSEAH</u>, VII-2 (1966), 75-77, 80-81. The attitude of
     Worcester is expressed well in Worcester, <u>Conditions
     in the Philippines</u>, his retirement speech given in Manila
     in 1913. See also Hayden's biography of him in <u>Philippines,
     Past and Present</u>.

108. Forbes, I, 166-67. Commenting in 1942 on the American
     efforts, Hayden, p. 264, stressed that "these four decades
     of provincial and local government afford an example of
     the extreme difficulty of altering the ingrained political
     habits of a people, especially in that part of the govern-
     ment which touches them the most."

109. Forbes, I, 98.

110. Friend, p. 20.

111. See Salamanca, pp. 94-95. Had it been in the character of
     the Americans to attempt significant interference into the
     economic base of the Filipino elite, it is quite likely that
     the latter would have offered forceful resistance.

112. Taft continued, "But we were anxious to give them as much
     power as could be trusted to them as a means of educating
     them to the responsibility of a self-governing people."

Taken from Taft's speech to the Brooklyn Institute of Arts and Sciences (November 19, 1913) in Forbes, II, 503.

113. RPC 1906, I, 140.

114. Worcester, Conditions in the Philippines, p. 18. He warned against any further accommodation and declared that such acts were futile gestures in the light of the constant demands of the Filipino politicians. Oscar Alfonso also contends that the early American administrators were often willing to sacrifice efficiency and honesty if the official in question was sufficiently pro-American. Alfonso, "Expediency . . ." pp. 250-52.

115. Hayden, pp. 277, 289.

116. Barrows, p. 59, pointed out, however, that "material improvements" were "not difficult to men who can draw upon the organized resources and trained effectiveness of the modern world."

117. See Hayden, p. 272, and Romani and Thomas, pp. 83-84, 122.

118. See Hayden, p. 272. After the Jones Law of 1916 there seemed to be a trend among the high ranking Filipino leaders to increase the centralization of the government begun by the Spanish and continued under the Americans. This trend culminated in the constitution of the Philippine Commonwealth, which made local governments little more than administrative units under the direct control of the Philippine President.

119. Salvador Lopez views the lack of an effort to build self-reliance at the local level as "one of the most glaring failures of the American colonial regime." Salvador Lopez, "The Colonial Relationship," The Philippines and the United States, ed. Frank Golay (Englewood Cliffs, N.J., 1966), p. 21.

120. See Spector, pp. 76, 80. Barrows, p. 74, attacked Forbes on this position and argued that "it seems idle to urge the Filipinos to diminish their interest in . . . political advance

of their race and unstatesmanlike not to recognize that the problems of consummate difficulty in the Philippines will continue to be political in character."

121. Quoted in Forbes, I, 154-55.

Conflict in the Philippine Legislature:
The Commission and the Assembly from 1907 to 1913

by

Frank Jenista, Jr.

The history of Filipino participation in the American colonial government of the Philippines dates from the earliest years of United States rule. Two months after the outbreak of Philippine-American hostilities in 1899, the Schurman Commission tried to stop the fighting by assuring the Filipino people of self-government in the future. In 1901 the promise began to be fulfilled with the institution of local autonomy under the Municipal Code of 1901. A year later the United States Congress took a further step and passed the Organic Act of 1902 which authorized the establishment of a bicameral Philippine Legislature two years after the completion and enumeration of the 1903 Census. In July, 1907, following the Governor-General's declaration that a state of peace and tranquillity prevailed in the Islands, elections were held. In October, eighty Filipino representatives met in Manila's Ayuntamiento building for the inauguration of the First Philippine Assembly.

Until October, 1907, all Insular legislation had originated in the Philippine Commission, a group of seven to nine Filipino and American administrators. The Commission retained sole legislative jurisdiction over the Special (i.e. Non-Christian) Provinces but shared its other law-making responsibilities with the new Philippine Assembly. The Assembly was comparable in many ways to the United States House of Representatives and was in most respects the equal of the Commission. Bills of either house had to be approved by the other to become law.

Soon after the opening session of the new bicameral legislature difficulties arose between the Commission and the Assembly and relations steadily deteriorated until the advent of the Harrison administration in 1913. These legislative skirmishes were important because they represented the political aspect of a larger conflict between American and Philippine concepts of government. The Philippine Commission had begun the work of creating in the Philippines a republic fashioned on the American model. The Commission, convinced of the moral propriety of its program and strengthened by seven years of legislative experience, was determined to see its foundational work continued. The Philippine Assembly, representative of a traditional aristocracy, was equally anxious to use its newly acquired power to control the course of Insular legislation. The Filipino elite wanted to gather as much political influence as possible in order to nullify unattractive Commission proposals and to ensure retention of their traditional positions as spokesmen for the Filipino people. The determination of both houses to realize their often antagonistic goals produced the conflict which marred the first five years of bicameral legislation in the Philippines.

When the Malolos government disintegrated under American pressure, the position of national leadership it had temporarily held was quickly assumed by the Philippine Commission. The American Commissioners during the Taft Era (1900-1913) were capable and sincere idealists, dedicated to a Kiplingesque mission of educating and uplifting the Filipino masses. They were persuaded that their aims for the Philippines were altruistic and would benefit the Filipino people. Convinced of the innate superiority of their republican institutions, the Commissioners attempted to transplant them bodily into the Philippine nation. The Americans paid little attention to traditions which conflicted with their intention to make the Philippines a testing ground for the democratic experiment in Asia. Without responsibility to a capricious but controlling electorate, the Commissioners were free to pass unpopular laws when such legislation was deemed beneficial to Philippine development. Modernization could be legislated whether or not it was desired by the Filipinos. Universal education was introduced in the mistaken hope that it would break down the aristocratic nature of the society and provide a truly independent electorate on which the proposed republic could be based. American officials in all areas tried to impress upon their Filipino wards the value of efficiency in government administration. This ideology of efficiency was applied in all areas and Filipino officials were expected to adhere to its principles. A merit-oriented civil service was established to alleviate the

problem of personal considerations in the conduct of official
business. Judicial procedures were reviewed in an effort to
avoid abuses. Roads and schools were built. Tax structures
were streamlined.

For the first seven years the Commission acted as overseer
for much of this nation-building. The Filipino Commissioners
constituted a significant minority and appear, for the most part,
to have accepted the standards of their American counterparts.
They supported with considerable zeal the same policy of modernization. It was a very rare occurrence, even during the stormy
period toward the end of the Taft Era, for Commission votes to
be divided along ethnic lines.

The reluctance of the Commissioners to abandon their program
of modernization in the face of Assembly opposition was not understood by their opponents in the Philippines or the United States.
The Commissioners' fervent dedication to what they considered
progress for the Philippines and their almost Quixotic egotism
was well expressed by W. Cameron Forbes, himself a Commissioner and Philippine Governor-General:

> The Commissioners, with their keen American minds,
> their sense of justice and dislike of delay, display, sham
> and subterfuge, were turned loose upon a world of
> medieval mismanagement and abuse like a group of
> knight-errants looking for wrongs to right and abuses
> to end. They found plenty of these and literally worked
> themselves sick in their efforts to bring into the Islands
> the blessing of the kind of administration to which
> Americans have become so accustomed.[1]

This cultural arrogance and impassioned dedication made
the natural conflict between the Commission and the Assembly
all the more inevitable. The Philippine press often railed
against the Commission's assumption that it knew what was best
for the Philippines. The Americans were genuinely "imbued
with a desire to serve the best interests of the Filipinos,"[2] but
their views of what was in the Filipinos' best interests differed
markedly from those of the Assembly.

The educated and nationalistic Assemblymen were sensitive
to the Commission's repeated intimations that it knew better than
the Assembly in matters of government, and the popular view of

the Assembly as "a harmless little debating society"[3] did not help to soothe the friction. The Commission accepted the necessity of working with the Assembly because it accepted the United States' declared goal of eventual Philippine autonomy, but subtly resented its formation because the existence of the Assembly made the process of legislation more difficult and decreased administrative efficiency.[4]

It was much easier for the Commissioners to accept the existence of the Assembly than to work whole-heartedly with some of the delegates who comprised it. A large number of the Assemblymen had been associated with the Malolos government and their presence caused some initial apprehension that the Assembly would become a center for revolutionary ferment.[5] The threat failed to materialize but it did contribute to Commission suspicions of any Assembly legislation which infringed on Insular authority.

Concerned as they were with honesty and efficiency, the Commission hesitated to welcome into the government men whose past records did not fit American conceptions of good citizenship. After the Assembly elections in 1907 the Insular government culled its files and produced a security profile on the elected representatives. This "Personal and Police History of the Deputies to the First Filipino Assembly" gave the Commission some cause for uneasiness. Several delegates had been requested to resign from previous positions in the Insular government because of malfeasance in office, the most notable among them the representative from Tayabas, Manuel Quezon.[6]

Suspicion of the Assembly's motives, distrust of certain delegates with records of previous misbehavior and a subtle resentment against the Assembly for its contribution to greater inefficiency exacerbated the difficulties between the two legislative branches from the start. Though the Commissioners evinced an apparently genuine desire to cooperate with the lower house,[7] the interests of the two houses were too divergent to permit the development of an overall unity of purpose. The Commission's legislative proposals were in keeping with its intention to construct a modern, efficient and essentially mass-based republic, while the Assembly reflected the values and traditions of a much different society.

Prestige and influence in Philippine society were traditionally based on kinship groups and their associated followers. Certain prominent, wealthy families exercised de facto control over the political activities of people within their municipality. These self-perpetuating elite groups spoke for the Filipino people. They were the patrons of the patron-client relationships common throughout Philippine society. They expected and received obligatory support from those indebted to them either economically or socially. Most of the members of this ilustrado clique seem to have supported the Philippine government at Malolos until American military strength fragmented it. This politically pragmatic elite then turned from Aguinaldo and cooperated with the new colonial government in the hope of retaining its property and social standing. The tactic was successful in preserving personal fortunes from the ravages of war and left traditional power bases intact. Though its highest offices were filled by Americans, the new government did not significantly alter the traditional social patterns which gave this indigenous aristocracy its influence. Certainly whatever changes did occur during the American interregnum had not taken place by 1901 when the Municipal Code was put into operation. The Filipino elite naturally gravitated toward the local and provincial offices opened to them and adopted the new American names for their traditional positions of local authority. Elective offices on the municipal or provincial levels were consistently filled by members of the leading families or by figureheads who held the office under elite aegis.

When the Assembly came into being in 1907 it provided another upward step in the Filipinos' attempt to regain primacy in Philippine affairs. Though the supreme powers of government had escaped them in 1899, the elite had managed to retain their influence in Philippine society. As each new office was opened to Filipinos, it was filled by members of this educated upper class. The ilustrados were continuing the abortive revolution through evolution. Once armed conflict had proved futile, the most obvious way for the Filipinos to retrieve their briefly-held positions of national leadership was to take full advantage of the Insular system and make it perform to their advantage. Until 1907 the elite had little ability to control Insular programs except insofar as they could be bent or evaded on the local level. The formation of the Assembly significantly increased Filipino capabilities to redirect American policy in the Philippines.

The Filipino delegates elected to the First Philippine Assembly in June of 1907 were, on the whole, young, aristocratic and well-educated. Many had been to Europe for schooling and fifty of the eighty were lawyers. Nine were under thirty years of age, the majority (47) were between thirty and forty and only ten were over fifty. The Speaker of the House, Sergio Osmeña, was thirty. [8]

The Assemblymen represented the educated upper class of the Philippines and seem to have been the direct descendents of the ilustrado group which developed in the last half of the nineteenth century. That the Assembly was in fact another extension of this politically pragmatic and socially conservative elite is apparent from the number of representatives who held office under the Spanish or Malolos governments. Twenty-one (26%) of the Assemblymen had held positions of varying importance during the Spanish period. Of these twenty-one, eleven were also in the Malolos government and two were in the revolutionary army. Nearly seventy-five percent of the delegates had served in civil or military capacities with the Malolos Republic, and seventy-three of the eighty had held office under the Insular government. [9]

The electoral qualifications established in 1901 by the Insular authorities on the advice of the educated Filipinos kept the number of eligible voters in each district small during the Taft Era. The smallest district had 165 voters, the largest just over 1,000. [10] There was no public opinion in the Western sense and the delegates often were elected to the Assembly by personal or family arrangement with other aristocratic members of the electorate. Class consciousness was pronounced. A number of Assemblymen in 1907 bore names still influential today, among them the Osmeñas of Cebu and the Singsons of Ilocos, an indication of the long-term political prominence of this elite.

While the Assembly did serve as a vehicle for the display of social standing and enabled delegates to reinforce their status as regional leaders, its most important contribution to Philippine advancement was the opportunity it gave Filipinos to originate, modify or reject Insular legislation. The centralized colonial administration had instituted changes from the top, changes which were usually beneficial but were often distasteful (strict quarantine for diseased carabaos, for example). Until 1907 the only recourse to undesirable legislation was evasion, a measure which varied in its effectiveness and always carried with it a distant threat of punishment. The existence of the Assembly gave the Filipino people, through their ilustrado representatives, an opportunity to tailor new laws to the Philippine situation. Nine years after they had lost formal Philippine leadership, a large number of Malolos officials were being given a chance to go beyond their local or regional power bases and regain some of their previous national authority.

That the Filipinos would eventually be reinstated as leaders of the Philippine nation was clear. The ideal of education and emancipation had been part of America's imperial rhetoric from the beginning. The increasing number of schools, the presence of Filipinos in important government offices and the establishment of the Assembly itself were all indications that the rhetoric was backed by actual intent. The question in Filipino minds was how long the period of tutelage would last.

William Howard Taft, then Secretary of War, answered this question in his address to the inaugural session of the Philippine Assembly. Taft praised the opening of the Assembly as a step toward more responsibility and eventual independence, but cautioned: "When I was in the Islands the last time, I ventured the opinion that it [independence] would take more than a generation. I have not changed my view upon this point. "[11]

This speech appears to have been a significant factor in the Assembly's attempt to achieve a larger measure of control over Insular programs. Prior to this time the Democratic Party in the United States had offered the hope of immediate independence at every election. Taft had carefully prefaced his remarks to the Assembly by saying, "I can not speak with the authority of one who may control policy, "[12] but his election to the Presidency the following year gave him the authority he lacked in 1907. The members of the Assembly who had favored a cooperative policy in the hope of quick autonomy had to reappraise their stand, and those who had advocated opposition to Insular policies gained new support for their arguments.

In its reassessment of the Philippines' future, the Assembly was faced with the problem of finding an evolutionary but effective way to obviate the long-term Republican intentions. Two different

routes to national prominence offered possible solutions. The
Assemblymen could try to open more offices at the highest levels
of government and move directly into positions of authority or,
alternately, they could continue their traditional policy of
strengthening Filipino control in the local/rural areas by
decentralizing the Insular government's administrative structure.
Both avenues promised some reward, but more options were
open to the legislators who concentrated their efforts on the
government's substructures.

The First Philippine Assembly faced a number of problems
universal to young legislatures. Though the delegates did not
lack education and carried out their duties with due regard for
the rules of parliamentary procedure, inexperience understandably and unavoidably created difficulties. As a result, a considerable amount of the Assembly's activity was dysfunctional. A large
number of bills drawn up and passed by the lower house were
returned by the Commission on the grounds that they were poorly
written. In the second session of the First Legislature, nine
separate Assembly bills were refused passage by the Commission
and their provisions were subsequently embodied in one bill
dealing with electoral law. Another five were likewise reordered
into one education act.[13]

Commission Secretary William H. Donovan expressed that
body's view of the problems bred by the Assembly's lack of
practical experience in government. Following the recess of the
First Legislature, he reported to the Governor-General that on
the last two days of the session sixty-four bills and resolutions
had been received by the Commission, compared to seventy-two
in the previous eighty-eight days.[14] The Commission responded
to the sudden surge of legislation by tabling most of it. Though
a number of the bills were hastily and inadvisably constructed,
Donovan noted that "had some of these bills been received earlier,
they might have been passed by the Commission with amendments
and be law by now."[15]

Not all of the bills rejected by the Commission were submitted during the rush. Soon after the beginning of the bicameral
legislative sessions, the Spanish-language newspapers began to
criticize the Commissioners for their intransigence. The validity
of the charge was obvious from the Commission's record. Seventy-
eight of the one hundred thirty-eight bills and resolutions received

by the Commission during the final session of the First Legislature were rejected.[16] The inexperience of the Assembly no doubt contributed to the high rate of attrition, but the percentage of Commission rejection was consistently above fifty percent during the Taft Era, indicating the presence of a more significant problem than Assembly inexperience.

The Filipino Assemblymen had been raised and educated under Spanish rule and seem to have accepted the traditional Spanish view of public office as a mandate for monetary and social aggrandizement. This perception was inevitably reflected in Assembly bills despite reprimands and repeated rejections of personal legislation by the Commission. On the first day of business, for example, the Assemblymen voted themselves a substantial and apparently unwarranted increase in per diem pay.[17] This action, because of its apparent universality among legislators, does not of itself indicate Assembly cupidity, but it may be significant when associated with other similar attempts to increase Assembly (and elite) revenues. Most of the ilustrados, in their Spanish positions as principalía (municipal leaders) had been in charge of tax collection and often had been exempt themselves. The new bureaucracy made taxation less easy to avoid and the Assembly passed a number of tax measures which would have enabled them to evade taxes again. The land taxes, in particular, were the focus of several Assembly bills. Bill 352 of the First Legislature proposed a five-year tax exemption for all uncultivated land outside Manila, a measure with obvious benefits for the holders of large unfarmed tracts.[18] Other tax bills exempted all land worth less than fifty pesos from land taxes and gave the provincial board (which was two-thirds elective) the right to suspend land taxes in the province for up to two years.[19]

It is difficult to differentiate between personal legislation and that submitted as part of the Assembly's political obligations. Given the unanimity of interests between the Assembly and the upper class which controlled electoral proceedings, tax measures could serve equally well as personal and class legislation. A large number of Assembly bills appear to have been political payoffs. It was to the Assembly's political advantage to have a watchdog Commission shepherding the new lower house. The Filipino representatives could propose legislation intended to fulfill obligations to their constituents with the confidence that the Commission would nullify irresponsible but politically attractive laws.[20] The Commission was aware of its role as a political foil and tried, unsuccessfully in the long run, to slow it down by allowing some of the questionable measures to pass if, in the words of Governor-General Smith, "there was no real damage to the general situation."[21] In one instance the Commission permitted an Assembly bill to pass which authorized 34,000 pesos to send a delegate to the International Navigation Congress in St. Petersburg even though by the time it reached the Commission it was impossible for a delegate to reach the Congress on time. Then, following their approval of the Assembly measure, the Commissioners submitted a bill of their own authorizing a more reasonable 4,000 pesos to send two representatives to a Tuberculosis Conference in Paris, a meeting which the Commission felt to be considerably more important for the Philippines.[22]

The poor construction of some Assembly bills, their susceptibility to manipulation and the frequent political gamesmanship contributed to the high rate of Commission rejection, but the most important measures to be turned aside by the upper chamber were those which tried to weaken the Insular administration's regulative power. These bills attempted either to open the highest government offices to Filipinos or to increase the administrative responsibilities of local political units.

The former approach was not often used during the Taft Era for it meant certain confrontation with a Commission which was determined to maintain what remained of its weakened authority. The most direct Assembly move in this area occurred during the second session of the First Legislature. The Assembly proposed that the Commission agree on Joint Resolution 26, a resolution which petitioned the United States Congress to dismantle the Commission and appoint a Philippine Senate in its place.[23] W. Cameron Forbes noted in the Journal of the Philippine Commission that in this measure the Assembly faced squarely the question of United States control in the Philippines, for control of the upper house would have given complete control of appropriations--and therefore the government--to the Filipinos.[24]

The clear opposition of the Commission to yielding immediate control to the Filipinos made such direct attempts to gain national authority rare. Since the Commission was sure to negate legislation designed to place Filipinos in the highest offices, the Assembly resorted to its alternative and tried to reduce the effectiveness of the government's centralized administration. The Filipino elite's strength usually came from local/rural areas where social institutions created an aristocratic class with considerable ability to determine regional politics. Diffusing the government's bureaucratic centralism was effective for it brought Insular activities within range of the elite's local influence. The most significant bills for the purpose of this study, therefore, are those which, if enacted, would have altered the ability of the Insular government to administer its programs efficiently.[25]

Under American rule the Philippine court structure retained most of its Spanish character. Local justices of the peace ruled on minor infractions of the law. More serious crimes were heard by circuit judges from the regional Court of First Instance. Assembly Bill 23 proposed to modify the judicial structure by instituting jury trial. The American officials who had elected to leave the Spanish system intact did so because they realized the dangers of jury trial to judicial equity in a society based on kinship ties and personal obligations. This Assembly measure would have exposed the litigants to the vagaries of Philippine social relations and would also have given the provincial board (which presumably reflected the will of the majority party) the authority to select the jurors from a list submitted by the elite-dominated municipal council. The net result of the act, if enacted, would have been to remove the administration of justice from the hands of appointed judges (who, though often partisan, were at least subject to Civil Service discipline), and place it in the hands of the local and provincial politicians.[26]

As attempts to bring political influence into the theoretically apolitical Civil Service became common, sharp differences emerged between the Commission, which saw itself as the last bulwark of good (i.e., efficient) government, and the Assembly, which felt it was legitimately attempting to regain Filipino supremacy in Philippine affairs. Since the bureaucracy controlled many government functions it was the natural target of most decentralization measures passed by the Assembly.

In 1908 the boldest infringement of this kind took place. Assembly Bill 197 would have effectively abolished the Civil Service Bureau's supervisory and disciplinary functions. The Bureau of Civil Service was to be changed into a "Division of

Civil Service" under the Bureau of Audits. Its major function
was to have been the administration of Civil Service examinations.
If the bill had become law, the Commission felt it would have
eliminated the central control which made the bureaucracy a
relatively efficient administrative tool during the Taft Era. [27]

In the years following the establishment of the Assembly,
Filipino efforts to entrench themselves within the Insular
administration accelerated. The bills of the Second Legislature
and the first session of the Third (up to the Harrison period)
increasingly pressed for the minimization of bureaucratic centralism. [See Appendix II for a more extensive listing of these
bills.] The elite found it could often exert sufficient pressure on
local officials to vitiate Insular intervention if supervision was
weak and threats of discipline were therefore lessened.

The conflict between the elite and the Commission steadily
increased until by 1910 the two chambers were at loggerheads.
The Assembly began to demand the right to initiate all appropriation bills and rejected such Commission bills as infringe-
ments on Assembly privilege. The Commission in turn refused
to give up the prerogative it had held since 1901. The resulting
deadlock[28] prevented the passage of annual appropriation bills
for the last three years of the Taft Era. In 1909 the Organic
Act which had created the bicameral Philippine Legislature was
amended by Congress, authorizing the Governor-General to use
the budget of the previous year until a new bill was passed.
Without this clause the conflict between the Commission and the
Assembly would have flared into a governmental crisis of the
gravest proportions.

This confrontation in the legislature was the political manifestation of a larger and more general conflict in the Philippines.
The Insular administrators and Philippine political leaders held
sharply divergent views on the nature of government and each
group's determination to be successful brought about an inevitable
clash. The brief period of Filipino rule under the Malolos government had contributed to the development of nationalism in the
Philippines. Nationalism provided a convenient and easily mobilized source of support for the ilustrado/Filipino attempt to
re-achieve national prominence during the American period.
Self-determination was the ultimate goal of the Filipino program,
but the upper class which articulated the nationalism and led the

movement was pragmatic enough to settle for pre-eminence in local affairs. The Assembly's attempt to defuse the revolutionary changes the Americans were administering was a traditional move to ensure de facto Philippine control in subnational affairs while pushing for increased representation on the national, policy-making level. During the Spanish era the Filipinos had learned that the obnoxious decrees of a central government could be evaded with sufficient local influence, and the lesson was applied during the first decades of United States rule. Philippine control of local affairs was strengthened initially by the American decision to place municipal government in Filipino hands in 1901. The movement of the Filipino upper class into positions of local author-ity was the continuation of a political pattern evident before and after the American interregnum, and was considerably more complex than a conflict between colonial authority and Philippine nationalism. Leaders of the Philippine nation, whether Spanish governors-general, Malolos ilustrados, American civil governors or Philippine presidents had consistently recognized the need for strong central control if administration policies were to be en-forced on the local level. An equally strong tradition of local autonomy pervaded the rural regions which were subject to the directives of the national government. Members of the principalía who lacked the ability to change the central authority's rulings tried to retain their traditional leadership and local status by building up political influence which, at the municipal or regional level, was superior to that of the national government. Only when concessions were made to this local/rural aristocracy could the policies of the central authority be effectively implemented in the subnational, elite-controlled areas.

This tradition of local autonomy and cacique domination pro-vided a naturally antagonistic force to the democratic idealism of America's program in the Islands. The Commissioners assumed that the Filipino tao wanted freedom from his "feudal" state. They failed to appreciate the complexities of social obligation and the beneficial aspects of traditional patron-client relations. The "white man's burden" articulated by Kipling and others fired the imagination of American zealots who came to the Philippines looking for a world to civilize. These administrators intended to reduce what they considered an oppressive, feudalistic aris-tocracy and construct in the Philippines an honest, efficient and mass-based Philippine Republic. Governor-General James Smith, President of the Philippine Commission, expressed that body's

view of its work in the Philippines in his opening day address to
the second session of the First Legislature:

> Until the great majority of the citizens, and not a
> small minority, have been prepared for the intelligent
> use of the franchise, until democratic customs and
> usages have permeated and become a part of the daily
> life of the people, . . . the best future of the Islands
> lies with the land which has given to the Filipino people
> freedom of speech, liberty of the press, freedom of
> religious worship . . . and many other rights, liberties
> and privileges not enjoyed by peoples which have led
> an independent national existence for hundreds of
> years.[29]

During the Taft Era most Insular administrators, and the
American Commissioners in particular, were convinced that
intervention with the goal of educating and then emancipating
the Filipinos held priority over national self-determination,
especially when an aristocratic class dominated the society to
the presumed detriment of the common people. The educated
Filipino upper class, supported by the vocal anti-Imperialists
in the United States, considered self-rule of paramount importance and made great efforts to achieve it as quickly as possible.
The Commission, though it did not fully realize it, had been
placed in an untenable position. Guilty colonial consciences,
sensitized by exposure to anti-Imperialist lectures on the
immorality of American tinkering in Philippine society, kept
American officials from developing the resolve necessary to
implement their declared goals of efficient administration and
mass-based democracy. The United States was determined to
create in the Philippines an American-style government based
on principles alien to the indigenous society while simultaneously
giving the Filipinos, who did not fully share its ideals, an
increasingly significant role in the formation of the new republic.
In the end, America's dedication to the ideology of efficiency and
its conviction that democracy had to become a Philippine reality
went for naught as the Commission's knight-errants found themselves tilting against the firmly imbedded windmills of Philippine
society and tradition.

APPENDIX I

DELEGATES TO THE FIRST PHILIPPINE ASSEMBLY:
CONTINUITY IN ILUSTRADO AUTHORITY

Previous Governmental Association		Number	Percentage
Spanish civil office		21	26%
Malolos government:			
civil officials	41[a]		
military officers	18	58[b]	73%
Spanish and Malolos positions		13[c]	16%
Neither Spanish nor Malolos offices		17	21%
Insular civil offices:			
provincial governors	10		
other provincial officials	31		
municipal officials	32	73	91%

[a] Includes 2 with revolutionary juntas overseas and three later with the autonomous government of Negros.

[b] One official with both civil and military authority.

[c] Includes 2 with the military during the Malolos period.

Sources:

LeRoy, James A. "The Philippine Assembly," The World Today, XV-2 (1908), 847-852. (WPC)

Nieva, Gregorio (ed.). Official Directory, Philippine Assembly, First Philippine Legislature (Manila, 1908). (WPC)

Tuohy, Anthony R. (ed.). Album Histórico de la Primera Asamblea Filipina (Manila, 1908). (WPC)

APPENDIX II

A SELECT LIST OF ASSEMBLY BILLS DISAPPROVED
BY THE PHILIPPINE COMMISSION:

MEASURES DECENTRALIZING INSULAR AUTHORITY

FIRST LEGISLATURE:

Bill Nos.

23   Jury trial to be established with provincial board exclusively empowered to select jurors from list prepared by municipal councils; jurors to be paid per diems of 2 or 5 pesos.

136   Power of enforcement for Bureau of Health regulations to be transferred from Bureau Director to provincial boards.

148   Administration of educational programs to be placed under control of municipal boards, including authority to decide language and curriculum.

191   Authority of provincial board to remove municipal treasurers to be taken away (not given to anyone else). Appointment of municipal treasurer to be by nomination of municipal council from list of civil service eligibles. (Previously appointed by Civil Service Bureau.)

197   Bureau of Civil Service to be abolished, reorganized as the "Division of Civil Service" under the Bureau of Audits; its primary duty to be the administration of Civil Service examinations. (Would have eliminated the Bureau's regulative capacity over its members.)

236   Election laws to be amended to allow municipal councils to fill their own vacancies. (Provincial boards had been given the authority because the above system had resulted in abuses.)

Bill Nos.

239   Amendment of Cattle Registration Law for the control of rinderpest and rustling. (Would have effectively nullified the law as a police measure.)

308   Assembly to be given the right to audit the accounts of the Insular Auditor.

310   All officers of the provincial board to be elective. (Would have removed the appointive position of provincial treasurer from Civil Service control.)

370   Assembly to be given responsibility for legislation over the Moro territories. (Hitherto governed by the Commission.)

518   Municipal bonds to be posted for police weapons. (Removed individuals from responsibility for loss of firearms entrusted to them.)

532   Duplicate cedula (tax) certificates to be issued upon declaration of loss or destruction of the original. (Only issued previously in special cases when lost or destroyed through no carelessness on the part of the taxpayer and where evidence that tax was paid existed.)

535   Municipal president to be empowered to appoint police in barrios, rural areas.

540   Provincial boards to be granted authority to suspend land taxes for up to two years. (Previously could request suspension for certain periods in cases of disaster, subject to approval of the Governor-General.)

559   Amount of public money expendable without approval of the district engineer to be quadrupled. (Would have resulted in the expenditure of a large proportion of provincial funds on projects needing scientific advice without consultation of an engineer.)

563   Standards for entrance to the Bar to be lowered.

Joint Resolution #25. Philippine Assembly to be authorized
          to legislate for all Special Provinces. (Hitherto
          Commission responsibility.)

Joint Resolution #26. A Philippine Senate to supersede the
          Philippine Commission as the upper chamber of
          the legislature.

SECOND LEGISLATURE:

Bill Nos.

84   Duplicate cedula certificates to be issued (cf. #532,
        First Legislature.)

141   Governor-General's control over provincial boards
        in the matter of road taxes to be eliminated.
        Provincial boards to be allowed to suspend taxes
        for up to two years at their discretion.

162   Provincial treasurer to be allowed to rule on legality
        but not advisability of municipal expenditures. (Would
        have removed control of municipal treasurer's
        expenditures from the provincial treasurer.)

170   Penalties assessed for counterfeiting receipts, stamps
        of the Bureau of Internal Revenue to be reduced.

270   Municipal boards of assessors to be empowered to
        revalue property upon request; provincial board
        prevented from modifying revaluation except on
        appeal. (Would have resulted in reduced revenue
        and control of local boards of assessors.)

303   Bureau of Health to be replaced by a Council of
        Hygiene. (Centralized authority of the Bureau
        would have been nullified; new Council had little
        enforcement capability.)

391   General land survey of the Philippines to be authorized.
        (No qualifications established restricting surveying
        activity to qualified personnel.)

Bill No.

487   Administrative functions to be removed from the
Bureau of Lands. (A further attempt to reduce
the Bureau's strict control of surveyors.)

505   Office of provincial engineer to be established.
(Would have placed responsibility for public works,
formerly in control of the Bureau of Public Works,
in the hands of a provincial official not responsible
to a central office.)

507   Imprisonment as punishment for failure to pay cedula
taxes to be abolished.

539   Municipal council to be given jurisdiction over the
thirty percent of municipal revenue spent within the
town. (Previously, the thirty percent was expended
within the municipality with the approval of the
provincial board.)

613   Office of provincial engineer to be established.
(Cf. #505, Second Legislature.)

660   Municipal control to be established over expenditures
supervised by the provincial board. (Cf. #539,
Second Legislature.)

727   Municipalities to be allowed to tax sand, gravel from
river beds. (Removed rivers from classification as
public domain, made possible local control of
navigable rivers.)

783   Governor-General's authority to disqualify public
officials subject to official investigation to be repealed.

888   Provincial boards to be permitted to remit, suspend
or postpone payment of 1912 land tax; Insular treasury
to reimburse provinces for land taxes collected in 1911.

916   New qualifications to be applied to heads of departments
in Manila. (Would have rendered non-Filipinos
ineligible.)

Bill Nos.

931   Court of Land Registration to be abolished; an
increased number of Courts of First Instance to
be substituted.

978   Restrictions preventing re-election to a provincial
or municipal office except after four years to be
removed.

994   Comprehensive survey of the Philippines to be
undertaken; Bureau of Lands to be abolished and
replaced with a Bureau of Land Registration.
(Would have done away with the strict Civil Service
qualifications for surveyors, taken regulative
capability from the Bureau of Lands.)

THIRD LEGISLATURE, FIRST SESSION:

Bill Nos.

25   Municipal board to be entrusted with disposal of
funds spent by the provincial board. (Cf. #539,
#660, Second Legislature.)

27   Property owners to be guaranteed a position on
municipal board of tax appeals.

66   Land tax of 1913 to be suspended; Insular government
to reimburse municipalities for lost taxes. (Cf. #888,
Second Legislature.)

90   Office of provincial engineer to be created. (Third
attempt to decentralize the Bureau of Public Works,
cf. #505, #613, Second Legislature.)

187   Appointment of chief of municipal police to be taken
from Provincial Governor, given to municipal
president.

212   Fee payments from Justice of the Peace Courts to be
restructured; fines to be paid to municipality.
(Previously paid to the Insular government.)

Bill Nos.

251   Rural guards to be established in all municipalities.
       (Would have interfered with Constabulary operations,
       set up unnecessary armed groups.)

262   Director of Agriculture or agents not to be permitted
       to adopt quarantine measures without the concurrence
       of the provincial board.

304   Municipal councils of provincial capitals to be able
       to fix salaries for municipal officials without regard
       to the limitations of the Municipal Code. (The Code
       based salaries on population, with increases not to
       exceed fifty percent of the established rate.)

312   Forcible occupation of land along public thorough-
       fares to be prohibited. (Intended to stay eviction of
       squatters or uprooting of trees encroaching on
       rights-of-way.)

319   Judges to be prohibited from issuing orders of
       arrest at hours of the night or on other than working
       days.

380   Municipalities to be authorized to let at auction
       municipal excise and other taxes.

Sources

Journal of the Philippine Commission, I-VI (Manila, 1908-1913).

WPC: "Bills of the Philippine Assembly, First Legislature:
    Tabled, Refused Passage, Indefinitely Postponed."
    (Typewritten, bound volume; apparently compiled by Dean
    Worcester, ca. 1910.)

WPC: Documents, Volume XI, Item 12, "Notes on Certain
    Assembly Bills Disapproved by the Philippine Commission
    and on Certain Commission Bills Disapproved by the
    Assembly."

WPC: Documents, Volume XI, Item 17, "A List of Assembly
Bills Disapproved by the Commission and Commission
Bills Disapproved by the Assembly from October 16, 1907
to February 11, 1913, Inclusive."

Notes

1. W. Cameron Forbes, The Philippine Islands (Boston, 1928), I, 141.

2. Ibid., I, 172.

3. Quoted in Dean C. Worcester, The Philippines Past and Present (New York, 1914), II, 772.

4. Charles B. Elliott, The Philippines: To the End of the Commission Government (Indianapolis, 1917), p. 123.

5. James A. Robertson, "The Philippines Since the Inauguration of the Philippine Assembly," American Historical Review, XXII-4 (1917), 817-8.

6. Worcester Philippine Collection (Harlan Hatcher Library, The University of Michigan), Documents and Papers, 1834-1915, Volume XI, Item 12, "Personal and Police History of the Delegates to the First Filipino Assembly." (Hereinafter referred to as WPC, Documents.)

7. Commission President James Smith noted during the first session of the Legislature that "to create in the minds of the Assemblymen . . . the impression that the Commission is an opposing body instead of a cooperative one would be most unfortunate." Journal of the Philippine Commission, II (Manila, 1909), 154. (Hereinafter referred to as JPC.)

8. James A. LeRoy, "The Philippine Assembly," The World Today, XV-2 (1908), 847-8.

9. For a statistical analysis of the delegates' previous governmental associations see Appendix I.

10. LeRoy, p. 849.

11. JPC, I (Manila, 1908), 14.

12. Ibid., 13.

13. WPC: "Bills of the Philippine Assembly, First Legislature: Tabled, Refused Passage, Indefinitely Postponed." (Typewritten, bound volume; apparently compiled by Dean Worcester, ca. 1910.)

14. Ibid.

15. Ibid.

16. Ibid.

17. WPC, Documents, Volume XI, Item 17, "A List of Assembly Bills Disapproved by the Commission and Commission Bills Disapproved by the Assembly from October 16, 1907 to February 11, 1913, Inclusive."

18. Ibid.

19. Ibid.

20. Forbes, I, 158-9.

21. JPC, III (Manila, 1910), 153-4.

22. Forbes, I, 160.

23. JPC, III, 454-8. The new upper house was to have been elected by an elite group of voters. Electors had to fill one of the following qualifications: owner of 10,000 pesos in property, tax payments of over 1,000 pesos per year, director or member of a banking or agricultural corporation, university professor, member of the Philippine Legislature, provincial official, municipal president by election.

24. Ibid., 482.

25. Tax measures are difficult to assess as instruments of decentralization and for that reason have been excluded unless they obviously contributed to Filipino abilities to control Insular functions.

26. WPC, Documents, Volume XI, Item 17, "Bills Disapproved..."

27. Ibid.

28. This is not to say that no legislation passed during the deadlock. When their goals agreed, the two houses worked well together. Education and public works rarely failed to get Assembly support and Commission rejections of such Assembly measures were usually caused by the inability of the Insular treasury to meet large Assembly appropriations.

29. JPC, III, 76.

Philippine Economic Development and American Policy:
A Reappraisal

by

Norman G. Owen

In the political history of the Philippines, 1898 is a clear
turning point, the end of three centuries of Spanish rule and the
inauguration of the "American period." It has often been
assumed by both the critics and defenders of American intervention that the same date also marks the beginning of significant
changes in the economic sphere, and that American policy was
directly responsible for the development of the Philippine
economy over the next forty-odd years. Certainly the United
States, by asserting sovereignty over the Philippines, assumed
a major share of the credit or blame for the society that emerged.
Clearly American rule was intended to affect the economy; the
first Philippine Commission proclaimed, as one of the "regulative
principles" of American policy: "Domestic and foreign trade and
commerce, agriculture, and other industrial pursuits, and the
general development of the country in the interest of its inhabitants will be constant objects of solicitude and fostering care."[1]
But it remains to be asked whether specific governmental programs actually shaped (or "distorted") the Philippine economy,
or whether the United States merely allowed it to develop in the
direction it was already heading under the Spanish. Too much
attention may have been paid to the transfer of sovereignty, and
too little to the continuity of development and the passivity or
ineffectiveness of American rule which allowed it.[2]

———————

The economy of the Philippines in 1898 was predominantly agricultural. Despite some pockets of estate tenantry, which included large holdings by religious orders in the rice lands of central Luzon, the agrarian landscape remained predominantly smallholder; there were few plantations on the Malayan or Caribbean model.[3] Four crops--sugar, abaca, tobacco, coconuts-- accounted for nearly 90% of export value; six crops--these four plus the major food crops, rice and corn--covered nearly 90% of the cultivated land.[4] The islands imported manufactured goods, especially textiles, and enough rice to make up the recurrent food deficit. The direction of trade had been far more dependent on world demands and prices than on the political connection with Spain, which accounted for less than 10% of the total trade of the Philippines as late as 1890.[5]

When the United States intervened in the Philippines in 1898, most Americans hardly knew where the islands were, much less the state of the local economy. But the economic structure which the first Philippine Commission discovered was very much to their liking. The Commissioners were concerned to increase the magnitude and efficiency of production, they were anxious to divert Philippine trade toward America, but they showed no real commitment to alter the basic shape of the economy. The underlying assumption of the United States, assiduously fostered by those Filipinos who had the ear of the Commission or Congress, was that the interests of the Philippines were identical with the interests of existing agricultural producers. In the interminable hearings on insular policy from 1898 through the Philippine Trade Act of 1946 and beyond, this assumption permeated both sides of every debate. The few voices raised in protest--Americans interested in plantation development or protection of domestic agriculture, Filipinos objecting to closer trade relations with the United States--were dismissed as acting in self-interest, or were simply ignored.[6] Despite the vague rhetoric of change, official policy during the American period can be characterized generally as ratification and rationalization of the status quo.

Land was the most important single factor in the Philippine economy, and American land policy was conservative in almost every respect. The Philippine Commission, hoping to see a

profitable plantation economy develop, asked Congress for permission to make large grants of public land; Congress, however,
refused, limiting grants to 1024 hectares (per corporation), well
below the optimum envisaged. But, on the other hand, no effective legislation to reduce the size of existing holdings was ever
passed by Congress or the Philippine Legislature. Expropriation
and redistribution of the Friar Lands would not have solved all
the agrarian problems of the Philippines, but at least it would
have pointed the way to a radical solution. Instead the land was
purchased, and most of it eventually went not to the cultivators
but to wealthy speculators, in violation of both the original aim
of the endeavor and the spirit of the Public Land Law. By the
Commonwealth period there was a growing rhetorical commitment to land reform, but little actual redistribution of land
occurred, and tenancy apparently worsened under American rule. [7]
Those interested in tracing the motives for land policy will find
a complex web of sincere principles and crass self-interest, but
those interested in results will find a simpler picture: the overt
formation of new plantations was discouraged, but old estates
were allowed to remain.

To make Philippine agriculture more efficient and equitable,
the United States attempted to introduce homesteading, regularize
land titles, and encourage migration to the "frontier," especially
to Mindanao. Programs for agricultural credit were devised,
and advanced agrarian technology (irrigation, fertilizers, machin-
ery, pest and disease control) was introduced. But most of these
programs were ill-planned, all were under-funded, and none of
them made substantial impact. [8] At the end of the American
period, the average tao lived where his grandfather had lived, [9]
was deeper in debt, remained without land title, and grew his
crops as inefficiently as anywhere in the world. [10] By the standards of 1898 there had been some slight progress (in land registration, frontier development, and crop yields), but meanwhile
the rest of the world had moved past the Philippines in harnessing
the opportunities of twentieth century agrotechnology.

Fiscal and monetary policies in the American period were
also designed to produce stability rather than change. The revenue
system was essentially the Spanish system with the obvious inequities removed; it was hardly progressive, much less redistributive. The tax structure did not force people into agriculture
nor automatically create inequality, but neither did it encourage

industry or destroy inequities. By tying the peso to the dollar, the Americans stabilized Philippine money, but they also removed the possibility of autonomous currency manipulation. A balanced budget was required; severe restrictions were placed on the level of bonded indebtedness. In all these respects the Philippines was no worse off than most independent non-socialist countries of the time; those that were not restrained by law were restrained by fear of losing their international fiscal reputation. Nor is there any reason to assume that a Spanish or Filipino administration would have pursued an essentially different policy. But American policy in this area clearly did not attempt any grand innovations or foster any noteworthy economic developments, beneficial or otherwise.

Outside the narrowly "economic" sphere, the American period saw many developments whose impact on the economy has yet to be assessed--population growth, exclusion of Chinese immigrants (but removal of many restrictions on resident Chinese), mass media, mass education, vastly improved transportation, the ideology of progress and democracy. Some direct connections between American policy and socio-economic developments can be posited--public health programs led to the acceleration of population growth, the rapid Filipinization of the government gave power to an elite which would have fought against fundamental reforms had the United States ever proposed them. Yet most of these developments fall largely under the rubric "modernization" rather than "Americanization." Despite all the shortcomings of Spanish rule, the late nineteenth century had seen great changes--a high rate of population growth, expansion of the transportation network, administrative reforms, new commercial institutions, industrial investment, more newspapers, wider circulation of modern ideas, and the rise of a new Filipino agro-commercial elite. The United States obviously changed the weight and rate of these factors, but in the search for the distinctive role of America (in contrast to the twentieth century) in Philippine economic history, we must examine tariff policy.

American tariff policy toward the Philippines has been the subject of numerous studies, most of them focussing on motives rather than consequences.[11] Within the American period, tariff

relations fall into three distinct stages. In the first, the United
States retained (largely because of treaty obligations) most of the
Spanish system of tariffs and export taxes, somewhat rationalized,
while applying the rates of the 1897 Dingley Tariff (or a substantial
percentage thereof) to Philippine products entering the United
States. With the Payne-Aldrich Tariff of 1909 and the Underwood
Tariff of 1913 came virtual free trade between the United States
and the Philippines, except for quotas (which were never met) on
sugar and tobacco from 1909 to 1913, and a continuing prohibition
on the export to the United States of manufactured goods containing
more than 20% non-Philippine raw materials. There were no
further restrictions on trade for over twenty years, although the
American (and world) agricultural crisis of the late 1920's and
1930's prompted a series of bills, beginning in 1929, proposing
import quotas, often in conjunction with swift political separation.
In 1934 the first such quotas were passed (in the Tydings-McDuffie
Act and the Jones-Costigan Amendment to the Agricultural Adjustment Act); there were soon duty-free or absolute quotas on sugar,
cigars, cordage, and coconut oil, which was also subject to a
processing tax. Though this quota system was designed to be
reduced until it disappeared with the coming of independence, in
fact it has persisted in various forms to the present.

The Congressional hearings throughout the period lay bare the
politics of the tariff and reveal the crude self-seeking of most of
the parties involved. The three major interest groups which regularly spoke loudest and longest were American domestic agriculture, American manufacturing, and Filipino export agriculture,
which was generally assumed to speak for the Philippines as a
whole. The compromises among these interests, complicated by
domestic politics on both sides of the Pacific, within the framework
of a colonial relationship with which no one was truly comfortable,
make fascinating political reading; this has often been to the detriment of economic analysis. It cannot be assumed that just because
small-minded men framed the tariff it automatically had a baneful
effect; we must attempt to assess to what extent it actually altered
the Philippine economy, with what results. [12]

One general tendency of tariff policy after 1909 is quite evident:
the discouragement of potential investment in Philippine industry.
The free entry of American goods into the Philippine market left
the local entrepreneur with only shipping costs as a comparative
advantage against the greater experience and capital of established

American firms. The prohibition on the export to America of
manufactured goods of over 20% non-Philippine materials prevented the development of a Japanese-style re-export industry.
When restrictions on trade were re-established in the 1930's,
they fell most heavily on processed products, such as cordage
(exports of which had increased 500%, 1920-1030) and coconut
oil, while the agricultural raw materials (abaca, copra) remained on the free list.

It is easy to see in this the most blatant type of imperial
exploitation; certainly a reading of the tariff hearings can support this interpretation. Yet in a sense the United States showed
restraint, in that she was generally careful not to violate perceived Philippine interests. Except for a few firms such as
Tabacalera and San Miguel, there was very little Filipino manufacturing when the Americans arrived. From the beginning most
Filipinos who spoke for the country encouraged, if indeed they
did not create, the definition of Philippine interests as perpetually
agrarian; in the absence of a significant Filipino industrial sector
there was no political faction to represent and fight for such a
sector. The tariff policy was predicated not just on American
capitalism, but on a joint Filipino-American assumption that the
exchange of American manufactures for Philippine raw materials
was an equitable quasi-permanent relationship.

Furthermore, it is not yet proven that the tariff did in fact
retard Philippine industrialization. The country was, in 1938,
almost as "agrarian" as it had been in 1902 (ca. 70-80%,
although the definitions are too imprecise for exact comparison),
but there was a perceptible shift toward manufacturing and processing in the non-agrarian sector, and in absolute terms there
was substantial growth. Moreover, developments since World
War II give no indication that there had been a critical mass of
Filipino capital and potential entrepreneurship which was ready
to explode into industrialization had it not been thwarted by
American policy; the evidence suggests rather that a long-term
unwillingness to tax or tamper with agriculture has been the
chief obstacle to development. Americans might indeed have
invested more in the Philippines, or the government might
consciously have promoted industrialization; but that they did
not is a sin of omission rather than of active exploitation. [13]

The free entry of Philippine products into the American

market, on the other hand, unquestionably had a substantial
impact on certain sectors of the Philippine economy. It was
intended as a developmental measure, a boon the Philippines
could derive from the colonial relationship;[14] it was attacked
on selfish grounds by American agricultural interests and on
theoretical grounds by critics of imperialism. Yet it can be
argued that its effect on the Philippine economy as a whole was
less profound, less sharply defined for better or worse, than
either its proponents or critics have assumed.

A tariff, of course, is of most commerical significance when
it creates a sharp price differential between the goods protected
and competing unprotected goods. Some historians have (seemingly)
assumed that the introduction of mutual free trade in 1909 automatically benefited all Philippine products at once. But the Payne-
Aldrich Tariff of that year began a slight downward revision of
American duties on the produce of all countries, a process which
was carried much further by the Underwood Tariff of 1913. If
Philippine products had easier access to the American market,
so did most competing products from the rest of the world. Sugar
was the major Philippine commodity that remained "protected" at
this time, and in 1913 a provision to eliminate even that tariff was
passed, although the abolition was never put into effect. Not until
the Fordney-McCumber Tariff of 1922 were tariffs raised against
coconut oil and cordage, and the differential between American
and world market prices for agricultural products did not reach
its peak until the Smoot-Hawley Tariff of 1930--by which time
Philippine independence was clearly just around the corner. Such
major Philippine exports as abaca and copra never received preferential treatment at all, staying on the American "free list"
throughout the period; if they were imported to the United States,
it was because that was their natural market. It is one of the
implicit ironies of colonialism that precisely those Philippine
products which competed with American goods benefited most
from the imperial tariff relationship.

Direct tariff advantage, then, was limited to sugar after 1909,
plus coconut oil and cordage after 1922, and such lesser exports
as tobacco and embroideries. Available export and acreage
statistics show that most of the Philippine agricultural economy
responded primarily to world market prices and local demand,
while these protected industries prospered in correlation to tariff
preference. Abaca flourished in the first quarter century of

American rule (particularly in the first decade, although it was subject to export taxes retained from the Spanish system), slumped in the 1920's under the international competition of other hard fibers (such as sisal) and wire rope, and recovered slightly as the Japanese began to develop interest and investment in it. The rise of coconut acreage and copra exports was continuous from the 1890's onward, as the international market in vegetable oils expanded with technological breakthroughs in the manufacture of soap, margarine, and nitroglycerine. Rice acreage kept pace with population growth, while the great expansion of corn acreage reflects increased population pressure, as corn was a distinctly less preferred grain, but one which could be grown on inferior land. The sugar industry, on the other hand, really took off after the passage of the Payne-Aldrich Tariff, and cordage and coconut oil followed suit in the 1920's, when they were favored by the Fordney-McCumber Tariff. Philippine tobacco, primarily used for cigars, grew less rapidly, due in part to a secular shift of consumer preference toward cigarettes.[15]

It is possible then to make some very rough estimates of the "distortion" in the Philippine economy caused by American tariff policy. Sugar was the commodity most obviously affected; the Philippine cost of production in the 1930's was estimated at more than twice that of Java, its natural competitor, at a time when Javanese production fell 80% in five years because of the world sugar crisis. The New York (protected) sugar price was from 30% to 150% above the London (world) price, whereas copra, for example, usually obtained a higher price in London than New York. On the other hand, Philippine sugar had competed successfully on the world market in the nineteenth century, and the United States had purchased as much as 66% of Philippine sugar in 1883-87, with no tariff preference; certainly not all of the Philippine sugar industry owed its existence to American policy.[16]

Yet even if one assumes for the sake of argument that the entire sugar and tobacco industries, plus the processing/manufacturing of coconut oil, cordage, and embroideries, were attributable to the imperial relationship, these "distorted" sectors hardly represent a majority of Philippine society. Nearly all statistics for employment or investment by industry are speculative, but the most educated guess is that those directly favored employed approximately 500,000 Filipinos in the 1930's, or some 15-20% of the population (assuming family sizes of 5-6 members).[17] Sugar and tobacco, the two crops directly affected, occupied only 8% of the total area in cultivation, although this was mostly prime land. More land and people, of course, were indirectly involved, in coconut and abaca growing, in trade and transportation of these commodities, etc.; on the other hand, a good share of this production went to domestic markets, and more might have been sold, if necessary, to other foreign markets. One can reasonably conclude that most Filipino farms and farmers were only indirectly and distantly affected by American tariffs, although there were certain regions where the investment in favored industries was very great, enough to cause severe local dislocation if the protection were abruptly withdrawn.

The share of available Philippine capital invested in these industries (ca. $250 million in 1938, 80% of this in sugar) must have been more substantial, although the absence of adequate definitions of or data on the total "capital" in the country makes percentages meaningless. But this was more than compensated for by the immense profitability of these industries; sugar alone, in the peak year of 1934, produced an estimated 40% of total crop value, 65% of export value, 30% of national income, and, directly or indirectly, 40% of total government revenue. The investors in these industries, presumably rational men, had plenty of time to recover their investments, and, from at least the Jones Act of 1916 onward, clear notice that an end to the largesse would eventually come. (In fact, when restrictions were imminent in 1929-30, sugar production was actually expanded, 80% in the next four years.) Even if independence had forced complete disinvestment in these industries, it is by no means clear that the initial investments would have been proven unsound, from either an individual or national viewpoint. In 1955 a distinguished economist could still assert: "As long as the Philippines have access to the sheltered United States market, sugar production is undoubtedly an economically efficient way to earn foreign exchange."[18] Critics of imperialism who suggested that, in view of the Philippines' chronic food deficiency, sugar land could have been more beneficially planted to rice were flying in the face of the facts; sugar was far more profitable per unit area.[19]

From a strictly economic standpoint, therefore, American tariff policy should have been beneficial rather than deleterious.

There would always have been some problems of adjustment
surrounding the reallocation of resources at both the opening
and closing of mutual free trade, but there was ample time to
prepare for both events, and a farsighted government could have
set aside some of the increased revenues generated to cushion
the shocks of transition. The fact that the United States took
over 75% of Philippine exports was of no great economic consequence in itself, so long as these provisions for transition were
made. There is no evidence that the protected industries produced greater social tensions than the unprotected ones; if
working conditions were bad on the sugar estates of Negros, they
were better than on the rice plains of central Luzon, where the
agricultural technology, the system of land tenure, and the
pattern of peasant revolts all antedated the arrival of the Americans.[20]   And although agricultural productivity for most crops
remained low by world standards, there is evidence that the
sugar industry was investing more in agrotechnology and was
improving yield more than non-protected industries were.[21]
Tariff policy created, in effect, an American consumer subsidy,
a "bounty,"[22] for certain sectors of the Philippine economy.
This can be seen as a form of foreign aid; even though it was not
as clearly oriented toward general economic development as the
carefully structured direct grant programs of today, it certainly
should have been better than nothing.

This argument might well lead to an apology for colonialism,
an assertion that up to World War II the Philippine economy was
doing well, that American policy had worked. But such a conclusion would be patently false. In 1941, the Philippine economy
was troubled, social tensions were increasing, and even before
the war there were serious questions as to how well the country
could face the shock of independence. The documentation is
extensive and damning, both for the 1930's and for the essentially
unchanged conditions of the 1950's. Overdependence on a few
exports, tenantry, indebtedness, low productivity, corruption
and inefficiency, undercapitalization, miserable working condi-
tions--all the symptoms of economic backwardness were present
at the end of the American period as they had been at the beginning. Some of them had been mildly alleviated, others were
much worse. Something had obviously gone wrong; the United
States had fallen far short of her noble principles and dreams.
But the crucial defect was not so much in what she did, as in
what she failed to do.

Some of the omissions of the Americans have been suggested already -- effective land reform, extensive private investment in industry, adequate governmental investment in agricultural credit and technology, etc. But the most symptomatic and profound failure of the American period was an inability or unwillingness to curb the Filipino agricultural elite, and to redefine Philippine interests as progressive rather than static. The tariff preference provided a windfall to the sugar planters and millers; this should have been tapped for the benefit of the whole country, to prepare for the day when that windfall would cease. But the Americans refused to allow export taxes (after 1909) and the Filipino legislators continually battled against any significant increase in taxation of agricultural lands or income. So the money remained in the hands of the wealthy. Some of it they spent on luxurious living; that is a privilege allowed in most societies. But some was also spent in obtaining and expanding political leverage -- directly and illegally through bribery, as well as indirectly and legally through lobbying. The wealthy agriculturalists succeeded in defining their own interests as those of the Philippines. They spoke for the Philippines, and neither American administrators nor Filipino "public opinion" ever successfully contested this right. Some of these plutocrats achieved economic ascendancy as a direct result of American largesse, but others inherited fortunes founded under the Spanish, and dealt in products unaffected by the tariff; there was no essential difference between them. The crushing inequality of wealth and power in the Philippines was not created during the American period, but neither was it removed or even reduced.

The political clout wielded by some of the wealthy has been abundantly documented; they kept down wages, oppressed workers, used local militia or constabulary to suppress dissent, and ignored all efforts at reform. Even Quezon, whose attitude toward landed wealth was far from radical, was frustrated when his Commonwealth reform programs, such as the Rice Tenancy Act, were consistently thwarted in practice by local barons who felt themselves above the law. Through their influence in the legislature, they prevented any serious attempt (throughout the American period, and since) to tap the immense agricultural wealth provided in part by the American tariff/subsidy. And there is some locational correlation between concentrated agricultural wealth and peasant discontent; in the Census of . . . 1939, five provinces accounted for 40% of all "farm equipment" by value, and four of

these (Negros Occidental, Nueva Ecija, Pangasinan, Tarlac)
were among the provinces most notorious for agrarian distur-
bances.[23] The problem of Philippine agriculture under American rule was not that it was economically unprofitable, but that
the profits increased problems rather than solved them.

There is no single point in time within the American period
of which one can say, "Here the economic battle was lost." The
Philippines did not then face the kind of population pressure
which made economic modernization seem hopeless in such areas
as India, China, or Java. Even after the sugar barons had spent
most of their profits unprofitably, it was perhaps not too late in
1941 to plan for a Philippine economy that could compete in the
world economy, one marked by increasing equality and diversification rather than by inequality and agricultural overspecial-
ization. But the political will was lacking on both sides of the
Pacific. The joint reaction to the devastation of the Philippines
in World War II illustrates this perfectly. The economy had
been virtually dismantled, which should have created a golden
opportunity to rebuild it on a more rational basis. Instead the
Filipino representatives insisted--as they had nearly half a
century before--that subsidizing existing agricultural interests
was the best way to benefit the Philippines as a whole. And
once more the Americans bought this argument, renewed the
preferential quota, and helped a shattered sugar industry, which
could not compete in the world markets of the 1930's, grow into
a major industry which could not compete in the world markets
of the 1970's.

It may well be argued that the Filipinos, knowing how badly
rehabilitation was needed, fought for the only kind of substantial
relief they were likely to get. After all, a tariff preference is a
subtle levy on the consumer through prices, politically far more
palatable than a direct levy on the taxpayer--although it should
be remembered that Congress approved massive aid for Europe
under the Marshall Plan just two years later. The key to the
Philippine question, however, is not that such substantial direct
aid was not granted, but that it was never seriously proposed.
In the long and acrimonious debates on the Bell Trade Act, the
participants all focused their energies on such issues as how
long the transition period should be, or whether the quotas should
be in long tons or short tons, rather than on what kind of Philippine economy they were trying to (re)build. The economic battle

may not have been over, but the political issue had long since been laid to rest. Perhaps as early as 1898-99, probably no later than 1909, the Americans had decided they would accept the Philippines as they found it, and Philippine interests as defined by existing Filipino leadership. So by mutual consent, American and Filipino leaders attempted to expand and to rationalize the economy, but not to change it.

One result of this policy has been that in Philippine economic history the "American period" is not very different from either the late Spanish period or the early Republican. In 1937, as in 1894, as in 1950, the same four crops accounted for nearly 90% of all Philippine exports, although the relative proportions had changed.[24] Specifically American inputs--tariffs, homesteading, etc. --had less impact on the economy than such international phenomena as population growth[25] and fluctuations in world prices. There is no accurate way of measuring whether or not the Filipinos were actually "better off" in 1941 than they had been in 1896; production had increased, probably average income had as well, but so had tenantry and population pressure.[26] The state of the economy in 1941 was certainly not good, but neither was it hopeless, and it is not reasonable to blame all the economic problems of the Philippines today on the colonial legacy. What the Republic of the Philippines has done and may yet do with the economy it inherited is another story. But the American failure to transform the economy, to produce the kind of change that might have justified intervention, is history. It was a failure to see beyond the Filipino elite definition of the society as static, irrevocably agrarian; a failure as much of politics as of economics; a failure born less of exploitation than of inertia.

APPENDIX I

ON USING THE PHILIPPINE CENSUS

Anyone seeking a statistical sense of Philippine society and economy in the American period will eventually turn to the three relevant censuses:

Census of the Philippine Islands: Taken Under the Direction of the Philippine Commission in the Year 1903 (Washington, 1905)

Census of the Philippine Islands: Taken Under the Direction of the Philippine Legislature in the Year 1918 (Manila, 1920)

Census of the Philippines: 1939 (Manila, 1940)

These are indispensable sources, for agricultural data as well as for population distribution. (They also contain material on "Industry," Education, Diseases, etc. to which some of the same general caveats may apply.) The sheer volume of statistical information provided is almost overwhelming; there seems to be almost nothing about the agricultural economy which cannot be computed from them. The censuses are nicely spaced, near the beginning, middle, and end of the period of effective American rule; it looks as if a profile of the national (or provincial) economy in 1902 (March 3, 1903, to be exact) can be directly compared with the same profile for 1918 (December 31, 1918) and 1938 (January 1, 1939). But there are pitfalls, some obvious, some less so, in attempting to compare data between these censuses--pitfalls which not all historians have successfully avoided.

Certain of these are common to any census, particularly one taken in an area where literacy is low and administrative control is incomplete. The population figures for "non-Christian" peoples are only rough estimates, particularly in the early censuses; and agricultural data for these areas just do not exist. Even for "Christian" areas the statistics are not totally reliable; any figures purporting to be accurate beyond two places are highly suspect. There is also a question of how representative even the accurate data are--the Census of . . . 1903 was taken during a period of drought, disease, and severe dislocation, which may

make it a misleading guide to the general situation in the early
American period; all three censuses were taken during the peak
season for labor migration, hence do not accurately portray the
"normal" provincial distribution of population. The best guides
through these routine problems of Philippine censuses are
H. Otley Beyer, Population of the Philippine Islands in 1916
(Manila, 1917), and Stephen Low, "The Effect of Colonial Rule
on Population Distribution in the Philippines: 1898-1941"
(unpublished Ph. D. dissertation, Fletcher, 1956).

But more troubling to the economic historian are the anomalies
within the various Agricultural Censuses, which render comparisons across the years difficult, if not impossible. Some of these
are annoying, but obvious: the early censuses include a "no rental"
category of occupancy (squatters? friends or relatives of the owner?)
and combine all part-owners and owners, while the Census of . . .
1939 omits the former and separates the latter; there are changes
in the size-classifications into which farms are grouped (e.g. 10-15
ha. and 15-30, vs. 10-20 and 20-50). Even more perilous are
differences which only appear in the small print--the earlier
censuses classify all farms according to total area, and again by
cultivated area; in the Census of . . . 1939 what appears to be an
identical table turns out to be classified by "cultivable" area.
There is a similar trap involving the minimum size of a "farm"--
in 1903, no minimum exists, so the census includes "small parcels
of land, many of them no larger than ordinary kitchen gardens";
in 1918, an official minimum is fixed at 200 square meters; in
1939, this figure is raised to 1000 square meters. But despite
all these discrepancies, it seems as if these data could still be
utilized by a historian who is willing to calculate/postulate some
"conversion factors" for the data affected and accept a somewhat
lower degree of precision in his statistics.

Yet the scholar who has come this far is still in for a cruel
shock when he reads carefully this short paragraph on page 898
of Part II of Volume II of the Census of . . . 1939:

> Comparability of data for previous censuses. -- Although
> a simple census of agriculture was taken in connection
> with the general censuses of 1903 and 1918, no compar-
> ative data are presented in this report as it is believed
> the data obtained in those two censuses are not compar-
> able with those of the 1939 Census because of the differ-
> ences in the definition for a farm, in the completeness

and accuracy of the enumeration, and because of differences in the accuracy and methods of compilation.

Very close comparison of "the definition used for a farm" in the various censuses will reveal that whereas in 1903 and 1918 each separate lot is counted as a "farm," in 1939 all the fragmented holdings of a given owner or tenant are grouped together and listed as one "farm."

This fact, which has been overlooked by many scholars (including, through nearly three months of research, this writer):

1. Completely invalidates all comparisons (between 1903 or 1918 and 1939) of the average size of farms or the number of farms, including the frequently drawn conclusion that agrarian conditions were demonstrably worsening because (seemingly) there were fewer and larger "farms" in 1939 than in 1918. (This may in fact be true, but it cannot be proved by the censuses.)

2. Renders suspect most conclusions about comparative rates of tenancy, except insofar as one can assume that fragmentation of holdings is as frequent among tenants as among owner-operators (a plausible assumption, but unsubstantiated). The apparent overall increase in tenancy from 1902 to 1938, however, is sufficiently great (from 18% to 35% of all farms) to be regarded as true in general, if not in detail.

3. Similarly upsets or destroys all other intercensal comparisons involving land distribution, correlations between farm sizes, types of occupancy, etc.

NEVERTHELESS, the censuses can and should be used when possible. Total farm area, cultivated area, population density, and crop distribution can, it seems, be profitably compared on both the national and provincial levels. It appears that crop productivity can also be compared, but for some unknown reason, all yield and production figures in the Census of . . . 1918 are so unreasonably high--often 50-100% above yields for 1902, the 1930's, or even the 1950's--as to render them presumptively invalid, although it should be noted that Richard Hooley and Vernon W. Ruttan ("The Philippines" in Agricultural Development in Asia, ed. by R. T. Shand [Berkeley and Los Angeles, 1969]) utilize them. In the attempt to see Philippine history quantitatively, the economic historian must continue to use the censuses--but with the greatest of care.

APPENDIX II

LAND, FARMS, AND POPULATION

Areas in thousands of hectares
Population in thousands
Percentages rounded to nearest 0.5%

	1902	1918	1938
Total Area	29741	29741	29741
Farm Land	2828	4564	6691
% of all Land	9.5%	15.5%	22.5%
Cultivated Area	1311	2416	3954
% of Farm Land	46.0%	53.0%	59.0%
Population	6988*	9492*	16000
Population/hectare	0.235*	0.316*	0.540
Population/agricultural hectare	2.47*	2.08*	2.39
Population/cultivated hectare ("nutritional density")	4.44*	4.10*	4.05

* Christian population only, for 1902 and 1918, since no agricultural statistics for non-Christian populations are available.

SOURCE: Censuses of 1903, 1918, 1939.

APPENDIX III

CROP DISTRIBUTION

Areas in thousands of hectares
Percentages rounded to nearest 0.5%

	Total(net)* Cultivated Land	Rice	Coconuts	Corn	Abaca	Sugar	Tobacco
1902	1311	593	148	108	218	72	31
% of total*		45.5%	11.5%	8%	16.5%	5.5%	2.5%
1918	2416	1058	400	364	393	147	72
% of total*		43.5%	16.5%	15%	16%	6%	3%
% of 1902	184%	178%	270%	337%	180%	204%	232%
1938	3954	1830	1051	827	291	230	58
% of total*		46%	26.5%	20.5%	7.5%	6%	1.5%
% of 1918	164%	173%	263%	227%	74%	156%	81%
% of 1902	302%	308%	711%	766%	134%	320%	187%

* The net area for cultivated land does not include double-cropping, whereas individual crop areas (specifically rice and corn) do. The percentages given are of the net area, and hence may add up to over 100%. The gross area, including double-cropping, exceeds the net area by 8% in 1918 and 15% in 1938.

SOURCE: Censuses of 1903, 1918, 1939.

APPENDIX IV

COMMODITY DISTRIBUTION OF EXPORT TRADE

Values in millions of U. S. dollars
Percentages rounded to nearest 0.5%

	Total Exports	Sugar	Abaca, Cordage	Coconut Products	Tobacco	Total of 4 Products
1873-77, Avg.	18.7	9.3	4.5	---[a]	2.3	16.1
% of total		49.0%	24%		12.5%	85.5%
1890-94, Avg.[b]	20.1	7.3	7.9	0.6[c]	2.2	18.0
% of total		36.5%	39%	3.0%	11.0%	89.5%
1908-12, Avg.	38.7	7.1	16.6	9.6[d]	3.6[e]	36.9
% of total		18.5%	43%	25.0%	9.0%	95.5%
1933-37, Avg.	120.0	56.5	14.2	29.9	5.0[f]	105.6
% of total		47.0%	12%	25.0%	4.0%	88.0%
1948-50, Avg.	301.5	37.3	33.5	200.5	1.3	272.8
% of total		12.5%	11%	66.5%	0.5%	90.5%

[a] The fourth export in value at this time was coffee, with 6% of the total.

[b] In the late nineteenth century pesos (silver) depreciated nearly 50% relative to dollars (gold); there was thus a far greater increase in the peso value of exports between 1873-77 and 1890-94 than the table shows.

[c] 1890, 1892-94 only.

[d] Copra only [coconut oil exports minimal at this time].

[e] 1908-11 only.

[f] 1937 only.

SOURCES: Legarda, pp. 197, 222; Census of . . . 1903, Vol. IV; Hugo H. Miller, Economic Conditions in the Philippines (Boston, c. 1920), pp. 362-65; Joint Preparatory Committee on Philippine Affairs, Report of May 20, 1938, Vol. I; Jenkins, p. 172.

APPENDIX V
AGRICULTURAL PRODUCTIVITY

International Crop Yields, 1930's

Sugar Cane, Quintals/Hectare 1929/30-1933/34

Philippines	361
Java (European plantations only)	1327
Formosa	683
Hawaii	1357
Cuba	381
WORLD (rough estimate)	400

Rice, Quintals/Hectare 1929/30-1937/38

Philippines	9.0-11.9
Cochinchina	10.1-14.1
Thailand	15.2-16.4
Japan	30.6-39.3
WORLD	14.6-16.0

Corn, Quintals/Hectare 1929/30-1937/38

Philippines	5.3- 7.0
Netherlands East Indies	9.5-10.0
Indochina	11.8-15.8
WORLD	11.4-14.9

Tobacco, Quintals/Hectare 1929-1937

Philippines	4.5- 5.9
Netherlands East Indies (European plantations only)	9.1- 9.7
Cuba	4.1- 5.1
U.S.A.	8.7-10.1
WORLD	9.2- 9.6

SOURCE: International Yearbook of Agricultural Statistics (Rome, 1940).

Philippine Crop Yield, Changes, 1910-1937

	1910	1937	% increase/ decrease
Sugar cane, pounds per acre	3968	9259	+134%
Rice, " " "	1534	2588	+75%
Corn, " " "	1093	1501	+37%
Abacá " " "	1027	1067	+4%
Tobacco " " "	1151	992	-14%
Coconuts, nuts per tree	88	73	-17%

SOURCE: Owen L. Dawson, "Philippine Agriculture, A Problem of Adjustment . . . ," Foreign Agriculture (1940), 405. Dawson also discusses the causes for low productivity in Philippine agriculture and crop processing. For productivity statistics derived from the Philippine Census, see Appendix I.

Notes

1. Proclamation, "To the people of the Philippine Islands,"
   April 4, 1899, Report of the [Schurman] Philippine Commission
   to the President (Washington, 1900), I [January, 1900], 5.
   It may be significant that this "principle" is only ninth in a
   list of twelve, well below (#1) enforcement of "the supremacy
   of the United States," (#2) the promise of "the most ample
   liberty of self-government" reconcilable with good government
   and American authority, and (#3) the guarantee of "civil
   rights of the Philippine people." The priority of political
   over economic goals can be reasonably inferred.

2. A growing number of socio-economic historians and geographers
   are framing their research across the apparent "discontinuity"
   of 1898--e.g., the dissertations of Jo Ann Roland, Canute
   VanderMeer, and Frederick Wernstedt, and the works in progress of John Larkin and David Sturtevant. (See bibliography.)

3. In 1902, six of seven provinces in which tenants occupied over
   30% of all "farms" were in central Luzon; the rate for the
   whole country was 18%; in many agricultural areas it was
   below 10%; in the rich abaca region of Albay-Sorsogon it was
   only 1 1/2%. Census of . . . 1903, IV, 190. Precise figures
   on the area of the "Friar Lands" do not exist, but the total was
   on the order of 172,000 hectares (6% of total Philippine "farm"
   land in 1902/3), of which nearly two-thirds was in the
   "immediate neighborhood" of Manila.

4. See Appendix III, IV.

5. In 1891, new protective regulations raised Spain's share of
   Philippine import trade considerably (from less than 10% to
   37% by 1894), although her share of total exports remained
   below 10%. Great Britain, British colonies in Asia (especially
   Hong Kong), and the United States took 80-85% of Philippine
   exports (1880-94), with a definite shift after 1890 away from
   the U.S.A. toward the U.K. Great Britain and British colonies

dominated the import trade, with America supplying less than 5%. Benito F. Legarda, Jr., "Foreign Trade, Economic Change, and Entrepreneurship in the Nineteenth Century Philippines" (unpublished Ph.D. dissertation, Harvard, 1955), pp. 215-39.

6. In 1909, the Philippine National Assembly protested the mutual free trade provisions of the Payne-Aldrich Tariff, which, they stated, "in the long run . . . would be highly prejudicial to the economic interests of the Philippine people and would create a situation which might delay the obtaining of independence." José P. Apostol, in a series of articles on "The American-Philippine Tariff," Philippine Social Sciences Review, III (1930-31), 42-47, 190-97, 254-63; IV (1932), 142-51, stresses such Filipino opposition to American policy. But this resolution was dismissed by the Commission as insincere and frivolous opposition for its own sake; the recent study of Bonifacio S. Salamanca, The Filipino Reaction to American Rule: 1901-1913 ([Hamden, Conn.], 1968), pp. 121-33, tends to substantiate this view. In any case, it should be contrasted with Filipino testimony in hearings before the Philippine Commission, Congressional committees, etc., which shows a persistent interest in prolonged and increased preference within the American market.

7. Although the figures are not directly comparable (see Appendix I), census enumerations of tenantry are indicative: in 1902, 18% of all "farms" were occupied by tenants, in 1938, 35%. See also James S. Allen, "Agrarian Tendencies in the Philippines," PA, XI-1 (1938), 52-65.

8. Karl J. Pelzer, Pioneer Settlement in the Asiatic Tropics (New York, 1948), pp. 93-110. Irrigation had been known in the Philippines for centuries, yet in the Census of . . . 1939 only 13% of the cultivated land was reported as benefiting from any type of irrigation (gravity, pump, etc.) at any season of the year.

9. By 1939, only 11-12% of the population lived outside the "ethnic area" of their birth. Stephen Low, "The Effect of Colonial Rule on Population Distribution in the Philippines: 1898-1941" (unpublished Ph.D. dissertation, Fletcher, 1956), pp. 254-55. Low, however, regards this as an "imposing" figure.

10. Philippine agricultural yields for most major crops ranged from 5% to 60% below world averages in the 1930's; see Appendix V.

11. ". . . the tug of war between conflicting interests, between idealism and a considerably narrower policy--between immediate advantage and ultimate benefit." Pedro E. Abelarde, American Tariff Policy towards the Philippines: 1898-1946 (Morningside Heights, N.Y., 1947), p. 1. See also José Apostol; Amado A. Castro, "Philippine-American Tariff and Trade Relations, 1898-1954," Philippine Economic Journal, IV-1 (1965), 29-56; and José S. Reyes, Legislative History of America's Economic Policy toward the Philippines (New York, 1923), on this subject; all these works cite the principal Congressional hearings extensively.

12. Cf. Frank H. Golay, "Economic Consequences of the Philippine Trade Act," PA, XXVIII-1 (1955), 55, on the Bell Trade Act of 1946:

> The present article reflects the belief that the adverse economic consequences of the Trade Act upon the Philippine economy have been relatively small and bear little relationship to the economic effects generally attributed to the Trade Act. This analysis should not be considered in any sense a defense of the Act since, in my opinion, the Trade Act was a hapless United States excursion into economic imperialism which has made American relations less smooth than they should have been, and has been made the excuse for propaganda damaging to the United States throughout the Far East.

13. Ibid., p. 60; Golay, The Philippines: Public Policy and National Economic Development (Ithaca, N.Y., 1961), pp. 183-86, 206-13; Stephen A. Resnick, "The Decline of Rural Industry Under Export Expansion: A Comparison among Burma, Philippines, and Thailand, 1870-1938," Journal of Economic History, XXX-1 (1970), 62n; A.V.H. Hartendorp, History of Industry and Trade of the Philippines (Manila, 1958), pp. 18-59.

14. After the devastations of both the Fil-American War and World War II, tariff preference was urged as a relief measure for the Philippines, by such disparate types as Taft,

McNutt, Osmeña, and Carlos Romulo; in both cases it was proposed in conjunction with direct rehabilitation/relief aid from the United States to the Philippines. Reyes, pp. 94-99; Shirley Jenkins, <u>American Economic Policy Toward the Philippines</u> (Stanford, c. 1954), pp. 42-63.

15. See Appendix II, III, IV. On the correlation between corn and population pressure, see Canute VanderMeer, "Corn on the Island of Cebu" (unpublished Ph.D. dissertation, Michigan, 1962), and Frederick L. Wernstedt, "Agricultural Regionalism on Negros Island, Philippines" (unpublished Ph.D. dissertation, UCLA, 1953).

16. Miriam S. Farley, "Sugar -- A Commodity in Chaos," <u>FES</u>, IV-22 (1935), 176; Charles O. Houston, Jr., "The Philippine Sugar Industry: 1934-1950," <u>UMJEAS</u>, III-4 (1954), 372; <u>International Yearbook of Agricultural Statistics: 1939-40</u> (Rome, 1940), "Summary"; Legarda, p. 229; Thomas R. McHale, "Sugar in the Seventies," <u>Solidarity</u>, VI-5 (1971), 6-10.

17. Statistical data for this and the following paragraph are drawn from the <u>Census of . . . 1939</u>; Catherine Porter, "Philippine Industries Today and Tomorrow," <u>FES</u>, VII-3 (1938), 144-45; Miriam S. Farley, "Philippine Independence and Agricultural Readjustment," <u>FES</u>, V-8 (1936), 71-77; Houston, pp. 370-72; Grayson L. Kirk, <u>Philippine Independence: Motives, Problems, and Prospects</u> (New York, 1936), p. 67; and Theodore W. Friend, "The Philippine Sugar Interests and the Politics of Independence, 1929-1935," <u>JAS</u>, XXII-1 (1963), 179-92. Figures for "crop value" and "national income" tend to be particularly gross estimates.

18. Golay, "Economic Consequences," p. 64.

19. According to figures in the <u>International Yearbook . . . 1939-40</u>, the average yield of Philippine sugar was 40 quintals per hectare, worth over 440 gold francs at New York prices; rice yielded only 11 quintals per hectare, an amount which could be purchased in Saigon for 72 gold francs. (Shipping and handling costs would, of course, decrease this differential.)

20. Friend, p. 181. Coconut farming, which enjoyed a boom in the American period second only to sugar (600% acreage increase 1902-1938) continued to be a smallholder industry relatively free from agrarian unrest; according to the Census of . . . 1939, tenants occupied only 21% of coconut farms, as opposed to 40% for rice and tobacco, and 60% for sugar.

21. See Appendix V; Houston, pp. 370-407, passim.

22. F. W. Taussig, The Tariff History of the United States (8th ed.; New York, 1964), pp. 398-99.

23. Census of . . . 1939, Vol. II, Part II, p. 1093. The fifth province, Davao, represents largely Japanese capital and labor; see Grant K. Goodman, Davao: A Case Study in Japanese-Philippine Relations ([Lawrence, Kansas], c. 1967). For general discussions of agricultural wealth and political power in the Philippines, see Houston, pp. 382-97; James Allen; and Akira Takahashi, Land and Peasants in Central Luzon: Socio-Economic Structure of a Bulacan Village (Tokyo, 1969), pp. 73-81.

24. See Appendix IV.

25. Although the population growth in the American period was quite high (2.0% p. a., 1903-1939), it was almost as high in the late Spanish period -- nearly 1.7% for much of the nineteenth century. For comparable developments elsewhere in the region, see C.A. Fisher, "Population Growth in South-East Asia," in The Economic Development of South-East Asia, ed. by C. D. Cowan (London, 1964).

26. "Nutritional density" (population per cultivated hectare) seems to have decreased only slightly between 1902, when agriculture was still disrupted by disease, drought, and the aftermath of the Fil-American War, and 1938; furthermore, some of this is accounted for by the expanded area planted to corn, which provides less nutritional value per unit area than rice. Although the area cultivated in rice increased from 600,000 to 1,800,000 hectares, the Philippines remained a net importer of grain. See Appendix II, III, IV.

American Internal Revenue Policy in the Philippines to 1916

by

Harry Luton

In most of the published studies of American rule in the
Philippines, little attention has been paid to fiscal policy,
particularly internal revenue policy (as opposed to import and
export duties). Yet the whole administrative program of the
United States--education, civil service, health, economic
development, local and national governments, etc. --depended
in part on the crucial questions of how much revenue was obtained, by what means, from what sources. This paper is an
exploratory attempt to describe the development of this internal
revenue policy up to 1916. In these years the foundations of
fiscal policy were developed which lasted not just for the remainder of American rule but for the postwar period as well. The
emphasis is on actual programs rather than motives; however,
the discussion would be incomplete without reference to the
Progressive ideology which was so significant a part of American
imperialism in that era, and which permeated almost every area
of decision-making. [1]

The development of tax-gathering institutions under American
rule shows clearly the conflicts that developed between various
Progressive theories and imperial realities. One basic commitment held by William Howard Taft and other colonialists of his
times was to decentralized government; this was a common
characteristic of many Progressives of the period. Thus, David
Barrows, who served as Director of Education for the Philippines,
wrote: "The American Commissioners had in view the American

county as a model, and were impressed with the evils of
'centralization' and 'autocracy.' They undertook to decentralize, and created provisional governments of the 'commission type' ostensibly autonomous in their powers." At the
same time, because of the necessities for control inherent in
the colonial situation, these men found themselves attracted
to highly centralized models of government, especially those
provided by the British systems in the Southwest Pacific.
Barrows continued, "However, these [decentralized provincial]
governments were never entrusted with important branches of
the service or utilized by the insular authorities as local agents.
Education, constabulary, forests, mines, lands, and posts
were committed to the insular bureaus with the headquarters
in Manila and representatives in all parts of the islands."[2]

The structure of the American revenue collecting agencies
showed a centralizing tendency which seems to have arisen more
from colonial necessities than from ideological commitment.[3]
The American revenue structure was basically a simplification
of its outdated, centralized Spanish predecessor. The Bureau
of Customs was charged with the collection of "all tariff duties
on exports and imports, and tonnage, wharfage, and immigration
taxes, and other charges on foreign trade, and interven[tion] in
the regulation of both foreign and coastwise shipping." While
the centralization of the Bureau of Customs in Manila was an
obvious necessity, since almost all foreign trade entered through
that port, the same cannot be said of the rest of the revenue
system. The Bureau of Internal Revenue, also in Manila, was
"charged with the supervision of the collection by provincial
treasuries, through their deputies, the municipal treasurers, of
all other taxes (i.e. not covered by the Bureau of Customs)
accruing in part or wholly to the insular treasury, also, the cash
poll tax, which is of general application, although the proceeds
accrue exclusively to provincial and municipal treasuries."[4]
Under this system, the provincial treasuries were left solely
responsible only for the collection of real estate taxes, municipal
licenses, school tuition and matriculation fees, and, under some
conditions, a road tax collected either in cash or labor.

The Reorganization Act of 1905 concentrated the responsibility
for tax collection still further. It gave the Collector of Internal
Revenue, head of a division of the Bureau of Internal Revenue,

supervisory powers over both internal revenue agents and provincial treasurers. He held review jurisdiction over the actions
of provincial boards in assessing the land tax, and over the
appointments of subordinate personnel of the provincial governments. Provincial functions were curtailed, and five provinces
were eliminated. [5] Actual collection of revenue was organized
under the Bureau of Internal Revenue in Manila, and most of the
funds collected went to the insular treasury. In 1906, the first
fiscal year that was affected by reorganization, 58.2% of all
taxes in the islands went to the insular treasury, 17.7% to the
provincial treasuries, and 24.1% to the municipal ones (including
Manila). [6] The distribution of tax revenues did fluctuate throughout the period being considered (1905-1916). For example, in
1913, only 53.3% went to the insular treasury, 27.1% to the
provincial, and 19.5% to the municipal treasuries. [7]

After 1913, the relative importance of the insular treasury
tended to increase, though slightly. In 1916, the last year with
which this study deals, 65.4% of all revenues were directed
into the insular treasury, and only 20.0% and 14.6% of the
revenues went into the provincial and municipal treasuries
respectively. [8] This pattern of centralized revenue collection
and use, furthered by the United States, has continued to the
present day. "Philippine governmental functions are relatively
centralized, and local government tax bases are restricted in
number and productiveness. Because of the high degree of
centralization, local governments are dependent on grants-in-aid
and allocations of revenues from the national government for
approximately 40 percent of their receipts. "[9]

While under the Spanish system revenue collection was also
theoretically centralized, the United States did make at least one
specific change which had major practical consequences in terms
of centralization, for, coupled with organizational consolidation,
went the elimination of the Church as a governmental institution.
Frank Golay points out that "It would be a mistake to minimize
the role of the clergy, who, during the Spanish period, provided...
[the] direct functions of local rule."[10] The local priest (often a
Spanish friar) handled the major part of tax collection on the local
(provincial and municipal) level, as the Inspector of Taxation and
Censor of the Municipal Budget. He was also the major dispenser
of funds for the locality, Inspector of Primary Schools, President
of the Health Board, of the Board of Charities, and of the Board

of Works.[11] The United States destroyed this system and centralized these functions in the hands of the civil bureaucracy, which was largely staffed by the Filipino elite.

Although the basic changes which were made in the tax gathering institutions by the Americans did not follow their original plan for decentralization, they did help fulfill another Progressive demand, for efficient and inexpensive government. For example, the "partial merging of the former office of the city assessor and collector in the Bureau of Internal Revenue, on August 1, 1904, and its complete merging, under the provisions of the Reorganization Act, on January 1, 1906 . . . resulted in a distinct economy to the city of Manila in the cost of collecting its taxes." Between the fiscal years ending in 1906 and 1907, these costs dropped from 4.2% to 3.7% of collected revenues.[12] Outside of Manila, this consolidation of the tax-gathering bureaucracy helped bring about a decrease in the cost of all collections (excluding expenses incurred by provincial governments) from 4.90 centavos for each peso collected in 1908, to 2.45 centavos per peso in 1914.[13] Thus American colonialism in the Philippines sacrificed Progressive decentralization to (Progressive) efficiency in government.

Whatever the complexity of forces, ideological and otherwise, which caused this centralization, it had important social and political consequences. First, it provided an important part of the modern infrastructure created by the United States, and one which was used by an elite whose power base was and still is concentrated in Manila. Secondly, it reinforced what has been termed the "parasitic" relationship between urban centers and rural agricultural areas.[14] Eric Wolf has described how this type of power concentration generally tends to encourage the breakdown of the traditional personalistic aspects of the relationship between landlord and peasant, and to encourage the development of purely economic ties.[15]

The evolution of the actual structure of internal taxes under American rule parallels the development of tax-gathering institutions. The colonialists came to the Philippines with an ostensible commitment to reform, to social justice as they saw it. Harold

Pitt, President of the Manila Merchants' Association, was merely echoing the reformist sentiments of such men as Taft, Elliott, and Barrows when he wrote:

> We started out to regenerate eight million people.
> Every authentic report on the subject declares that
> we are making a good job of it. . . . [We] have
> built roads and bridges, improved water ways,
> constructed wharves and carried out an elaborate
> scheme of harbor improvement at the principal ports
> as well as arranging for the building of railroads on
> the important islands, all of which has stimulated
> industry by providing better facilities for communica-
> tion and marketing of products: and, most important
> of all, we are giving the Filipinos Opportunity which
> they never had under the domination of Spain. [16]

The Americans came to the Philippines ostensibly committed to "uplifting the natives." This drive was manifested in many areas, including that of internal revenue reform. The Americans were going to replace the "repressive" Spanish system with a new one which would discourage various forms of "immorality," bring social justice to the "whole Filipino people," and grant these people opportunity by encouraging economic development. In the main, these goals, like that of decentralization, were not achieved by American policy.

The causes of this failure, however, are perhaps more com-plex than those which doomed decentralization. While the inability to decentralize can be traced to the problems inherent in ruling any colony and to the nature of the institutional system which was inherited from the Spaniards, the failure to implement many tax reforms can be attributed as well to the symbiotic relationship which developed between the Filipino elite and the Americans, to the "class fears" basic to much of the thinking of these two groups, [17] and to a basic and perhaps necessary misunderstanding by the American colonialists of the dynamics of the economics of colonies.

The Americans inherited a system of taxation from the Spanish which they left largely intact until its reorganization in 1905. The tax structure which the Americans encountered was both overly complex, and in many respects, archaic. [18] In fiscal year 1894-95, internal revenue collections amounted to about ₱8,745,300.

Of this total, 76.1% came from direct and 23.9% from indirect
taxes. The most important source of direct taxes was the
cédula and its variants: the Chinese poll tax, and the tributes
from the wild tribes. These three taxes accounted for 76.3%
of direct taxes and 58.0% of all internal revenues collected. The
most important sources of indirect taxes were receipts from
two state monopolies: the opium contract and the lotteries. These
provided 70.8% of the receipts for indirect taxes for the fiscal
year 1894-95, and 16.9% of all internal revenue tax receipts
for that year.

The cédula was the most important single tax, accounting
for 52.4% of all internal revenue tax receipts. This was more
than twice the percentage of the rest of the direct taxes combined
(23.7%) or of the combined percentage of all indirect internal
revenue taxes (23.9%). The cédula had archaic roots, growing
out of an earlier head tax required from natives who had submitted
to Spanish rule as a "recognition of vassalage." By the time of
American occupation, it had grown into a rather complicated,
roughly graduated, but still basically inequitable system of taxation. Under its terms, every resident except the Chinese, and
the inhabitants of Palawan and Balabac was required to carry a
cédula personal, or certificate of identification. The goberna-
dorcillos, cabezas de barangays, religious and military personnel,
paupers and prisoners received these certificates free. The
heads of households had to pay for cédulas for those members not
excluded from this tax. The required payment varied from one-
half peso to 37 pesos, "determined by occupation, status, amount
of other taxes paid, and income."[19]

The Chinese poll tax was a discriminatory form of the cédula.
In the words of Charles Eliott, "The authorities seem to have
been in constant fear that they were not imposing on the Chinese
all that the traffic would bear."[20] This tax was never a major
source of revenue under the Spanish system (in fiscal year 1894-95,
it accounted for only 5.5% of all internal tax revenue), but its
social effects were disproportionately great. It was one form of
repressiveness in the Spanish system to which the American
colonialists never ceased pointing. (The Americans, by the way,
were quick enough to discriminate against Chinese immigration
to the islands.) The tributes from wild tribes were collected
from non-Christian tribes in lieu of the uncollectable personal
cédulas.

The Industria, or commerce and industry tax, was a tax on business determined not by the income of the enterprise but by "the kind of goods manufactured, the size and arrangement of the shop in which the business was transacted and the importance from a commercial point of view of the town in which it was located." Like the cédula, the effects of this tax were roughly graduated. Although in its actual operations it was probably a more equitable tax than the cédula, it was still designed to encourage capital investment into agriculture and was highly discriminatory against the Chinese.[21] The urban property tax was an assessment against commercial property in towns. This, of course, favored agricultural enterprises, since commercial agricultural property was not so taxed.

Several observations concerning the general operations of the nineteenth century Spanish internal revenue system are necessary. The system, dependent on various collection schemes, such as "farming out," was both racially discriminatory and overly complicated. This made its collection costs high both in social and monetary terms. Moreover, the system was inflexible and therefore incapable of dealing properly with the Philippines' rapidly emerging export economy. Elliott, perhaps the most knowledgeable American writer on the Spanish fiscal system, argued that such a system was adequate for the Filipino economy prior to the mid-nineteenth century. For example, the cédula and the commerce and industry taxes were roughly graduated, and were the most that could be achieved by way of an "income tax" in a country at that level of socio-economic development.[22] However, this system proved inadequate to the task of dealing with the rapidly changing situation which began in about the mid-1800's. Most importantly, the system discriminated heavily in favor of the cacique elite--the class on which both Spanish and, later, American rule rested. Although the cédula was a roughly graduated income tax, 37 pesos was almost nothing to a wealthy landlord, while one-half peso was a lot to a peasant. Furthermore, urban property was taxed, while rural agricultural land, the economic base of the caciques, was untouched. Finally, and most blatantly, the cabezas de barangays, the group from which the caciques developed, were exempt from most forms of taxation altogether.

Faced with this tax system, the Americans moved to "reform" the internal tax structure of the Philippines. American reformism

in this area reflected diverse concerns, many of which were
addressed to specific problems in the Spanish system. First,
the new colonialists attempted to simplify and rationalize the
tax collection system in order to shape it to the economic reality
of a rapidly emerging market economy. They also tried to
make the tax structure more equitable. However, their sense
of equitability was rather limited; they failed even to attempt
the types of redistributive measures which today seem almost
mandatory for dealing with the social consequences of an
expanding export economy. Finally, in their efforts at reforming the Spanish tax structure, the Americans displayed a type
of Progressive moralism, akin to that which stimulated Prohibition in the United States. All three of these concerns figured in
American tax reforms in the Philippines, although not all with
equal importance. Certainly most pressing to the colonialists
themselves was the need to rationalize tax structure. The
Americans showed a surprising lack of real commitment to
equity in taxation, even in their own terms, especially in view
of their professed aim of uplifting the "whole Filipino people."

Minor and piecemeal modifications in the tax structure of
the islands were made as early as 1899. The collection of
customs was greatly simplified; charges for the coinage of
money were ended; the government lottery and opium contract
were eliminated, as was the repugnant discriminatory Chinese
poll tax. [23] However, basic changes in the Philippine tax structure were not attempted until the passage of the Internal Revenue
Law of 1904. The commissions and omissions of this law are
important, because it established the basic tax policies which
were to continue through the American period and to a large
extent until the present day, and because it represented an
attempt to solidify the modus vivendi which had developed between
the American colonialists and the Filipino elite.

That the 1904 law strengthened the relationship of the cacique
elite and the Americans is illustrated in a description of its
drafting given by John S. Hord, one of its chief architects. [24]
The original draft was prepared in June and July of 1903, in the
United States by Hord and Henry Ide. Hord took it back to the
Philippines, where it "was considered an important piece of
legislation, and, following an established precedent in such
cases, the Commission set a day for a public discussion of the
proposed law and all interested were invited, by announcement

in their daily papers, to attend the public sessions and to join
in the debate before the Commission." The day was set for
April 6, 1904. Not much criticism was expected, as the writers
considered their work a fine example of new and enlightened tax
policies. "It developed, however, that the proposed measure
had been weighed in advance, and had been found wanting, by
those whose interests it affected . . . [none of whom] had a good
word to say for the bill. . . . Criticism of every detail of the
bill was permitted, and in fact invited, by the Commission. All
of the oral arguments were taken down verbatim."[25]

After meeting several days to hear such testimony from the
Filipino elite, the Commission adjourned and the revenue law
was rewritten. Several regulations were simplified and certain
penal provisions and proposed taxes were abolished. The amended act was then again publicized, a public discussion was held,
a few minor amendments were made, and the law was enacted
on July 2, 1904.[26]

The two taxes which were deleted completely from the final
version of the Revenue Law of 1904 illustrate the kinds of compromises which the colonialists made with the Filipino elite.
One was a proposed tax on corporations. The exclusion of such
a tax is perhaps understandable in terms of American economic
goals: "It was believed that to tax corporations, as such, might
discourage investors and keep out of the islands capital urgently
needed for their development."[27] The colonialists, who looked
forward to growing American investments in the islands, were
understandably willing to make this concession. However, it
must also be stressed that the corporation tax was originally
considered and proposed as a Progressive measure -- and was
thought to represent an example of the type of good government
which Progressive Americans were supposed to be bringing to
the islands. Such a corporation tax would have been progressive
and equitable in the more technical sense, and therefore surren-
dering it must be considered an abandonment of certain Progressive goals.

The second proposed tax which was eliminated in toto was a
legacy and inheritance tax. Since this tax would not in fact have
been disadvantageous to United States investment aims in the
country, the willingness of the Commission to dispense with this
particular measure cannot be explained by colonial economic

interests. In fact, the tax exemplified the type of reform measure
to which Progressive colonialists were purportedly ideologically
committed. According to Hord, "The proposed inheritance tax
was similar to the more modern systems lately adopted by several
of the States, providing liberal exemptions to next of kin, and a
graduated rate of tax increasing as propinquity of relationship
decreased and the amount of the inheritance increased. Under
ordinary conditions this tax is most equitable and imposes scarcely
any burden." But Mr. Hord found that ruling the Philippines did
not make for ordinary conditions. "Due to the fact that in the
Philippine Islands estates of descendants consist largely of lands
and city property and that it was not the general custom to parti-
tion such estates, and also for other weighty reasons, the
Philippine Commission wisely decided that a tax on inheritance
would impose undue burden and it was eliminated from the proposed law."[28] This decision represents an obvious concession
to the landed elite. The elimination of this tax betokens another
failure--along with failures which accompanied many proposed
judicial, land, and suffrage reforms--to effect changes in the
Philippine social system which would have lessened the power
of the caciques and thus would have provided a necessary, if not
sufficient, condition for balanced economic growth. Certainly
the inheritance tax, like the rest of the aforementioned reforms,
would not in and of itself have provided all that was necessary to
bring about such social change, but it could at least have been a
step; the failure to take such a step is a clear reflection of the
nature of the cooperative relationship which was developing
between the colonialists and the native elite.

Of course, the actual provisions of the Revenue Law of 1904
are more important than its omissions. These provisions, like
those made earlier in the period, served the causes of efficiency
and flexibility in the newly existing Philippine market economy,
rather than the cause of real and necessary social change. The
changes in the Industria (commerce and industry) tax serve as
an example. Hord writes concerning the old Spanish system,
"Neither the value of the merchant's stock, nor the extent of
his business, nor the amount of his profits, were used at all as
a basis for assessing the old Industria tax. All merchants in a
given line of business paid the same tax. The new internal
revenue law repeals this inequitable system." This analysis
does the old system somewhat of an injustice, however, for, as
mentioned earlier, the Spanish system was a complex, roughly

graduated system adequate for dealing with a non-expanding economy. However, the economy had begun to change rapidly long before American arrival and by the time of United States seizure of the Islands this tax had become cumbersome, expensive, and inadequate. The Revenue Law of 1904 modernized this business tax, making it more efficient and slightly more equitable. It imposed a percentage tax on sales payable quarterly. "The tax rate is 1 peso on each 300 pesos worth of sales; the small merchant pays a small amount as taxes and his tax payments increase in direct proportion to the increase in his business."[29]

The percentage of total revenue that businessmen were paying did not, however, change drastically during the American period. Under the Spanish system in 1894-95, this tax amounted to 15.1% of internal tax receipts. Under the American system, the "merchants, manufacturers, and common carriers" licenses amounted to 12% in 1906, had dropped to 9.6% in 1914, but had risen again to 22.2% in 1916. Adding the licenses for dealers in alcohol and tobacco, this percentage increased from 16.3% in 1906 to 24.7% in 1916. These figures seem to indicate a more impressive increase both in terms of percentages and in absolute values. However, to the Spanish figure should be added a portion of the Chinese poll tax, which was in actuality an indirect business tax, bringing that total percentage to roughly 17 or 18%. Thus only in 1915 and 1916 did the new American revenue system begin to change the tax burden substantially.[30] Furthermore, this tax, unlike one on agricultural land, for example, was easily shifted onto the consumer and thus, in itself, did not encourage social and technological changes in the form of "economies of production."

The Revenue Act of 1904 also included changes in the documentary stamp tax. These provide an additional example of reforms which aimed at increasing efficiency, but which did little to make the tax structure more equitable. John Hord asserted that formerly the tax had been unjustly high, thereby discouraging personal industry and that it had been overly complicated and petty. It therefore "often caused vexatious delays and unduly harassed business and professional men."[31] To eliminate such problems, the Revenue Act of 1904 exempted sums less than 30 pesos from such taxes, deleted a "multitude" of documents, and radically reduced the rates on others. This action in turn reduced the collections of stamp taxes from what they had been in the

Spanish period both in gross amount and percentage of total
collections. In 1894-95, ₱ 510,550 was collected. In fiscal
year 1906, only ₱ 166,167 was collected. The percentage of
total collections in the Spanish year 1894-95 was 5.8%, while in
1906 this number was 1.5%. By 1916, the percentage of total
collections represented by the documentary stamp tax fell to
0.9%. While this drop in percentage between 1906 and 1916
rarely reflected a drop in the absolute value of collections, in
no year did collections from this tax keep pace with the rapidly
expanding collections from more important taxes.[31] The
decreasing importance of this tax bears out Hord's claims to its
low levels of taxation.[32] These levels were especially low
considering that many of these taxes stood in lieu of any sort of
income or corporation tax. This tax reform was an explicit
attempt to make the revenue system more efficient. It also
aimed at stimulating economic prosperity by stimulating
"enterprise." However, it was not a reform which was concerned
with legislating social change or making the tax structure more
progressive.

The changes in the _cédula_ tax offer a third example of the
American failure to use fiscal policy as an instrument of reform.
"By various general orders of the Military Governor and acts of
the Philippine Commission during the first five years of American occupation, the cedula personal tax was reduced in amount
from an average of 5 pesos per adult male to a straight tax of
1 peso."[34] As a consequence of these measures, the percentage
of total revenue for which the _cédula_ was responsible declined
from 52.4% in 1894-95 to 15.5% in 1906. In 1908 the _cédula_
accounted for 22.9% of internal revenue, but by 1916 only 14.6%.
In monetary terms this meant the _cédula_, which produced about
4.6 million pesos in fiscal year 1894-95, accounted for only
about 1.75 million in fiscal year 1906. It grew throughout the
period under consideration but by 1916 collections had not yet
quite risen to the old Spanish level. In that year the _cédula_
accounted for about 4.5 million pesos.[35]

While this decline in the importance of the _cédula_ is pointed
to by both Hord and Taft as a progressive step, it was not really
as progressive as is often assumed. Under the Spanish system
the _cédula_ had been roughly graduated. Even granting that 37
pesos was little for a landlord while one-half peso was a great
deal to a peasant, the American "reform" of making the _cédula_

a flat one peso was definitely not a step in the direction of equity. Furthermore, the American internal revenue system depended on the cédula tax more heavily than would be supposed merely by considering the figures which were given in the reports of the Bureau of Internal Revenue. Roads were built chiefly by cédula labor (the peasants, under the American system, could pay their road cédulas in labor). The road cédula was levied by the provincial boards under the provisions of Act. No. 1652. It was a less repressive, updated version of the Spanish polo (forced labor). This act allowed the provincial governments to double the amount of the normal cédula, and keep half of it for construction and repair of roads. By the calendar year 1913, this act was in force in 33 Philippine provinces, in which resided 95.6% of the cédula-paying population.[36]

While reforms which have already been discussed were not particularly progressive in effect, one tax change accomplished by the 1904 Internal Revenue Act was in fact a definite move in the direction of equitable reform. "The most radical change made by the new internal revenue law . . . consisted in the shifting of the bulk of the taxes . . . from articles of necessary consumption to the articles of luxurious, or optional consumption."[37] Under the Spanish system necessities such as imported rice and cloth were rather heavily taxed, thus forcing the poor to carry a major part of the burden of excise taxes. When the United States occupied the Philippines, the colonialists moved immediately to eliminate such "ultra-regressive" taxes. True to much of the Progressivism of the period, they shifted heavy taxes to the rather decadent luxuries of life--tobacco and liquor--figuring that if a man could afford to drink, he could also afford to pay a heavy tax for the privilege. Under American rule the excise taxes on alcohol and tobacco (including taxes on domestic production and on imports) became the most important single revenue collecting device in operation. In 1906, it accounted for 38.1% of total collections, in 1913, 38.6%, and in 1916, 30.5%.[38]

While this new system of excise taxes was definitely more equitable than that of the Spaniards, it was also--like similar Progressive measures in the United States--a method of justifying a basically regressive system of taxation upon moral grounds. For, unfortunately, the consumption of alcohol and tobacco does not necessarily increase with income, and thus such a tax weighs more heavily on the poor. While it is understandable that members of the American upper class, such as Forbes or Hord, or of the

the Filipino elite saw their position as morally based, it was also a position which allowed the elite to carry less than its fair share of the tax burden.[39]

This is not to say that such moralism was a sham. Sincere moralistic beliefs motivated several fiscal reforms. For example, the lottery, which was a governmental monopoly under the Spanish system, was abolished. Cockpits, by far the most important revenue source included under the American tax on "Occupations, trades, and professions," were always under attack.[40] The most important of these moralistic Progressive fiscal reforms involved opium use. When the Americans seized power, they moved almost at once to eliminate the Spanish opium monopoly, though opium trade with China continued. After various earlier attempts, on March 8, 1906, the Philippine Commission finally took definite action to end the opium problem with the passage of Act No. 1761, the "Opium Law."[41] Typical of much of Progressive thinking, the Opium Law was an attempt to tax opium use out of existence. The plan was based on slowly raising the price of opium to the consumer, especially by increasing indirect taxes on it. The rise in price, in turn, was expected to cause the demand for opium to fall. This would facilitate the stage-by-stage, orderly prohibition of the drug's use.[42]

While there is some question as to the opium law's effectiveness in legislating morality, it was successful in legislating itself out of existence as an important source of revenue. By the end of 1913, William T. Nolting, then Collector of Internal Revenue, could write that, "In the early days of the enforcement of this Law, the revenue features of [it] were of considerable importance to, and were inseparably connected with the general scheme and purpose of the law. . . . [However,] after March 1, 1908, . . . due to [the] absolute prohibition of the use of opium, except for medicinal purposes, the revenue features of the law became insignificant."[43] Nolting's statement is supported in the records of revenue collections. In 1907, the first full year of its operation, the Opium Law accounted for 4.6% of total revenue collections. This is somewhat lower than the 6.9% brought in by the opium monopoly in 1894-95. By 1914, receipts from the law amounted to 0.2% of collections and never thereafter made up as much as 0.1% of total revenue collections. This drop represented as well a decline in the absolute money value of collections from the Opium Law. In 1907, the law accounted

for ₱ 589,600, but by 1916, it brought in only ₱ 1,700.[44]
Nevertheless, although Progressive moralism was an important part of the justificatory ideology of American colonialism,
and although it was often incorporated into fiscal policy, it was
not really integral to that policy, and did not significantly affect
the total tax structure on which the administration was based.

Of greater economic importance were -- or could have been --
the decisions made with regard to agricultural production and
real estate, the bases of the whole Filipino economy and of elite
wealth. First, all agricultural products were exempted from tax
payments by either the producer or the exporter.[45] This exemption, like a similar one under the Spanish regime, encouraged
export agriculture. It favored, both economically and politically,
the cacique elite, whose power base was in agriculture. Real
estate, on the other hand, was taxed in an ostensibly new way by
the Revenue Law of 1904. Under the Spanish system, the land
tax was determined solely by the use to which the property was
put. But under American rule "The tax on real estate, or 'land
tax' as it came to be called, was an even more significant departure from Spanish revenue methods than the taxes on alcoholic
liquors and tobacco. Following American practice, the land tax
was levied on the capital or market value as assessed against all
privately owned land, buildings, and improvements."[46] However,
if the methods of assessing land taxes differed greatly from the
Spanish system, the net effects did not. Under the American
system, land -- especially that in rural estates -- continued to be
undertaxed. The tax was not even collected between 1904 and
1907, due to resistance from the caciques, and, when it was
collected, large amounts of assessed tax were waived, and non-
payment was generously forgiven.[47] Furthermore, the real
estate assessment was a local and not a national tax. The net
effect of this was that "the full possibilities of this tax base as
a revenue source have never been realized."[48]

Although several progressive taxes -- including a personal
income tax and an inheritance tax -- were enacted later,[49] the
basic tax structure of the Philippines during the American period
was formulated by the end of 1904. By this time the Americans
had reformed many of the aspects of the earlier Spanish system.
Simplified tax schedules and a modernized tax bureaucracy made

the revenue systems more efficient and economical. The elimination of such revenue sources as the opium monopoly and
especially the Chinese head tax decreased certain social costs
of the internal revenue system. Finally, the American colonialists eliminated many ultra-regressive aspects of the Spanish
system. For example, the burdensome excise taxes were shifted
from articles of necessity, such as rice, to "luxury" items,
particularly alcohol and tobacco. More importantly, the idea of
taxation for all was accepted. Under the Spaniards the goberna-
dorcillos and cabezas de barangays were specifically exempt
from much of the tax, while under the Americans they were
taxed along with the peasants.

Singly, any of these reforms might be called progressive.
However, on a broader level, the overall tendency of American
revenue policy was not to produce a truly progressive system of
taxation. Throughout the period under study, two undeniably
regressive taxes, the excise tax on alcohol and tobacco, and the
cédula, accounted for over 45% of all internal revenue. Moreover, most of the more progressive taxes, like that on "merchants, manufacturers, and common carriers," etc., were in
the main taxes which could be easily shifted onto the consumer.
The tax which had the single greatest possibility as a progressive
assessment on real wealth, the land tax, was largely ignored.
This failure was particularly significant because of the concentration of land ownership in the hands of the caciques, who
therefore largely escaped their share of taxation under the American internal revenue system in the Islands. [50]

Judged by their own standards, the American fiscal policy
makers failed in a basic way to make taxation an instrument of
Progressive aims. There is another sense, at least, in which
American internal revenue policies were a failure--they did not
encourage economic development. Much has been written concerning the effects of free trade on Filipino economic development,
but internal fiscal policy, though frequently ignored as a factor,
was also very important. Taxation is more than just a revenue
producer; it can also provide incentives to increase productivity.
In the Philippines, the low levels of property tax failed to create
a situation in which the landlords were encouraged to increase
agricultural productivity. Since agriculture was so important
in the Philippine economy, such a failure did have ramifications
for all sectors of the economy.

Moreover, the internal fiscal policy of the Americans did much to actually discourage economic diversification, by encouraging concentration on market agriculture. Like its Spanish predecessor, the American system supported export agriculture through low levels of taxation of it. In the American case, produce was left entirely untaxed, while land, though taxed, was underassessed. This made the more modern sectors of the economy carry a disproportionate share of the tax burden. It is important to note in this regard that many progressive revenue measures enacted by the Americans, such as the income tax of 1913, were most effective in taxing the more modernized sectors of the economy.[51]

The failure to use the powers of taxation to promote economic development can be traced in part to a mistaken idea on the part of the colonialists as to what in fact would bring such development. John Hord, W.C. Forbes, and Harold Pitt, among others, show in their writings that they considered the agricultural export sector as the crucial one in promoting growth, and thus felt that low levels of taxation of this sector would encourage such growth and thus bring economic prosperity.[52] Perhaps these men felt this way because they perceived a basic, though false, analogy between the nature of economic development in the United States, and that which they considered was necessary for the Philippines. Their positions as colonial officials were also a clear influence on their thinking in such matters. Probably all the American policy makers felt that the best relationship for both the metropolitan and colonial structures would be one in which the latter would export its raw materials and import goods manufactured in the metropolis. Their failure to see the inherent limitations for the Philippines of such a relationship was very much a function of their position as representatives of the colonial power.

Also significant in the failure to use the powers of taxation to encourage development was the nature of the political hold of the United States in the Philippines. The Americans ruled through some of the most conservative elements in Filipino society--"elements" which supported the supremacy of an agricultural elite, and thus were ultimately committed to a colonial type of underdeveloped export economy. In this respect, American fiscal policy must be seen as a concession to a group whose favor was necessary for successful rule.

Thus, in the final analysis, American colonial rule failed to bring promised social change because it was colonial rule. As such, order was more important than change, agriculture was desired over industry, and stability was more necessary than development. The Americans found themselves in alliance with the group which was at the same time most able to keep the peace and most committed to retaining the status quo ante. The United States, though ruling in the name of uplifting the natives, found herself entirely committed to the ascendency of a Filipino elite whose members wanted the rest of the "natives" to stay right where they were.

APPENDIX I

INTERNAL REVENUE RECEIPTS FOR FISCAL YEAR 1894-95[a]

| Type | Figures in thousands of Pesos | | |
	Receipts	% of Category	% of Total
Direct Taxes	6,659	100 %	76.1%
Cédula	4,586	68.9	52.4
Chinese poll tax	483	7.2	5.5
Tributes from "wild tribes"	12	0.2	0.1
Industria	1,323	19.9	15.1
Urban property tax	110	1.7	1.3
10% tax on railroad tickets	35	0.5	0.4
10% assessment on "certain salaries"	70	1.1	0.8
10% premium on certain taxes[b]	40	0.6	0.5
Indirect Taxes	2,086	100 %	23.9%
Opium contract	602	28.9	6.9
Stamps and stamped paper	511	24.5	5.8
Lotteries	873	41.9	10.0
Profits on coinage[c]	100	4.8	1.1
Total	8,745	----	100 %

[a] Constructed from Elliott, pp. 266-67, and George Arthur Malcolm, The Government of the Philippine Islands: Its Development and Fundamentals (Rochester, N.Y., 1916), pp. 82-83. This table omits several types of revenue receipts which either fall outside the scope of this paper or lack reliable statistics. In the former category are customs receipts (₱4,565,000, or 36% of all revenues) and profits from the sale of forest products and state lands, etc. (In 1880-81 the Spanish collected ₱220,000 from such sales, or approximately 1.5% of total revenues for that year; D. Gregorio Sancianco y Gosón, El Progreso de Filipinas [Madrid, 1881], pp. 16-25.) In the latter category are provincial and municipal taxes, which Malcolm, pp. 86-87, estimates at ₱2 million for 1895-96, of which Manila accounted for ₱667,538. No figures for Church revenues or expenditures are included.

[b] Premiums were charged for the collection of the urban property tax, the Industria, the cédula, and the Chinese poll tax.

[c] Estimated by Elliott.

APPENDIX II

INTERNAL REVENUE RECEIPTS FOR SELECTED YEARS, 1906-1916[a]

Type	Figures in Thousands of Pesos						
	1906	1907	1908	1913	1914	1915	1916
Cédula	1,756.8	1,919.7	3,285.5	4,081.3	4,090.1	4,296.8	4,480.7
% of total	15.5	15.1	22.9	18.4	18.1	15.7	14.6
Merchants, manufacturers, and common carriers	1,365.4	1,374.2	1,305.3	2,140.9	2,175.6	5,116.2	6,819.8
% of total	12.0	10.8	9.1	9.7	9.6	18.7	22.2
Alcohol, tobacco dealers	494.3	511.4	502.2	689.4	715.8	815.0	768.9
% of total	4.3	4.0	3.5	3.1	3.2	3.0	2.5
Excise on alcohol, tobacco	4,328.1	4,736.1	4,990.6	8,567.2	8,658.7	8,507.0	9,370.3
% of total	38.1	37.1	34.8	38.6	38.4	31.1	30.5
Opium tax	81.4[b]	589.6	312.0	88.6	39.2	10.7	1.7
% of total	0.7	4.6	2.2	0.4	0.2	c	c
Documentary stamp tax	166.2	181.1	182.7	280.9	261.1	250.8	282.1
% of total	1.5	1.4	1.3	1.3	1.2	0.9	0.9
Occupations, trades, and professions[d]	308.2	380.2	417.2	668.9	717.1	846.1	859.2
% of total	2.7	3.0	2.9	3.0	3.2	3.1	2.8
City of Manila taxes[e]	2,465.8	2,668.0	2,859.3	3,676.7	3,709.2	3,782.1	3,852.0
% of total	21.7	20.9	20.0	16.6	16.4	13.8	12.5
Income tax	----	----	----	----	285.9	481.0	529.6
% of total					1.3	1.8	1.7
Inheritance tax	----	----	----	----	----	----	5.9
% of total							c

Other[f]	400.4	388.6	544.0	1,991.4	1,897.5	3,382.7	3,761.4
% of total	3.5	3.1	3.3	8.9	8.4	11.9	12.3
TOTAL	11,366.6	12,749.0	14,399.8	22,184.9	22,550.1	27,338.4	30,731.6
% increase from previous year	----	12.2	12.5	----	1.6	21.5	12.2

Total increase 1906-1916: 170.4%

a Source: "Summary of Collections" in RCIR, 1906, 1907, 1908, 1914, 1916. This table does not include revenues collected by the Bureau of Customs nor fees collected by other bureaus, nor revenues collected by any provinces nor municipalities except Manila.

b Three months only.

c Less than 0.1%.

d While by its title this tax appears to be a (progressive) tax on the educated elite, this is not actually the case. "Proprietors of cockpits" paid 64% of this tax in 1906, 72% in 1908, 69% in 1916. "Lawyers, doctors, civil engineers and surveyors" paid only 16% in 1906, 14% in 1908. (No figures for 1916.) The remainder was paid by other licensees, including owners of race tracks.

e Includes land tax, market receipts, liquor licenses, rentals of city property, vehicle licenses, Board of Health fees, and Justice of the Peace fees.

f Includes "Banks and Bankers," forest products, excise on fuel (1915-16 only), mining concessions, taxes on insurance companies, playing cards and movies, franchise taxes, fees from weights and measures, and income from the San Lazaro estate. Of this, forest products amount to ₱ 165-495 thousand, or 1.3-2.0% of the total.

150

Notes

1. Cf. William J. Pomeroy, <u>American Neo-Colonialism: Its Emergence in the Philippines and Asia</u> (New York, 1970), pp. 99-149; and William E. Leuchtenburg, "Progressivism and Imperialism: The Progressive Movement and American Foreign Policy, 1898-1916," <u>The Mississippi Valley Historical Review</u>, XXXIX-3 (1952), 483-504. Both authors argue that Progressivism was intimately linked to the imperialist surge.

2. David P. Barrows, <u>A Decade of American Government in the Philippines: 1903-1913</u> (Yonkers, N.Y., 1914), p. 17.

3. Cf. Rhoads Murphey, "Traditionalism and Colonialism: Changing Urban Roles in Asia," <u>JAS</u>, XXIX-1 (1969), 70, 83, for one discussion of this centralizing tendency. Murphey argues that in Asia, seaport cities were "beachheads of an exogenous system which became the nuclei for penetration and rule."

4. William Cameron Forbes, <u>The Philippine Islands</u> (Boston and New York, 1928), I, 258.

5. Barrows, pp. 17-18.

6. <u>Second Annual Report of the Collector of Internal Revenue, Fiscal Year 1906 (John S. Hord, Collector of Internal Revenue)</u> (Manila, 1906), p. 6. Figures rounded to the nearest 1/10 of a percent. (Hereinafter these <u>Reports</u> referred to as <u>RCIR</u>.)

7. <u>RCIR 1914 (James J. Rafferty)</u>, p. 6. Even these figures, of course, reflect a high degree of concentration of revenue use.

8. <u>RCIR 1916 (James J. Rafferty)</u>, p. 6.

9. Frank H. Golay, The Philippines: Public Policy and National Economic Development (Ithaca, N.Y., 1961), p. 205.

10. Ibid., p. 16n.

11. Alleyne Ireland, The Far Eastern Tropics: Studies in the Administration of Tropical Dependencies (Boston and New York, 1905), p. 222.

12. RCIR 1907 (John S. Hord), p. 7.

13. RCIR 1914 (James J. Rafferty), p. 8. It is important to note that Filipinization was also important in lowering costs. "This substantial progress toward the Filipinization of the service, with the incidental saving on the salary roll, . . . also resulted in a more systematic and logical arrangement of its work." RCIR 1913 (William T. Nolting), p. 10.

14. Golay, p. 14; Murphey, p. 84. Murphey points out that in Southeast Asia and specifically in the Philippines, the urban area serves both to transform the hinterland, and to drain the surplus which is thus created there.

15. Eric R. Wolf, Peasants (Englewood Cliffs, N.J., 1966), p. 56. Wolf concludes that there is often a critical social failure in such situations. "Such a system is self-limiting in that it reduces incentives by reducing the cultivating populations' consumption to the biological minimum. Thereupon the cities benefit from the surpluses drained off from the countryside by urban rent collectors, without generating expanded rural productivity."

16. Harold M. Pitt, The Facts as to the Philippine Islands: Compiled for the Enlightenment of the American People (Manila [1914?]), pp. 29-30.

17. Golay, p. 183.

18. See Appendix I for internal revenue taxes and receipts 1894-95, the last year under Spanish rule in which collections were not disrupted by the Philippine Revolution.

19. Charles Burke Elliott. The Philippines: To the End of the Military Régime (Indianapolis, 1916), p. 252.

20. Ibid., p. 253.

21. Ibid., pp. 256-57.

22. Ibid., p. 258.

23. Forbes, I, 248, 254.

24. John S. Hord, "Internal Taxation in the Philippines," Johns Hopkins University Studies in Historical and Political Science, XXV-1 (1907), 7-45.

25. Ibid., pp. 20-21.

26. Ibid., pp. 23-24.

27. Ibid., p. 23.

28. Ibid.

29. Ibid., p. 32.

30. See Appendix I, II. Some of the increase in the percentage of the collection on "merchants, manufacturers, and common carriers licenses" is probably due to the collection of a corporate income tax. On March 1, 1913, corporate income was subject to 1% tax. In 1916 the tax was increased to 2%. Golay, pp. 192-193. The "merchants, manufacturers, and common carriers licenses" accounted for 24.2% of total internal revenue in 1917, 28.4% in 1918, 25.9% in 1919, and 23.4% in 1920. RCIR 1917 (James J. Rafferty), p. 5; RCIR 1918 (W. Trinidad), pp. 5-9; RCIR 1919 (W. Trinidad), pp. 5-9; RCIR 1920 (W. Trinidad), pp. 5-9.

31. Hord, pp. 10-11, 32.

32. See Appendix I, II.

33. Hord, pp. 26-28. A glance at selected documentary rates also bears out Hord's claims to its low levels of taxation.

Certificates of stock, whether on organization or
reorganization, on each 200 pesos, or fractional
part thereof, of face value . . . 20 centavos.
(1 centavo = 1/2¢ American.)

Drafts drawing interest, and payable otherwise than
at sight or on demand, on each 200 pesos, or fractional part thereof of face value . . . 2 centavos.

Promissory notes, other than issues for circulation,
or any renewal thereof, on each 200 pesos, or
fractional part thereof . . . 2 centavos.

Lease or rent of any real estate, tenement or part
thereof for period of 1 year or less . . . 20 centavos.

34. Ibid., pp. 10-11.

35. See Appendix I, II.

36. RCIR 1913 (William T. Nolting), p. 25.

37. Hord, p. 33.

38. See Appendix II.

39. It is interesting, in this respect, to note that John Hord saw
that many of the tax reforms in the Philippines would have the
same effects as many Progressive reforms in the United
States: that of concentrating economic power in the hands of
the "better class" of large manufacturers. (Cf. Gabriel
Kolko, The Triumph of Conservatism: A Reinterpretation
of American History, 1900-1916, [Chicago, 1967], for a
discussion of this aspect of Progressivism in the United
States.) Hord wrote that the American licensing procedures
would force the "smaller and more ignorant manufacturers
of vino, cigars, and cigarettes" to operate illegally. This,
in turn, would cause the larger manufacturers to support
governmental actions against these smaller competitors.
The effective operations of the law, Hord felt, would tend to
decrease the number of stills operating and increase their
efficiency. (Hord, pp. 37-38.) His predictions were essentially correct.

40. See Appendix II, note d.

41. The full title of this law was: "An Act gradually to restrict and regulate the sale and use of opium pending the ultimate prohibition of the importation of opium into the Philippine Islands in whatever form except for medical purposes as provided by the Act of Congress approved March third, nineteen hundred and five, and prohibiting any of their several forms or any derivative or preparation of any such drugs or substances, except for medicinal purposes, and to repeal Act Numbered Fourteen hundred and sixty-one, and for other purposes." RCIR 1912 (William T. Nolting), p. 39.

42. RCIR 1913 (William T. Nolting), p. 42.

43. Ibid.

44. See Appendix I, II.

45. Hord, p. 31.

46. Forbes, I, 254-55.

47. Ibid., I, 256.

48. Golay, p. 206. For an analysis of postwar conditions see Ibid., pp. 207-09.

49. See Appendix II. A personal income tax was enacted in the Philippines in 1913. In fiscal 1914, it amounted to 1.3% of total revenue; in 1915, 1.8%, and in 1916, 1.7%. Golay writes "The rates of the Philippine personal income tax are moderately progressive. . . . The personal exemptions . . . are excessively liberal." Because of a lack of tax discipline, "only a small part of the potential revenues from this source" is realized, most of which is "accounted for by withholding tax assessed against employees of enterprises and civil servants." The end result, he writes, is that "The Philippine personal income tax as presently administered is a travesty on tax equity." Golay, pp. 187-92. Also enacted in 1913 was a corporate income tax (see note 30, above); collections on an inheritance tax were first made in 1916.

50. For a parallel argument about a later period see Golay,
    p. 209. He writes, "Failure to levy and collect a realistic
    real property tax in the Philippines is particularly unfor-
    tunate because of the concentration of land ownership and
    absentee landlordism. Ownership of agricultural land is
    a reliable index of agricultural income and wealth, and in
    the Philippines these largely escape taxation." The approach
    of this paper owes much to the general arguments found in
    Golay.

51. For a similar argument about a later period again see
    Golay, pp. 190-91, 209.

52. Cf. Hord, pp. 13-15; Forbes, I, 249-51; Pitt, pp. 1-18.

Quezon's Role in Philippine Independence

by

Joseph F. Hutchinson, Jr.

On February 10, 1933, a tired, tubercular man delivered
to a meeting of Philippine Provincial Governors and Treasurers
a succinct denunciation of the Hare-Hawes-Cutting Act, an act
for Philippine Independence which had recently been passed by
the United States Congress over President Hoover's veto. The
speaker's once jet-black sideburns were now a hoary white, but
his elegant style still radiated charm and force. He attacked the
trade provisions of the act as unfair to the Philippines; he
claimed that the proposed Commonwealth did not give the Filipinos
"the opportunity, the means, the power to legislate for themselves"; he denounced the proponents of the act for "behaving
as though we are engaged in an electoral campaign, accusing
those who do not agree with [them] as traitors to the country."[1]
What was remarkable was not the substance of the speech, but
the fact that it was made by Manuel Quezon, leader of the
Nacionalista Party and symbol of the Philippine demand for
independence. Now he stood as an apparent opponent of the
independence that had for so long been his publicly avowed goal,
stood in opposition not only to the United States Congress but
also to his close friends and long-time colleagues in the leadership of the Nacionalista Party.

This paper is not a biography of Manuel Quezon or a chronicle
of Philippine independence; it is, rather, a study of how a
remarkable man used political power. At one of the most crucial
points in Philippine history--when the reality of independence
was at hand in 1932-33--Quezon, the leader of that nation, was
seemingly willing to block the decades-old dream of attaining
independence in order to ensure his continued hegemony in

domestic politics. This is a study of how Quezon used this opportunity to strengthen his political position, and how the Filipino socio-political system allowed such an action to occur.

Quezon's most dominant characteristic was his ability to manipulate people; he had a proud, volatile, and charismatic personality which he used skillfully to mobilize Filipinos behind him. His personal flair and political force quickly made him a prominent national figure, and his keen understanding of the intricacies of Philippine politics enabled him to build up a permanently loyal following. By publicly advocating immediate, complete, and absolute independence for the Philippines, he became a national symbol to his people. Filipinos were mobilized into a more viable polity by their admiration for Quezon's dynamic personality. He made himself the embodiment of national unity, will, dignity, and desire for independence, and Filipinos responded by praising his ability to mingle with other world leaders and by reveling vicariously in his political pomp and grandeur.

Quezon's personality was also mercurial, however, and to understand him it is necessary to study the sly, ambivalent, and sometimes ruthless side of his personality. Quezon's private correspondence[2] shows how he manipulated the Filipino people so that he could continue his rule over them. He also deceived his own friends and lied to politicians in order to further his political ambitions. But he was extremely careful in his chicanery--he seldom allowed his lies to catch up with him publicly and undermine his position.

This study will focus on Quezon's opposition to the Hare-Hawes-Cutting Act, and the explanations he advanced for thus rejecting the very issue he had been publicly advocating for so long. It may lead us closer to an understanding of Quezon's own motivation, his rationalization of his action--was it pure political ambition, or a sincere belief that the Hare-Hawes-Cutting Act was inferior to an independence bill he himself might be able to obtain from Congress?

Manuel Quezon was born on August 19, 1878 in the small town of Baler in the province of Tayabas (now Quezon Province). He had a good education, culminating in study at the College of San Juan de Letran in 1894. After fighting the Americans as an insurrecto, Quezon passed his bar exams and was appointed Fiscal (prosecuting attorney) of Mindoro in 1903; in 1904 he was transferred to Tayabas. Later that year he resigned from the bureaucracy and set up a private law practice. At this time, Quezon began his illustrious political career.

There were then in the Philippines several underground pro-independence parties; three of these[3] were to merge to form the Partido Nacionalista (Nacionalistas) not long after the ban on such parties was lifted in 1906. Quezon plunged into action in this formative period of Filipino politics and became a close friend of Sergio Osmeña,[4] who would emerge as leader of the Nacionalistas. In the 1907 elections for the Philippine Assembly, the Nacionalistas rolled up a decisive plurality over all other parties;[5] Osmeña was elected Speaker, with Quezon's backing. Osmeña asserted his claim to leadership in Philippine politics by his fiery invective against American rule, claiming the Filipinos' right to immediate, complete, and absolute independence.[6]

In 1909 Osmeña sent Quezon to Washington as the Philippine Resident Commissioner to the United States. Quezon disseminated the Filipino desire for immediate independence to both Congress and the American people at large. He created a newspaper, The Filipino People, with the support of the American Anti-Imperialist League and "many important figures in the Democratic Party."[7] When he addressed Congress in 1910, instead of chiding the United States with a frontal attack on colonialism, he praised American conduct in the Philippines, while noting that the Filipinos were capable of controlling their own destiny. In response to a question about the desire of the Filipinos for independence, the young Commissioner replied, "Ask the bird, Sir, who is enclosed in a golden cage if he would prefer the cage and the care of his owner to the freedom of the skies and the allure of the forest."[8]

A swing in American politics toward the Democratic Party produced both the "Filipinization" of the Philippine bureaucracy under Governor-General Francis B. Harrison and a growing Congressional sentiment in favor of Philippine independence. In 1912 Democratic Congressman William Atkinson Jones introduced a bill providing for Philippine Independence, but it failed to get out of committee. In 1914 another "Jones Bill" passed the House but was rejected by the Senate. In 1916 it was reintroduced once more, this time with the Clarke Amendment attached,

which guaranteed that independence would be granted within five
years. Quezon had lobbied for the Jones Bill since 1912 but
did not support the Clarke Amendment. In this he was backed
by Osmeña; neither politician seemed over-anxious for a
definite early date for Philippine independence. [9]

The private memoranda of General Frank McIntyre, Chief
of the Bureau of Insular Affairs of the War Department, show
Quezon's growing concern that immediate independence might
be detrimental to the Philippines and to ilustrado control.
Despite his public espousals of immediate independence since
his rise to national prominence in 1907, Quezon now privately
proposed a new organic act which would give the Islands their
independence in twenty-five years. McIntyre wrote that Quezon
"said that there would perhaps be a little more difficulty in
getting an agreement to this now than there would have been a
few years ago, in that independence now had acquired an attractive sound to the ears of the Filipinos." When Quezon had
expressed his fear to Congressman Jones that the Jones proposal
for independence in three years would give the Philippines
independence too early, McIntyre recorded that Quezon "was
afraid that he had impressed Mr. Jones unfavorably in standing
out against that."[10]

Nevertheless, Quezon returned to Manila claiming sole
credit for the Jones Act (which had passed without the Clarke
Amendment)[11] and was greeted as a national hero. The Filipino
people believed that Quezon had done his best to obtain immediate
independence, but had been limited to the Jones Act by the United
States Congress. The credit awarded Quezon for this achievement made him a threat to Osmeña's power, but Osmeña skillfully managed to obtain the leading position in the newly created
Council of State, thus reaffirming his control of the party and
temporarily thwarting Quezon's advance in domestic politics.
In 1919 Quezon returned to Washington as head of the first
Philippine Independence Mission, hoping to obtain further
concessions from the Democrats which might enable him to
supplant Osmeña. He took with him the "Declaration of
Purposes" passed on March 17, 1919 by the Philippine
Legislature, which reiterated the demand for independence.[12]
Quezon pleaded the Filipino case to Secretary of War Newton
Baker with the help of Governor-General Harrison, then vacation-
ing in the United States. Baker gave the Mission a sympathetic
hearing and said that Wilson would work for Philippine independence

when he returned from Versailles.[13] In December 1920 Wilson
told the Congress (after a Republican electoral landslide)
that a "stable" government existed in the Islands, and that it
was the duty of the Congress to keep its "promise to the people
of those Islands by granting them the independence which they
so honorably covet."[14] But Wilson's efforts were fruitless,
and Quezon found he could do little else to promote the independence issue, so he decided to return to the Philippines to
challenge Osmeña directly.

The tactless rule of newly-appointed Governor-General
Leonard Wood gave Quezon the opportunity he sought. Wood's
constant pressure on the Filipino elite caused dissension within
the Nacionalista party. Quezon publicly blamed Osmeña for the
disintegration of the party, which, he asserted, stemmed from
Osmeña's pretentious assumption of a dictatorial role in both
the party and the Legislature. These attacks upon Osmeña's
"unipersonalistic" rule were ultimately successful, and
Quezon was elected President of the Senate. He thereupon
turned around and obtained a rapprochement with Osmeña
which lasted for a decade.

Quezon, now the most powerful Filipino politician, sent
several independence missions to Washington, but Presidents
Harding, Coolidge, and Hoover were impervious to any such
pleas. Late in 1927 Quezon was incapacitated by tuberculosis
and he was forced to convalesce at a sanatorium in Monrovia,
California. For three years he tried to maintain his power by
corresponding from his sick bed to Manila and Washington. His
enforced isolation allowed him to take an overview of the
Philippine-American situation. During his illness his views on
the possible problems of a premature independence began to
solidify. A new set of variables complicated the independence
issue even more. Quezon watched the growing militarism of
Japan and the worsening Depression; he was one of the first
Filipinos to recognize that these phenomena had profoundly
altered American policy toward the Philippine Islands. Independence was becoming a real possibility, no longer just a political
and rhetorical issue.

Before 1929, despite the increasing trade between the United States and the Philippines, Americans tended to overlook the economic realities of imperialism and to see the Philippines primarily in political and administrative terms. But with the coming of the Depression, every sector of the American economy began to suffer. Many Americans began to see the Philippines as a liability; the Islands became a scapegoat for American fears and hostilities. The Western states had begun lobbying to restrict Filipino immigration because their unemployed labor pool already exceeded the critical limits. The large labor organizations not only wanted Filipino immigration halted, but they also proposed that the free entry of Philippine goods be curtailed. Labor felt that any foreign goods successfully competing with the goods produced by the American worker would only add momentum to the snowballing Depression. Certain Congressmen, mainly from the agricultural states, also began to propose tariff and import quotas on Philippine goods. Groups such as dairy farmers, cottonseed oil producers, cane and beet sugar growers, cordage manufacturers, and sundry "patriotic" societies began to lobby for Philippine independence so that the Islands would lose their special status and become a foreign country susceptible to import quotas.

In January, 1930, Senator William King of Utah presented the Senate with a bill for immediate independence. In March, Senator Harry Hawes of Missouri and Senator Bronson Cutting of New Mexico introduced a bill which provided for the popular election of a Philippine constituent assembly to construct a constitution. By the provisions of the Hawes-Cutting Bill the Philippines would remain under lenient American control for five more years, during which time the free trade between the United States and the Philippines would gradually be abrogated by the introduction of steadily increasing tariff walls. A similar bill was introduced in the House by Congressman Butler B. Hare of South Carolina.

Quezon increasingly realized that the Philippine economy would be periled if there was no trade protection by the United States in an independence bill. [15] In a letter to Osmeña, Quezon wrote that Philippine free trade with the United States was not resting on a solid foundation, because it "depends not at all

upon our will but exclusively on the will of Congress."[16]
Although both politicians believed that immediate independence
would be a mistake, they dared not abandon their "immediate,
complete, and absolute" independence platform at this time,
professing instead to educate the Filipino people gradually about
the dangers of a premature independence.

Quezon, who had only partially recovered from his illness,
had returned to the Philippines late in 1929. Although the
political battle wounds of 1922 were not entirely healed, Osmeña
and Quezon became extremely close political comrades.
Quezon's will was by far the stronger of the two and Quezon
could usually get Osmeña to follow his lead. Osmeña and
Quezon were intimate enough to trust each other and to exchange
private political thoughts. It was not until later that their
divergent views on the independence issue drove them to ruthless political slander against each other.

Early in 1930, Osmeña and Manuel Roxas[17] had been sent
by the Philippine Legislature to Washington to lobby for independence. Osmeña returned to Manila after a brief stay in
Washington to confer with Quezon. After discussing the economic
issue, Osmeña proposed that he return to Washington to support
the Hawes-Cutting Bill and the Hare Bill. Quezon agreed to this
plan.

Roxas had remained in Washington to continue the fight for
independence and to espouse the Filipino position at the Senate
hearings on the Hawes-Cutting Bill. Roxas cabled Osmeña,
who was on his way to meet him, a statement made by Henry
Stimson which concerned the Senate's possible approval of an
independence bill, but Roxas assured Osmeña that no action
seemed likely to be taken in Congress in that session. Roxas
also met with Secretary of War Hurley and Senator Bingham,
Chairman of the Senate Committee on Insular Affairs, and
discovered that while both men were apprehensive toward the
Hawes-Cutting Bill, the sentiment of Congress was leaning
toward independence. Osmeña relayed Roxas' observations to
Quezon, who gave Roxas carte blanche in the pending Senate
hearings.[18]

Roxas was the first witness called to testify. He explained
that sovereignty over the Philippines was an unnecessary
financial burden for the United States. Roxas then claimed that

independence was owed to the Filipino people since they had
fulfilled the "stable" government provision of the Jones Law.
He went on to say that "under the present circumstances, aside
from any duty to free the Philippine Islands in accordance with
the desire of their people, the United States could be more
helpful to them if she were to withdraw her sovereignty, rather
than to permit their progress to lurk in stagnation." But Roxas
realized that "with the granting of tariff autonomy serious
difficulties may arise."[19] To Roxas, as to Osmeña and Quezon,
political independence was desired but economic independence
was not. They realized that not only would the Filipino people
as a whole be hurt by discontinuing the special trade agreement
with the United States, but also that they would personally lose
money and status if this relationship with the United States was
severed.

American farm and labor leaders were the next to appear
before the Committee. Although some of the witnesses demonstrated that their support of Philippine independence was purely
on economic grounds, most of the farm and labor witnesses
claimed that the group they represented had, in fact, always
supported Philippine independence. But the Committee soon
realized that many of the farm and labor witnesses only testified
because of the worsening economic conditions.[20]

The Philippines Chamber of Commerce, the American
Asiatic Association, and various American exporters to the
Philippines spoke out against independence.[21] These groups
based their arguments on idealistic and moral persuasion, but
the Committee continually directed its questions to the economic
problem. The Committee had discovered that American concern
with independence rested very heavily on the economic issues
involved, even though the moral argument had some prominent
proponents: A New York Times reporter, Nicholas Roosevelt,
argued that the duty of the United States was to watch over and
guide the Filipinos to a stable society, and therefore, the
United States should not modify the status quo, other than to set
a date for eventual independence. A different argument came
from Secretary of State Henry Stimson, who claimed that
independence would "inevitably create a general unsettlement
of affairs in the Far East."[22]

Stricken again with illness in the Philippines, Quezon followed
the Committee's proceedings by cablegrams from Roxas and

Resident Commissioners Guevara and Osias. Early in January,
1930, Quezon decided that a Philippine convention for independence in Manila could be useful in assisting the efforts of the
Filipinos in Washington. He wrote Maximo Kalaw, Dean of
the University of the Philippines, and Osmeña, suggesting that
Kalaw organize an Independence Congress to meet on February
22, Washington's Birthday. Due to Quezon's illness, Osmeña
was to take his place.[23]

The Independence Congress lasted for two days, and was
attended by a well-chosen group of two thousand from "all
sectors of the Philippine population."[24] The First Independence
Congress had two plenary sessions with speeches from various
delegates. The Congress authored a unanimous Manifesto,
which was subsequently disseminated throughout the Islands.
It declared that "no matter how lightly an alien control may rest
on a people, it cannot, it will not, make the people happy."[25]
The Independence Congress, while discussing the pending
difficulties facing the Philippines if independence should be
granted, still decided to support an "immediate, complete,
and absolute" independence platform. Quezon had submitted
a letter to the Independence Congress upon the request of
Maximo Kalaw stating that Filipinos should fight heartily for
independence, but with "self-control" and "patience."[26] Although this might have seemed like political blasphemy to the
delegates of the Congress and a breach of the "immediate"
independence proposal which Quezon had publicly professed
for so long, the letter seemingly generated no objections,
probably because the remainder of the letter was rather vague
and Quezon had not really expressed a specific platform.

While the financial crises of the Depression relentlessly
intensified, the Senate Committee hearings were drawing to a
close. Secretary of War Patrick Hurley, the spokesman of the
White House, submitted a report to the Committee on May 19,
1930. He strongly urged that independence not be "tampered
with" at this time and that the status quo should prevail.[27] He
believed that the Filipinos were not ready to govern themselves
and said that "it would be inexpedient and hazardous to attempt
to anticipate future developments by fixing any future date for
ultimate independence."[28]

Meanwhile, Senator Hawes, whose bill was under consideration in the Senate Committee, wrote Quezon in disgust

concerning an article in the St. Louis Dispatch which quoted
Quezon as proclaiming that a protectorate with a thirty-year
transition period would be necessary before Philippine independence could be conceivable. Quezon cabled back a
denunciation to the accusation and stated that he earnestly
hoped Congress would "now enact the laws granting the Islands
their independence." Quezon did not qualify the terms for
independence in this correspondence, and Senator Hawes was
consequently unaware of Quezon's growing apprehension toward
the termination of free trade. [29] When the Hawes-Cutting Bill
was favorably reported by the Senate Committee, Roxas cabled
Quezon that Stimson and Hurley made such damaging reports
at this time, that Quezon should cable Hawes and Cutting
reassuring them that the Filipino people coveted immediate,
complete, and absolute independence. Quezon did this on
May 24, saying that Filipinos "crave their national freedom."[30]

The Senate Committee, which consisted primarily of farm-
state Republicans and Democrats, favorably reported the
Hawes-Cutting Bill on June 2. [31] The Committee resolved that
since "the interests of Americans are concerned in Philippine
trade, it will be more simple to grant independence at an early
date than when their investments have a deeper and more far-
reaching contact with the Philippines."[32] The Bill provided for
the drafting of a democratic constitution. Upon ratification of
the constitution a Commonwealth government, run exclusively
by Filipinos, would function under the ultimate control of the
President of the United States. This commonwealth status would
exist for nineteen years with gradually increasing tariffs. [33]
The United States would give independence to the Philippines if
a plebiscite, to be taken after the transition period, was affirma-
tive. The Hawes-Cutting Bill was not considered again until
December, 1931, due to the more urgent domestic problems
that confronted Congress.

In the eighteen-month interim, the severe Depression
generated financial chaos and with this development farm and
labor lobbying intensified. The Republican setback in the 1930
elections produced a nearly evenly-balanced Congress, the first
stage of a political reversal which would reach its peak in the
1936 election. [34] During this interim, while the befuddled
economists tried to solve the financial dilemma, a portentous
incident occurred--Japanese armies attacked Manchuria in
September of 1931. United States opinion became emphatically

and fervently anti-imperialistic, and many more Americans proposed divestment of the Philippines. Although Japanese aggression did not frighten the mass of the Filipinos, Quezon saw the imminent danger of Japan and accordingly became more overtly against "immediate, complete, and absolute" independence. But throughout 1930 and 1931 (as at other times) Quezon was far from consistent in his public proclamations.

When Congress had adjourned in the summer of 1930, Roxas returned to Manila with a scheme he had devised to strengthen the Philippine argument for independence. Roxas founded an allegedly non-partisan elite group to carry the independence issue directly to the people. The group, called Ang Bagong Katipunan (The New Association), stressed economic progress, racial equality, the unification of a national culture, and the disbanding of political parties so that a unified polity could approach Washington with the plea for independence. [35] There was great debate in the Philippine press as to whether this solution should be considered by the Philippine Legislature, but Roxas' faction was not strong enough to sway Osmeña's and Quezon's comrades. [36] The Nacionalistas had no intention of disbanding, and Ang Bagong Katipunan died a natural death very shortly after its inception. Roxas was not hurt politically, because the Filipino politicians assumed that he was trying to bolster the Filipino cause rather than attempting a political power play. They automatically assumed that Roxas was too intelligent to attempt a coup of both Osmeña's and Quezon's factions at once.

Although the 71st Congress met in late 1930, Resident Commissioners Osias and Guevara cabled Quezon, who had returned to Monrovia, that there was no chance for any Congressional action on Philippine independence in that short session. [37] At this point Quezon wrote the Commissioners that the Hawes-Cutting Bill was "most like" the kind of independence he desired, and that the fight for independence should be vigorously continued by the Commissioners. Quezon also solicited the support of Senator Wheeler. Although Quezon knew there would be no action this session, he asked the Senator to use his influence to bring the Hawes-Cutting Bill up for debate and possible vote. [38] It is unclear whether Quezon actually approved of the economic provisions in the Bill, or whether his support of it was a politically expedient move, but it is clear that Quezon came more and more to favor the kind of limited independence that the Hawes-Cutting Bill provided.

As independence increasingly had seemed a tangible reality, uncertainties over what kind of independence bill Quezon wanted became more pronounced. Quezon privately supported the Hawes-Cutting Bill with its transition period and economic provisions but still espoused "immediate" independence in his public political pronouncements. [39] He also publicly denied the Philippine press allegations, which had accused him of abandoning "immediate" independence; the opposition press even dared to accuse Quezon of being anti-independence. [40] Quezon was not anti-independence, but was merely unsure of the optimum solution to his problem -- should he publicly support the relatively conservative economic provisions of the Hawes-Cutting Bill and thus sacrifice his political program by discarding the "immediate" independence issue? [41] Should he support the limited independence of the Hawes-Cutting Bill even if this might mean a decline in his political power? It would be several months before he formulated an answer to his dilemma.

In the early summer of 1931, Secretary Hurley and Senator Hawes decided to journey separately to the Philippines to examine the political context upon which successful independence would rely. Quezon and Hurley met several times in Monrovia before Hurley sailed for Manila. Hurley and Quezon came to an agreement which was to be submitted to Congress by Secretary Hurley; both had compromised their seemingly irreconcilable positions. Quezon stood firm as to what kind of independence he considered necessary for the Philippines; he publicly discarded his "immediate" independence platform, and instead offered a plan which had very similar provisions to the Hawes-Cutting Bill. Quezon's plan had political liabilities because it called for a ten-year transition period under a Governor-General. Quezon also agreed to a plebiscite after ten years, a raw sugar quota of 800,000 to 1,000,000 long tons, and the continuation of the present coconut oil quota. [42] Since these were high quotas and would essentially constitute free trade, Quezon had clearly sacrificed his political independence platform for more satisfactory economic provisions. Osmeña and Roxas had also agreed to this threefold plan for commonwealth status before Quezon had offered it to Secretary Hurley. [43]

Quezon, Roxas, and Osmeña had made a negotiation shift; they had publicly become the conservative element in the fight

for Philippine independence. Independence was no longer vague
political claptrap, but was a concrete proposal with definite
economic and political provisions qualifying it. Roxas had said
that Filipino leaders were compelled to use "radical statements"
for "immediate, complete, and absolute" independence to
"maintain hold of the people."[44] Quezon brought the new proposals to the people by reasserting his proposal to the First
Independence Congress of a year earlier in more explicit terms;
he said that "haste and unreasoning passion will sweep us into
danger" and that for this reason the Filipinos must "go slow."[45]

Quezon's revised ideas generated sharp criticism from
Filipino politicians. General Aguinaldo and Senator Juan
Sumulong of the Democratas considered the proposal a breach
of the debt of gratitude which the Nacionalistas owed the
Filipino people for electing them. The Philippine papers
that were not controlled by the Nacionalistas also lashed out
against the plan. The Democratas labeled Quezon a "reactionary"
and a "traitor to his pristine ideals of complete and immediate
independence."[46] But these accusations did not affect the
popularity of the Nacionalistas, who were re-elected en masse
on July 13, 1931. The entrenched party structure, based on
personal loyalties, remained more influential than any issues
yet raised in Philippine politics. Quezon was re-elected Senate
President, Roxas speaker of the House, and Osmeña Majority
Floor Leader.[47] The Filipino people had apparently felt that
the Nacionalista leaders had not reneged on their commitment.

With Quezon's commonwealth plan as the accepted proposal
of the Filipino people, the Philippine Legislature presented the
visiting Secretary Hurley with a resolution asking for the
"immediate political separation" from the United States.[48]
The support of Quezon's dominion plan was implicit in this
resolution which called specifically for political independence,
but no longer called for "absolute" independence. Hurley
reported to the President that even though Filipinos wanted
independence, it would not be feasible either politically or
economically. President Hoover agreed with the report, and
on October 26, 1931, Hoover emphasized this attitude in a
speech. Hurley's War Department was undoubtedly influenced
by the Japanese invasion of Manchuria in September, and he
believed that the abandonment of vital military and naval
installations in the Pacific would be an incalculable mistake.[49]

Quezon sent a belated confirmation of the commonwealth proposal to Commissioners Osias and Guevara, who reacted favorably. [50] Osmeña and Roxas enjoined the Legislature to finance a trip to Washington to permit them to work with Osias and Guevara for "political independence."[51] Quezon, now back in Manila but still ill, remained at home and rendered no specific instructions to the Mission. While the Mission was in Washington occupying itself with "winning friends for the Filipino cause, in solidifying friendships already won, and in mapping out a thorough campaign for independence,"[52] Quezon again changed his mind on the kind of independence he thought the Filipinos needed.

Quezon saw that his people were becoming more "active and radical" and that they really did seem to want absolute independence. He sensed that the increasing number of independence parades and rallies proved the Filipino people's desire for complete and absolute independence. [53] As a result, he may have overreacted to this situation, believing that to keep his power and position he needed to maintain a hard-line independence stand. Aside from being influenced by the changing Filipino mood, Quezon was also influenced by the fact that he was sitting on the sidelines watching Roxas and Osmeña sail for Washington and for the resulting glory of success.

Quezon knew that the new American Congress which would take up the Hawes-Cutting Bill in December was very sympathetic to Philippine independence because of the Democratic victories, the worsening Depression, and the Japanese invasion of Manchuria. Quezon saw that there was a good chance that his potential political rivals would receive credit for achieving Philippine independence. When Hurley asked Quezon in December if any solution to the Philippine problem had to include guaranteed independence, Quezon answered affirmatively. [54] Quezon had reneged on his commonwealth status agreement of the previous summer with Secretary Hurley.

Quezon's ambition not only prompted him to go back on his agreement with Hurley, but also to turn against the OsRox (the press and cable abbreviation for Osmeña-Roxas) Mission in Washington. Quezon wrote Resident Commissioner Osias that he still favored immediate independence but said he realized the termination of free trade would be disastrous to the Philippine economy. He added, however, that if immediate independence could not be achieved with a proposal for economic protection, then the Philippines would accept independence regardless of the circumstances.[55] Quezon said that he would "take independence under the most burdensome conditions if necessary" and if independence were impossible he would take "anything" he could get "that means an advance in our fight for freedom."[56] Quezon assured John Switzer and Senator King that the Philippines would accept independence even if there were no trade agreement at all.[57] From the beginning, Quezon had attempted to undermine the position and authority of the OsRox Mission in Washington, but the Mission relentlessly fought for the approval of the Hawes-Cutting Bill in the Senate and the Hare Bill in the House of Representatives.[58]

When the Hare and the Hawes-Cutting Bills had become the basis for discussion for an independence bill in the American Congress, Quezon had formed two definite concepts about Philippine independence. First, Quezon wanted to be the leader of a politically autonomous Philippine Legislature but wanted the Philippine economy to have United States protection. Second, Quezon was willing to undermine his political comrades' efforts to attain independence because he felt that he alone should liberate his people. Quezon continued undermining the OsRox Mission for the next two years until the political battle between Quezon and the OsRox Mission, called the pro- anti- fight, ensued in 1933.

The pro- anti- fight was waged to determine two things: on the superficial level it was to decide what course Philippine independence would take, and on the more profound level it was to decide who would become the leader of the Filipino people. Whoever brought independence to the people would be able to control the Legislature; for this reason Quezon did not want Osmeña to return to Manila with an independence bill. When this did happen he attacked the bill, claiming that the clause allowing the United States to retain its naval and military bases on the Islands was deleterious to the neutrality of the Filipinos. Quezon contended that a much better bill could be obtained easily from the American Congress which was only beginning to grapple with the consequences of the Depression.

Even before the bill was reintroduced in the American
Congress in December, 1932, "Quezon's imagination seized
on means not of improving but of defeating the Hare-Hawes-
Cutting Bill."[59] After the Hare Bill had been reported favorably by the House Committee on Territories and Insular Affairs
and passed by the House in April,[60] Quezon asked the OsRox
Mission to return to Manila to explain the issues to the people
and to help Quezon in the financial trouble that plagued the
Legislature. The OsRox Mission refused to return and said that
the independence issue was more important and that they would
agree with whatever Quezon decided. Quezon, not wishing to
force the issue and cause a public rift with the OsRox Mission
at this time, replied, "if you still believe that it is your duty
to remain there rather than take part in the discussion of all
these matters, I shall defer to your judgment and advise the
Legislature accordingly."[61] Encouraged by Quezon's acquies-
cence, the OsRox Mission and the two Resident Commissioners
to the United States asked Quezon to come to Washington to help
lobby for the Hare and the Hawes-Cutting Bills, but Quezon did
not go.[62]

Expecting a Democratic victory in the American Congress
in November of 1932, Quezon believed that if the Senate did not
pass the Hawes-Cutting Bill the new Democratic Senate would
pass some kind of independence bill. Quezon realized that Os-
Rox would eventually be successful and that he could not alter
this by traveling to Washington. Preparing for a political battle
at home, Quezon tried to purge the civil service and judicial
systems of Osmeña's followers. The Quezon faction claimed
that this was done to increase efficiency, but Osmeña and Roxas
correctly saw it as an offensive move to weaken their forces in
Manila.[63]

Both the Hare and the Hawes-Cutting Bills specified that
during the Commonwealth the American President would have
the right to intervene in case of an emergency, and that American
naval and military bases would remain on the Islands. Quezon
had never made this a real issue to the OsRox Mission, but early
in November, 1932, Quezon publicly denounced the Hare and Hawes-
Cutting Bills because they did "not grant independence." Quezon
then noted that he objected chiefly to the intervention and military
clauses and the low tariff quotas, but that he would be willing to
postpone independence for ten years "provided in the meantime

there is established in the Philippine Islands a government
autonomous in name as well as in fact. "[64] Quezon had set
the stage for the political battle. The military and intervention clauses and the low trade quotas were, in fact, somewhat
objectionable to Quezon, but he magnified their importance so
that he could publicly fight the OsRox Mission and begin to
mobilize his political forces.

In the meantime the OsRox Mission said it agreed with
Quezon's objections and would "seek further expert opinion
and [would] favor wording which most limits power intervention [by the President of the United States]." But later the
OsRox Mission noted that for independence to be at all possible
in the near future, the naval and military bases would have to
remain on the Islands because many members of the House and
Senate whose support was "indispensible" believed that these
military reservations were "necessary."[65]

In late November, Quezon informed the OsRox Mission he
was sending Senator Benigno Aquino to Washington "with special
instructions." Although Quezon publicly spoke out against the
military provisions of the two bills, he enjoined Aquino to inform
Osmeña and Roxas not to accept a bill unless Presidential
intervention was restricted and a higher sugar quota was provided (1.2 million tons).[66] Since Quezon clearly knew that the
American Congress would not accept these terms, he was trying
to force the OsRox Mission to get the bills tabled. He wrote to
a Mr. Ansberry that Aquino was sent with these instructions
because Quezon wanted to wait until the Democratic 73rd
Congress convened and an independence bill more favorable than
the Hawes-Cutting or Hare Bills could be passed.[67] With his
health slowly returning, Quezon knew he would be well enough
by that time to go to Washington and fight for a new independence
bill that he could give to his people.[68]

The Hare and the Hawes-Cutting Bills were both reintroduced
into Congress in early December, 1932. There were two amendments to the Hawes-Cutting Bill which genuinely angered Quezon.
Senator Hiram Johnson introduced an immigration exclusion
amendment and Senator Huey Long proposed an amendment
cutting the free trade quota on raw sugar to half of what the
Filipinos desired (585,000 tons). Quezon wrote to Osmeña and
Roxas that he was sure he was voicing "the unanimous sentiment of our people in urging you to press for immediate

independence and if this is impossible let there be no bill"
because a better bill would be possible in the new Congress.[69]
In a press release dated December 16, Quezon said that "the
last dispatches from America clearly show that the fight in the
Senate is not to give independence and freedom to the Philippines
but to close American doors to Filipino labor and Philippine
products. . . . America should grant independence to the
Philippines at once."[70] But Osmeña and Roxas ignored Quezon
and decided to continue lobbying for the acceptance of the Hawes-
Cutting Bill.

The lobbying of farm and labor groups pleading for relief
from the Depression was a powerful ally for Osmeña and Roxas.
The Hawes-Cutting Bill was passed on December 17, 1932, in
the Senate without a record vote. In the conference between the
House and the Senate on the Hare and Hawes-Cutting Bills the
Senate yielded quickly to the Hare Bill provision for a one
million ton per year sugar quota, and a token Filipino immigration quota of fifty persons per year. The two Houses also
settled on a ten-year transition period.[71]

After the conference the two bills became known collectively
as the Hare-Hawes-Cutting Bill (abbreviated H-H-C by the press),
although many Filipinos continued to refer to it as the Hawes-
Cutting Bill. This bill had to be signed by Hoover and accepted
by the Philippine Legislature to become law. It stipulated that
the Legislature must convene a Constitutional Convention to
write a constitution which would be republican in form and would
assure American rights and principles of government. The
constitution would have to be approved by the President of the
United States and, if acceptable to him, would then have to be
approved by the Filipino people in a national plebiscite. All
American property, except naval and military bases, was to
go to the Philippine government. The H-H-C Bill also provided
for a ten-year transition period during which time the Philippines
would be run under an autonomous Commonwealth government.
The President of the United States would have the final say on all
foreign policy and would appoint a High Commissioner to the
Islands with limited powers. The tariff rates would remain the
same for the first five years of the Commonwealth but would
increase 5% annually for the second five years. Independence
would come on July 4 ten years after the inauguration of the
Commonwealth of the Philippines.

Osmeña and Roxas immediately cabled Quezon announcing
that they "would not commit ourselves a priori in favor" of the
bill so that the Legislature may have an "absolutely free hand to
accept or reject" the measure. Quezon cabled back that the
H-H-C Bill was not satisfactory to the Filipino people. Quezon
wrote that there were no "signs that our people will be discouraged if there is [a] deadlock among [the] conferences or [a]
presidential veto because they are ready to force the immediate
independence issue upon the next Administration."[72] After
Hoover had been handed the H-H-C Bill by Congress, Quezon
continued to malign the bill, calling it "the work of the National
City Bank" and a "joke that is unfair and harmful to us, but
profitable to American manufacturers and exporters, [and] to
Cuban sugar and beet sugar interests." Quezon also said that
he would "oppose" the H-H-C Bill if it was "signed by the
President."[73]

The OsRox Mission tried to persuade Hoover to sign the
bill but on January 13 he vetoed it because he considered the
bill inconsistent with Republican policy.[74] Both houses of
Congress passed the H-H-C Bill over the veto on the same day,
and the bill became law.[75] Osmeña and Roxas had achieved
independence for the Filipino people but it was far from the
immediate, complete, and absolute independence which Filipino
leaders had publicly espoused for the last thirty years and which
Quezon now publicly professed.

Even though Osmeña and Roxas knew that Quezon's forces
in Manila had been trying to purge Osmeña's followers out of
the civil service and courts in November and were aware that
Quezon had previously accepted the provisions of the H-H-C
Act and then came out against them, Osmeña and Roxas were
either too slow to act or were naïvely unaware of Quezon's
motives for rejecting the measure. Since the OsRox Mission
felt that Quezon's objections to the act's provisions for Presidential intervention, the retention of military and naval bases,
the relatively low tariff quota on sugar, and the limited Filipino
immigration clause, were the real reasons Quezon castigated
the act, the OsRox Mission challenged Quezon to come to
Washington and see if he could obtain any further concessions.[76]
On January 28 Quezon agreed to come to Washington via Europe
and arrive in late March.[77] It would be several weeks before
Osmeña and Roxas realized that Quezon was waging a battle for
the leadership of Philippine politics.

In the two-month interim Quezon prepared for the ensuing
political battle with Osmeña and Roxas by campaigning against
the H-H-C Act. In a radio broadcast transmitted from overseas
to the United States, Quezon declared that the H-H-C Act was not
really an independence bill but a tariff quota and an immigration
exclusion act to help the American citizen. He also broadcast a
message on KZRM radio to his own people claiming that "the
Philippines would remain a conquered province of the United
States, just as we are now, but she [the United States] would be
under no moral or legal obligation to look after our interest and
to protect us from foreign invasion."[78]

Having heard the public attacks Quezon was making against
the achievements of the OsRox Mission, Osmeña and Roxas
decided to launch a counteroffensive against Quezon. Osmeña
entreated his followers in Manila to create a League for the
Acceptance of the Hare-Hawes-Cutting Law. The League disseminated pamphlets and had Osmeña-controlled newspapers
campaign, not only for the acceptance of the H-H-C Act but also
against the leadership of Quezon. As a reaction to this Quezon
made more and more public appearances denouncing the act and
Osmeña's attacks on Quezon's leadership. For the next month
there was little correspondence between the Independence
Mission and Quezon. In a "heat of temper"[79] Quezon wrote a
letter to Secretary of War Parker claiming that since the Philippines had a "deficit in legislative appropriation" the OsRox
Mission must "return as soon as possible." He added that
Parker should "inform them that their per diems will not be
paid after fifteen days of notification."[80]

Quezon chose a handpicked mission that was supposedly
"mixed" in sentiment over the H-H-C Act to journey to Washington. Quezon suggested that Osmeña and Roxas meet him in
Paris and they agreed. [81] Quezon and Osmeña and Roxas came
to an agreement on board the Ile de France which was taking
them to Washington. On April 25 Quezon, fearing that he could
not defeat Osmeña, agreed to accept the H-H-C Act provided that
the military and naval bases near Manila be evacuated, and that
either the transition period be reduced from ten to five years or
the tariff clauses be modified. [82] But Quezon reneged and the
agreement was dissolved. Quezon did this apparently because
the cables sent to him showed that his followers in Manila
believed they could easily defeat Osmeña and thus became dis-
enchanted with him for accepting the "common program."[83]

José Clarin and Quintin Paredes headed Quezon's faction
in Manila and Benigno Aquino and Maximo Kalaw headed
Osmeña's. Following the typical pattern of Philippine politics
the factions were split according to family and geographic
affiliations. José de Jesus, Quezon's personal secretary,
wrote that "we can readily see that it is in the Visayas Group
[home of Osmeña and Roxas] where the supporters of the bill
are centered." De Jesus also reassured Quezon by telling him
that the pros (the name that Osmeña's forces were called
because they wanted the H-H-C Act accepted) were waging an
"intensive" but "unfruitful" campaign against the H-H-C Act.
De Jesus mentioned that Aquino led the most vicious attack by
"mercilessly bombasting the opponents of the bill," and that
the battle in the Philippines press between Clarin and Aquino
reached a "low level." He also told Quezon that the National
Information Committee on the Hawes-Cutting Bill had been
established by one of Quezon's men, Representative Diokno,
and that it was working "full blast" and making pamphlets
for distribution throughout the Islands. [84]

The antis (or Quezonistas as Quezon's followers were
sometimes referred to by the Philippine press) formed the
Anti Hawes-Cutting League which was "to send orators and
debators to all parts of the province around Manila at their
own expense to counteract the propaganda launched by the
agents of the proponents of the Law." The League considered
the H-H-C Act "an assassination to the hope of Philippine freedom."[85] Paredes cabled Quezon that due to this kind of
strenuous campaigning a "majority" of the Legislature was
"anxious" to reject the measure but was "awaiting your
advice."[86] But Quezon's position was not this strong--
his followers had overestimated the effects of their efforts
and, in fact, the pro and anti forces at this time were about
equal in strength. [87] After several public debates between the
pros and the antis, the Filipino leaders returned.

The OsRox Mission and the "Mixed Mission" had decided
not to go back to the Islands by the same route; but they met in
Hong Kong and, refusing to accept the separate receptions prepared by the two camps, returned to Manila together. They did
not publicly attack each other until a few days after their
arrival. [88]

The pro- anti- fight was intensified by the return of the leaders of both factions. Before leaving for Europe Quezon had been the first to express publicly an opinion about the H-H-C Act; but Osmeña was the first to use personal slander. Knowing that he had ground to make up after a one-and-a-half-year absence, Osmeña aggressively attacked Quezon's patriotism. To many Filipinos this was seen as an act of <u>walang hiya</u> (base ingratitude); this allowed Quezon "to adopt a stance he loved well: injured innocence defending slandered patriotism."[89]

Osmeña obtained the support of a powerful newspaper chain (<u>Tribune</u>-<u>Vanguardia</u>-<u>Taliba</u>), but Quezon had only a few isolated papers supporting him. To remedy this Quezon bought the other major newspaper chain on the Islands (<u>El Debate</u>-<u>Mabuhay</u>-<u>Herald</u>-<u>Monday Mail</u>) for ₱300,000. The chain had been neutral but Quezon placed Carlos Romulo, an anti, to run it.

Since the University of the Philippines endorsed Osmeña and Roxas, Quezon charged the President of the University, Rafael Palma, with "abusing what should be a neutral office" and cut back the budget of the University by one third. Both Palma and Maximo Kalaw, Dean of the College of Liberal Arts, quickly resigned, and Quezon appointed an anti, Jorge Bocobo, to head the University. Although the newly-appointed American Governor-General, Frank Murphy, did not enter the pro- anti- fight, Quezon had previously persuaded the former Governor-General, Theodore Roosevelt, Jr., to allow the pros to be replaced by antis. Quezon was able to do this because he proposed a re-organization of the courts if the H-H-C were rejected, which Roosevelt believed would save money.[90]

Quezon not only had the power of his office and of his long-standing political prestige to fight Osmeña, but also the power of his personality and the knowledge of the intricacies of Filipino politics. At this time Quezon solicited the support of a proud independent, Vicente Vera, who was thinking of joining Osmeña. Quezon said, "Look here, <u>chico,</u> your leading opponent for leadership in this region is José Surbito--and he's an Osmeña man. If you go over to Osmeña, I'll take Surbito who, after all, is closely related to my former secretary, Felipe Buencamino. So you might as well join me." Not only did Vera join the antis, but Surbito did also. When Quezon was campaigning against the H-H-C Act in Tanawan, Batangas (country dominated by José P. Laurel, of the OsRox faction), he was greeted coolly. Quezon spotted a cross-eyed man and said, "Hey, putang ina mong duling . . . What are you doing here?" People gathered around Quezon, thinking that he knew one of their neighbors. When Quezon was asked later who the cross-eyed man was he said, "I'll be damned if I know his name. . . . This is the first time I've ever seen him in my life! "[91] In July, Quezon wrote to ex-Governor-General Harrison asking if Quezon publicly could "refer to Osmeña's visit to you [Harrison] trembling with fear when the Clarke Amendment [1916] was discussed in Congress as something you have told me in a private conversation."[92] Thus, Quezon had not only betrayed his friendship with Osmeña and Roxas when he made public a private conversation over a dead issue, but he also transcended the traditional trust supposedly sacred to ilustrado politicians. Neither Osmeña nor Roxas could compete with Quezon's political skill and they were confounded "by the intricate steps he took in his political dances."[93]

In carrying out his political maneuvers, Quezon was able to raise more money from his supporters than was Osmeña. Quezon was successful in raising substantial funds to fight the H-H-C Act. He received over ₱100,000 from his long-time friends, the Elizaldes and Sorianos. Since Quezon publicly claimed that the H-H-C Act did not sufficiently protect Philippine sugar trade he won strong support from "the majority of sugar centralistas." Senator Claro Recto said later that the antis were able to raise a million pesos in all "to get a new independence bill." Recto revealed that the largest contributor was the Elizalde family because, he said, "They had to save Quezon's face. They were very close friends of his."[94]

Quezon used an entirely different tactic to gain further support. In addition to saying that the H-H-C Act did not do enough to protect the Philippine economy (and in this way winning over the conservative business elements), he also continued to attack the act for failing to grant immediate independence, thus winning the radicals over to his camp. In this way he convinced Judge Sumulong, General Aguinaldo, and Bishop Aglipay, who had all fought for immediate independence throughout the American occupation and who were, unlike Quezon, consistent about its implementation. Since Quezon also strongly influenced a majority of the upper middle-class ilustrados, by the middle of the summer of 1933, he had won out over Osmeña in all sectors of the society. All that Quezon

had to do now was to use his power to purge Osmeña and Roxas
from the Government, have the Legislature reject the H-H-C
Act, and then head his own independence mission to Washington
to achieve an independence bill more to his liking and with his
name associated with it.

With Quezon holding most of the cards, Osmeña made a
final effort to uproot Quezon from the leadership of the Filipinos.
He challenged Quezon by suggesting that both combatants resign
from the Senate and take the issue to the people. Knowing that
he controlled the Senate, on July 20, 1933, Quezon offered his
resignation in a speech to the Philippine Senate. He said, "I
can not submit my judgment to them nor should they submit
theirs to mine," and added that it was up to the Legislature
"which has the authority to determine who should be at the head
of our national leadership."[95] Quezon made it clear that he
really did not want to take the issue to the people, but was
offering his resignation as a political power play so that the
Quezon-controlled Senate would make the obvious choice as to
who it would keep as head of the Legislature. Osmeña delivered
a speech to the Senate demanding that it accept Quezon's resignation. Osmeña used the same line of attack that Quezon had
used eleven years earlier to dethrone him--he castigated the
autocratic character of Quezon and his presumptuous rejection
of the H-H-C Act; he protested against "a personal leadership
gained through intrigue and machinations."[96]

Osmeña's diatribe did not succeed. The Senate voted 16 to 5
to reject Quezon's resignation and then accepted Osmeña's
resignation, 15 to 2. One of Quezon's most ardent followers,
Representative Buencamino, led the fight against Roxas in the
House. After a frenzied scuffle in the House caused by Roxas'
student followers, Roxas was voted out of office by the Quezon-
controlled House, 50 to 29. Quezon replaced Osmeña and Roxas
with antis--Paredes and Clarin.[97] He said that these changes
in the leadership of the Legislature were "unpleasant" but that
"changes in the national leadership are nothing abnormal in
democracies. . . ."[98] But Osmeña saw Quezon's actions as
both abnormal and undemocratic; he said that Quezon was
"insistent in the support of his pernicious, anti-democratic and
subversive principles of the stability of our institutions."[99]

Quezon was genuinely offended by Osmeña's continuous
attacks and asked him to leave the Nacionalista party ranks.

Quezon said that "as a matter of political honesty I would not
have as my associates in the leadership of the Legislature and
the Party men who have denounced me in private and in public
as conniving with imperialists to deprive my own people of their
liberty." Quezon then challenged Osmeña to form a new party:
"Let us have two parties and then the Senator [Osmeña] and I
will prove to the country that we mean what we say when we
affirm that we believe in the need of two political parties."[100]
The pros formed a party called the Partido Pro-Independencia
Nacionalista with the same ideology as the Nacionalistas except
that the Pros wanted the H-H-C Act accepted. The Pros elected
Osmeña as President and Roxas as Vice-President of the Party,
which was joined by former members of the recently disbanded
Democratas.[101]

Osmeña directed his minority group against Quezon, who
was waiting for the American Congress to settle its pressing
domestic problems which were consuming its time,[102] before
he would direct the Legislature to formally reject the H-H-C
Act and head his own independence mission to Washington.
Osmeña pressed Quezon to honor his previous agreement to
hold a plebiscite so that the Filipino people could decide on the
H-H-C Act. Quezon was afraid that the people might accept the
H-H-C Act and therefore fomented a fight with Osmeña over the
form the plebiscite would take. Osmeña wanted a straight "yes
or no" question and Quezon proposed a purposely ambiguous
set of questions, both to render the plebiscite useless and to
frustrate Osmeña. In effect, Quezon proposed that the plebiscite ask: "Do you want the H-H-C Act or do you want a better
independence act?" Osmeña finally conceded and no plebiscite
was held. In later years, Osmeña said he did not push the issue
because a bitter campaign would have ensued and it would have
divided the people.[103]

After Quezon and Osmeña had signed an agreement that a
plebiscite would not be held because they could not agree on the
form, the Philippine Senate decided to vote on whether to accept
or reject the H-H-C Act. On the morning of October 17, 1933,
the Philippine Legislature in a concurrent resolution declined
to accept the independence offered by the United States.

Quezon sailed for Washington in November to try to attain
the better independence bill he had promised his people. Quezon
had written Governor-General Frank Murphy seeking his support

for either a change in the H-H-C Act or "new legislation."
Quezon now desired political independence in three years with
economic protection. He wanted a yearly quota of not less than
one million long tons of sugar, 200,000 tons of oil, and not
less than the maximum amount of cordage ever exported to the
United States. He also specified that there should be no American "military reservations" in the Philippines but "if the
United States should feel that it must have and maintain naval
reservations, it should be in common accord with the Philippine
Republic and the bay and port of Manila." Quezon also naïvely
desired a treaty between the United States, France, Great Britain,
and Japan guaranteeing the neutrality of the Philippines after
independence.[104]

Quezon's aims were not revolutionary; indeed, they were
very similar to the provisions of the H-H-C Act. Quezon had
apparently suspected all along that Congress might be reluctant
to change its mood toward the Islands in less than two years. As
a result of this, Quezon still desired a continued economic protection by the United States but political autonomy in the Far
East without the interference of Japan. The American Congress
proved even more reluctant than Quezon had prognosticated and
he, therefore, had to utilize all his skill in political maneuvering
and manipulating.

The new Filipino delegation was not greeted enthusiastically
in Washington. Since the first New Deal legislation was sputter-
ing, Congress had more urgent measures to consider than
Philippine independence. Henry Stimson and Harry Hawes were
disillusioned by the rejection of the H-H-C Act and cautioned
Quezon not to ask too much of Congress--there might be no
independence bill rendered at all.

When Quezon arrived in Washington he discovered that the
pros had sent Camilo Osias to talk with President Roosevelt.
Osias told Roosevelt that the Filipino people were in favor of
the H-H-C Act, but that it was blocked due to Quezon's political
maneuvers. Roosevelt gave his support to Quezon, however,
and decided to allow Quezon to lobby Congress for the modifica-
tion of the H-H-C Act.[105] Osias was dismissed as Resident
Commissioner by Quezon's followers and the antis took complete
control of the independence bill negotiations.

Quezon presented a proposal to Senator Millard Tyding

Chairman of the Senate Committee on Territories and Insular Affairs. The proposal was very similar to the one he had earlier submitted to Governor-General Murphy. Tydings, having been influenced by Osias, rejected the proposal and stated that the acceptance date for the H-H-C Act would be extended another nine months. Quezon used his dignified charm to win a concession from Tydings. Knowing that better economic provisions were impossible, Quezon emphasized his objection to the military reservations. Tydings soon agreed that the army bases would be expunged and the naval bases would be subject to negotiation at a later date. [106]

But during this time, Quezon was trying to find a more advantageous avenue to a better independence bill. He told Senator King he would accept King's immediate independence bill. He entreated the support of Joseph Tumulty, Senator Robinson, and former Senator Hawes, who all believed Quezon was in favor of a bill similar to the H-H-C Act. Quezon implored ex-Governor-General Theodore Roosevelt, Jr., who was now in Washington, to support a dominion plan for the Islands. Quezon had not openly reneged on his agreement with Tydings which he later signed. He realized that Tydings held the real power over the fate of Philippine independence and that these other avenues to a better independence would most probably prove to be dead ends. [107] The President agreed to the Quezon-Tydings plan and sent a message to Congress asking for a new Philippine independence bill.

The King bill for immediate independence and full tariff, Dickenson's bill with a five year transition period, and Vandenberg's bill with a two-year transition period and eight years of economic protection were all quickly defeated. Congress had failed to change its mood and passed the Tydings bill in the Senate and a similar measure, the McDuffie bill, in the House. President Roosevelt signed the bill on March 24, 1934. The Tydings-McDuffie Act was, despite Quezon's efforts, almost a carbon copy of the rejected Hare-Hawes-Cutting Act. The economic provisions remained the same; the only political change was the abolition of American army installations and the promise of a later review of the naval bases.

Quezon was greeted as a national hero when he returned to Manila. His homecoming was enhanced by a throng of Filipinos shouting "Viva Quezon!" Quezon spoke to the

Philippine Legislature shortly after his arrival claiming sole
credit for the independence of the Philippines. He said, "There
is no other colored people in the Far East that has the same
benefits or anything like them that the Filipino people have to-day
and this victory of ours will be a stimulus to them. . . . Seven
years in the United States have proven to me that America is the
best friend that the Filipino people ever had or could ever
have."[108] But Osmeña rightly claimed that the Tydings-McDuffie
Act was "his" H-H-C Act with Quezon's name associated with it.

Six weeks later the elections determined who the people
wanted to rule the Legislature. The antis won a landslide victory over Osmeña's forces. This election was the last political
event in the system created by the Jones Law of 1916. Both the
antis and pros were now faced with constructing a commonwealth
government. Quezon saw that it would be to his and to the country's advantage if a union between the two camps was implemented.
At first Osmeña was reluctant, but finally acquiesced for three
reasons. He realized that he and Quezon held identical views on
almost all political issues and that the pro- anti- fight was really
a test to see who would become the political leader. His group
loyalties were such that he saw that only harm would come to the
ilustrado ruling elite by being bitterly divided at the time of
independence. Osmeña also realized that his personal power
would be stronger as second in command in a one-party system
than head of a relatively weaker opposition party. Many members
in the lower tiers of government felt that this was a breach of
utang na loob; they had strenuously fought each other at the local
level and knew a union would be extremely difficult. Senator
Juan Sumulong also vehemently protested the union. But Osmeña
was won over, as he had been in 1922, and the Nacionalistas
were reunited on June 16, 1935, under the direction of Quezon
and Osmeña. The union assured that the existing ilustrado elite
would continue to rule unchallenged during the Commonwealth
and the future Republic. A formidable ticket of Quezon for
President and Osmeña for Vice-President won an overwhelming
victory at the polls in the election for the Commonwealth
Government of the Philippines in 1935.

This study has attempted to show that Quezon was successful in the pro- anti- fight primarily because he both understood
the traditional personalism of Philippine politics and how to
manipulate modern political institutions by his charisma and by
his astute political judgment. He saw himself as a living bridge
for his people between a new, somewhat alien, modern world
and a traditional social system based on factions, kinship, and
family alliances of his peasant-based society. His success lay
in his ability to blend these relationships into a strong and
unified leadership. Quezon's mercurial personality and his
keen understanding of key issues enabled him to put off independence until a later date, to defeat Osmeña and Roxas, to regain
independence, and to continue in power over the Filipino people.

Part of Quezon's success lay in his ability to become the
leader of the Filipino politicians. Often resorting to ruthless
political trickery or to overt lies, Quezon built up the most·
powerful political machine in the Islands. Quezon's ability to
detect and thwart any threats guaranteed his position as leader.
Perhaps even more important than his political maneuvers was
his forceful personality which won much respect and many
followers among the ruling elite. Quezon's personality and his
use of patronage made most of the other politicians feel they
owed him _utang na loob_.

However, Quezon's role in Philippine independence cannot
be seen solely as an ambitious use of power. While it is true
that Quezon's ego thrived on ceremonies and the praise political
power awarded him, he also loved his people. Quezon delayed
independence because he believed, like Louis XIV, that he was
the state and that, therefore, he, and only he, should present
independence to the people. Quezon realized that his charismatic leadership was the crucial unifying force for his people
at the difficult time of formulating a Commonwealth government.
Quezon knew how to give the peasant something tangible to
believe in and to follow. Since Quezon could mobilize the
peasants and unite the politicians, he gave the Philippines the
kind of leadership necessary to make a successful transition
from a traditional society to a modern political system.

In 1932 and 1933, Quezon was truly a harbinger of how
other national leaders might attempt to mobilize their people

on a mass basis. Like Quezon, Nkrumah and Sukarno, for
example, clamored for independence and, after it was achieved,
were able to keep their people united and interested in politics.
They did this in part by filling a political void and by projecting
their personalities as symbols of their nations. Some leaders
were more successful and lasted longer than others; Quezon
was one of the first and one of the most successful.

Quezon's achievement in winning independence has not been
forgotten in the Philippines. Indeed today, Quezon is more than
just a historical hero who brought independence to the Islands;
Filipinos now see Quezon as the great emancipator of the Filipino people from the yoke of Western imperialism. Thus,
Quezon's proudly dynamic personality has made it possible for
him to be remembered and loved for the ends he produced, while
the means he used have been largely overlooked by most Filipinos.
As one Filipino historian noted: "No Filipino has equalled his
oratorical prowess, and his intuitive knowledge of Filipino mass
psychology led him from one political triumph to another without
meeting a single defeat."[109] Quezon, who was concerned for
his historical image, can be said to have fought and won what
he called "the good fight."

Notes

1. Manuel L. Quezon, "Our Peaceful Struggle for Independence," The Philippine Social Science Review, V-1 (1933), 71-86.

2. The Quezon Papers, which consist of Quezon's cablegrams, telegrams, radiograms, letters, and speeches, are at the Philippine National Library and are available on microfilm at the Michigan Historical Collections, The University of Michigan. (Hereinafter referred to as QP.)

3. The Partido Urgentista, the Comité de la Union Nacionalista, and the Partido Independista Inmediatista. Bonifacio S. Salamanca, The Filipino Reaction to American Rule:1901-1913 ([Hamden, Conn.] 1968), p. 160.

4. Sergio Osmeña was born in Cebu City on the island of Cebu in the Visayas on September 9, 1878. He received his A.B. degree from the College of San Juan de Letrán, and his Bachelor of Laws in 1903. He was elected Governor of Cebu in 1904 and in 1907 was elected the first Speaker in the Philippine Assembly.

5. The election results were: 32 Nacionalistas, 16 Progresistas, 7 Independistas, 4 Inmediatistas, 20 non-partisan, 1 Catholic. See Gregorio F. Zaide and Sonia M. Zaide, Government and Politics of the Government of the Philippines (Quezon City, 1969), p. 46.

6. Ibid., p. 53.

7. Grayson L. Kirk, Philippine Independence (New York, 1936), p. 42. From 1898 on, the Democrats had been the party more inclined to oppose (Republican) imperialism; this had been a major campaign issue in the elections of 1900 and 1902.

8. Manuel L. Quezon, The Good Fight (New York, 1946), p. 117.

9. This seeming anomaly was mentioned in only one important Philippine newspaper, La Nacion. Isabelo Caballero and M. de Garcia Concepcion, Quezon (Manila, 1935), p. 173.

10. Salamanca, pp. 172-73.

11. As it was passed, the Jones Act promised independence but set no specific date. The preamble said that independence would be granted when the Filipinos had formed a "stable" government. The ambiguity of this term proved explosive when the Republicans returned to power in 1921.

12. H. R. Rep. No. 511, 67th Cong., 4th sess., 1920.

13. Quezon, The Good Fight, p. 36.

14. Kirk, p. 48.

15. QP, Quezon to Mr. Pond, undated letter [1930?].

16. QP, Quezon to Osmeña, undated letter [early 1930?].

17. Manuel Roxas, born in 1894, was, like Osmeña, from the Visayan Islands. The youthful Roxas came to national prominence when he was elected Speaker of the House in 1922.

18. QP, Roxas to Osmeña, cables, Jan. 5, 7, 1930; Osmeña to Roxas, cable, Jan. 12, 1930.

19. Hearings Before the Senate Committee on Territories and Insular Affairs, 71st Cong., 2nd sess., 1930, pp. 10-17.

20. Ibid., statements of Chester H. Gray, p. 69; W. C. Hushings, p. 113; C. W. Holman, p. 453; Frederic Brenckman, p. 110; J. S. McDaniel, pp. 293-313.

21. Ibid., statements of Charles P. Perrin, pp. 540-67; Charles D. Orth, p. 179; John M. Switzer, pp. 377-437; D. F. Webster, p. 251; John H. Pardeo, p. 251; A. G. Kempf, p. 216; J. F. Comins, p. 209.

22. Ibid., statements of Nicholas Roosevelt, pp. 341-77; Henry Stimson, pp. 658-82.

23. QP, Quezon to Maximo Kalaw, letter, Jan. 4, 1930, and Quezon to Osmeña, letter, Jan. 4, 1930.

24. Gregorio F. Zaide, The Republic of the Philippines (Manila, 1963), p. 261.

25. Proceedings of the First Independence Congress (Manila, n.d.).

26. Ibid.

27. Hayden Papers, "Secretary Hurley's report to the Chairman of the Committee on Territories and Insular Affairs." (Typewritten.) (Hereinafter collection referred to as HP.)

28. Dapen Liang, The Development of Philippine Political Parties (Hong Kong, 1939), p. 209.

29. QP, Quezon to Hawes, letter, Mar. 17, 1930.

30. QP, Roxas to Quezon, letter, May 23, 1930; Quezon to Hawes, letter, May 24, 1930.

31. Sen. Rep. No. 751, 71st Congress, 2nd session, 1932, Part 1.

32. Kirk, p. 107.

33. The transition period was later changed to ten years.

34. Angus Campbell, et al., The American Voter (New York, 1964), p. 277.

35. Maximo Manguiat Kalaw, Introduction to Philippine Social Science (Manila, 1933), pp. 499-500.

36. Joseph Ralston Hayden, The Philippines: A Study in National Development (New York, 1942), p. 349.

37. QP, Osias and Guevara to Quezon, letter, Nov. 28, 1930.

38. QP, Quezon to Osias and Guevara, letter, Nov. 21, 1930, and Quezon to Senator Wheeler, letter, Dec. 3, 1930.

39. QP, Quezon to Guevara, letter (not sent), Mar. 23, 1931.

40. QP, Quezon to Osmeña and Roxas, cable, Mar. 19, 1931.

190

41. When Senator Bingham asked Quezon if he would accept a "dominion status," Quezon declined. QP, June 6, 1931; Quezon to Senator Bingham, letter, June 11, 1931.

42. QP, Quezon to Osmeña and Roxas, cable, Aug. 26, 1931.

43. Theodore Friend, Between Two Empires (New Haven, Conn., 1965), p. 65.

44. Carlos Quirino, Quezon: Man of Destiny (Manila, 1935), p. 56.

45. Ibid., p. 69; QP, draft of an interview of Quezon for the Philippine press, Nov. 13, 1931.

46. Friend, p. 60; Quirino, Quezon, p. 65.

47. QP, Osmeña to Quezon, cable, July 13, 1931.

48. New York Times, Sept. 18-20, 1931.

49. Friend, p. 77.

50. QP, Quezon to Guevara, and Quezon to Osias, both letters dated Sept. 18, 1931.

51. QP, joint resolution in both Houses of the Philippine Legislature, Sept. 24, 1931.

52. Caballero and Concepcion, p. 300.

53. QP, M. Kalaw to Quezon, letter, Oct. 5, 1931; Quezon to Osias and Guevara, letter, Nov. 6, 1931.

54. QP, Hurley to Quezon, and Quezon's reply, both letters dated December, 1931.

55. QP, Quezon to Osias, letter, Sept. 17, 1931.

56. QP, Quezon to Guevara, letter (not sent), Dec. 14, 1931.

57. QP, Quezon to John Switzer, letter, Oct. 2, 1931.

58. The major difference between the bills was that the Senate bill provided for a nineteen-year transition period and the House bill called for a five-year transition period.

59. Friend, p. 103.

60. The Hare Bill provided for a five-year transition period under an autonomous commonwealth status with no plebiscite after the five years; it also called for liberal trade relations. See QP, OsRox to Quezon, cable, Mar. 6, 1932. The Senate did not vote on the Hawes-Cutting Bill until December, 1932.

61. QP, Quezon to OsRox, cables, July 6, 9, 11, 13, 1932; OsRox to Quezon, cables, July 6, 13, 18, 1932.

62. QP, OsRox to Quezon, cable, Sept. 10, 1932; Osias to Quezon, cable, Sept. 19, 1932.

63. Hayden, p. 356; Liang, pp. 211-12.

64. QP, Quezon to the Independence Commission, letters, Nov. 3, 5, 1932. The Independence Commission consisted of several Philippine legislators who desired the right to vote on any independence bill offered by the United States.

65. QP, OsRox to Quezon, cable, Nov. 7, 1932.

66. QP, Quezon to Aquino, radiogram, Nov. 14, 1932.

67. QP, Quezon to Mr. Ansberry, letter, Nov. 16, 1932.

68. Quezon had chosen Aquino to inform the OsRox Mission of Quezon's instructions because he was an "Osmeña man" and Quezon thought Osmeña and Roxas would listen to him. But Osmeña convinced Aquino that the Hawes-Cutting and Hare Bills were the best possible arrangements for independence. From that time on, Aquino fought with the OsRox Mission versus Quezon. QP, Aquino to Quezon, cable, Dec. 13, 1932.

69. QP, Quezon to OsRox, letter, Dec. 10, 1932.

70. QP, Quezon, press release dated Dec. 16, 1932.

71. Kirk, p. 119.

72. QP, OsRox to Quezon, cable, Dec. 19, 1932; Quezon to OsRox, cables, Dec. 19, 21, 1932.

73. QP, OsRox to Quezon, cable, Dec. 31, 1932; Quezon to OsRox, letter, Jan. 2, 1933.

74. Hoover was also influenced by the report by the War Department which called the H-H-C Bill "fundamentally unsound." HP, "Report to the President by the Secretary of War on the Hawes-Cutting Bill Granting Philippine Independence," dated Jan. 11, 1933.

75. Quezon was so much against the H-H-C Bill that he asked Senator King and General Wheeler to vote against the overriding of the veto. QP, Quezon to Senator King, cable, Jan. 16, 1933; Quezon to General Wheeler, cable, Jan. 16, 1933.

76. QP, OsRox to Quezon, cables, Jan. 20, 28, 1933.

77. QP, Quezon to Osias, cable, Jan. 28, 1933. Quezon to Osmeña, letter, Feb. 9, 1933.

78. QP, "A Message to the American People: Speech Delivered by Senate President Quezon over the Columbia Broadcasting Station, transmitted from Station KZRM, Jan. 30, 1933"; "Address of Senate President Manuel L. Quezon over Station KZRM at 9:00 P.M., Mar. 16, 1933."

79. Liang, p. 213.

80. QP, Quezon to Secretary Parker, letter, undated [Mar. 20, 1933?]; Quezon to Paredes, letter, Mar. 18, 1933. This applied to everyone under Osmeña and Roxas but not to the leaders themselves.

81. QP, OsRox to Quezon, radiogram, Mar. 28, 1933.

82. QP, untitled document on Willard Hotel stationery, April 25, 1933; Quezon to Clarin, cables, April 27, 28, 1933.

83. Quezon later consented to the April 25 agreement but again reneged. See QP, Quezon to de Jesus, letter, May 22, 1933.

84. Quezon would often refer in speeches to Osmeña as the Senator or gentleman from Cebu instead of by name. QP, de Jesus to Quezon, letter, April 1, 1933.

85. QP, Hilarion Dugenio to Clarin, letter, April 20, 1933.

86. QP, Paredes to Quezon, cable, April 25, 1933.

87. QP, Clarin to Dugenio, letter, April 29, 1933.

88. Liang, p. 215; Friend, p. 113.

89. Friend, p. 122.

90. Ibid., pp. 114-16.

91. Carlos Quirino, "Anecdotes about Quezon," Historical Bulletin (Manila), VI-3 (1962), 239-43.

92. QP, Quezon to Harrison, letter, July 2, 1933.

93. Caballero and Concepcion, p. 326.

94. Friend, pp. 117-19.

95. QP, "Speech of Senate President Quezon to the Philippine Senate," July 20, 1933.

96. Sergio Osmeña, Diario de Sesiones, quoted in Friend, p. 127.

97. QP, Quezon to Governor-General Murphy, letter, Aug. 2, 1933.

98. QP, "Speech by Senate President Quezon to the Philippine Senate," July 21, 1933.

99. Caballero and Concepcion, pp. 322-23.

100. QP, "Speech by Senate President Quezon to the Philippine Senate," Aug. 1, 1933.

101. Liang, p. 226. The leader of the Democratas, Juan Sumulong, had disbanded the party in order to join with Osmeña and form a viable opposition party.

102. Congress at this time was swamped with Roosevelt's first New Deal legislation.

103. Friend, pp. 129-31.

104. QP, Quezon to Governor-General Murphy, letter, Nov. 3, 1933.

105. Liang, p. 225.

106. Friend, p. 140.

107. Quirino, Quezon, p. 77; Friend, p. 140; New York Times, Jan. 18, 1934.

108. Caballero and Concepcion, p. 160.

109. Quirino, "Anecdotes about Quezon," p. 239.

Joseph Ralston Hayden: The Education of a Colonialist

by

Ronald K. Edgerton

When Joseph Ralston Hayden first visited the Philippines in 1922 he was strongly critical of the one-party, elitist political system which he perceived to be developing there. When, after four visits and after studying the Islands in considerable depth, Hayden published his work entitled The Philippines: A Study in National Development, he did not abjure his earlier criticism. His point of view had, however, changed in the interim. For by 1942 Hayden was prepared to accept the Philippine system of government as being "in harmony with the political personality of . . . [the Filipino] people." Although his discussion of Philippine politics was never without caveats, he came to concentrate his criticism not on the political system itself but on the weaknesses within it. As he wrote in The Philippines:

> The establishment of the type of leadership which President Quezon exercises is a natural and inevitable result of the grant of complete autonomy to the Philippines. This is what 'Filipinization' means, and not merely the replacement of American by Filipino officials. . . . It would be folly to criticize adversely a system of government because it is in harmony with the fundamental political conditions under which it operates; or to judge an administration by foreign rather than native standards. [1]

The evolution which occurred in J. R. Hayden's thinking resulted from his prolonged analysis (both as a scholar and an administrator) of the impact of American colonial rule in the

Philippines. Perhaps more than any other American, Hayden
came to grips with the problems involved in the effort to initiate
change. In his studies of Philippine government between 1922
and 1945 he revealed a growing awareness of the Philippine
elite's capacity for adapting American initiatives to benefit its
own interests. In his own thinking he may thus have captured
the gradual change in American colonial policy in general -- a
change away from stereotypes towards a more complex interpretation of America's purpose and a more realistic conception
of her capabilities in the Philippines.

Hayden did not actually visit the Islands until very nearly
his thirty-fifth birthday. [2] His uncle, Ralph Hayden, who had
fought Commodore Dewey in Manila Bay and who regaled young
Ralston with accounts of his adventures in the Islands in 1898,
had stimulated in Hayden an early interest in the Philippines. [3]
He did not, however, pursue this interest until much later.
Rather he took his first job after graduation from high school
as a reporter and later as city editor for his home-town newspaper, the Keokuk, Iowa, Constitution-Democrat. Giving this
up in 1906 he set out for Knox College in Galesburg, Illinois, to
study medicine. Four years later he entered the University of
Michigan Graduate School where he held down an Assistantship
in American History under Professor Claude H. van Tyne. His
career took still another twist in 1912 when he became an
Instructor in Political Science and when he began to concentrate
his efforts on the study of international relations.

On August 25, 1917, two years after receiving his Ph. D.,
Hayden married Elizabeth Olivia Hall of Ann Arbor, Michigan.
Later that same year he went to war as senior officer of a unit
of ninety-six men of the Michigan Naval Militia. [4] Not until he
returned to Ann Arbor did he begin writing about colonial
governments, and in December, 1920, his first article on
American colonialism appeared. [5] He had at last settled on the
subject to which he would devote the rest of his life.

When J. R. Hayden first departed for Manila with his family
in 1922, as an exchange professor at the University of the
Philippines, he was a staunch exponent of the concept of limited
government. Always wary of governmental encroachment on
individual freedoms, he vigorously defended the principle of
separation of powers. And although he was to become more and
more convinced of the need for social welfare legislation, in

1922 he considered the regulation of competition and the protection of free enterprise as the most basic purposes of good government. He had voted for Woodrow Wilson and his "New Freedom" in 1912, but in the next five presidential elections he favored the Republican over the Democratic nominee. "I am, and always have been a Republican," he wrote in 1933, although by that time he admitted that he could best be described as an "Independent Republican."[6]

This political point of view put Hayden in close agreement with General Leonard Wood, the newly-inaugurated Governor-General of the Philippines whom he had known "for a number of years" before coming to Manila. He had even campaigned for the General when Wood sought the presidency in 1920, describing him as "the inevitable candidate of those who believe in the fundamental importance of a strong, economical, democratic, and efficient administration of our national government."[7] As an Exchange Professor, and again in 1926 when he accompanied the Colonel Carmi Thompson Mission to the Islands, Hayden "came into close enough touch with him [Wood] to gain that feeling of personal admiration and loyalty which he inspired in so many people."[8] Despite Wood's penchant for making enemies, Hayden never lost his respect for the old "Rough Rider." Looking back in 1935 on the Wood administration, he was to observe that Wood's task was "more difficult than that which any Governor-General has ever faced, and he performed it magnificently."[9] And in comparison of the different Americans who had resided in Manila's Malacañan Palace, he concluded in 1936 that "Wood was the great Governor-General. What he accomplished, --and sacrificed, --made it easy for his successors."[10]

In addition to holding great personal regard for Wood and his administrative achievements, Hayden hailed the years of Wood's governorship as a period of growing democracy in the Philippines. Contrasting Wood's policies with those of former Governor-General Francis Burton Harrison, he admonished Americans in 1924 not to forget that "the powers of government which General Wood has been seeking to exercise . . . [were] surrendered by his predecessor not to the people of the Philippines but to a very small group of Filipino politicians."[11] According to Hayden, this "small group" was endangered during the Wood administration by "the steady development among the Filipino people of the capacity for democratic self-government."[12]

Indeed, the legislative elections in 1922 did appear to usher
in a new era of democracy for the Philippines. The Philippine
House of Representatives, which had formerly been dominated
by the Nacionalista Party, went to work in 1923 with a member-
ship divided between thirty-two Colectivistas (supporters of
Manuel Quezon), twenty-six Democratas, and only twenty-one
Nacionalistas (Sergio Osmeña supporters). "The American
leaven is working," exclaimed Hayden. He contended that the
existence of a genuine opposition party spelled real danger
"for the men who have dominated Filipino politics since 1907."
He also noted in 1924 that the Democrata Party "so far at least
has refused to sell out the people and threatens to sweep out the
old bosses in the next election."[13]   And while he considered the
development of an opposition party to be the sine qua non of a
successful representative government, Hayden also believed
that as more and more young Filipinos filled the ranks of the
Nacionalista and Colectivista parties, the personal power of
men like Quezon and Osmeña would diminish.[14]   That such a
development was already occurring seemed evident from the
intensity of the attacks made by these leaders on Governor-
General Wood's policies.[15]

General Wood was not, in Hayden's opinion, an unusually
arbitrary Governor-General.[16]   In an interview with Wood, published in February 1924, he had posed the question, "Isn't the use
of . . . [your] ultimate authority almost beyond the possibilities of
practical politics?"   Answered Wood: "Yes it is. We wouldn't
be backed up at home. And they [Filipinos] know it."[17]   Even
Manuel A. Roxas, Speaker of the House after 1922, had admitted
that "we could not have a better chief executive at this time than
General Wood,"[18] and Juan Sumulong, Democrata Party chief,
had criticized Wood not for refusing to collaborate but for
cooperating too much with Quezon, Roxas and Osmeña.[19]
According to Hayden, the real Filipino grievance which led to
the break in July 1923 "was not that General Wood used the
powers of his office arbitrarily, or harshly, or even unwisely,
but that he exercised them at all."[20]

In view of this strong Filipino opposition to any assertion by
a governor-general of his powers, Hayden began to contemplate
alternatives to the colonial policy with which Leonard Wood had
become identified.[21]   Writing in 1924, he noted that "we cannot
permanently turn back the clock of political progress in the

Philippines no matter how necessary it was in 1921 to do so
temporarily."[22]

"When a Government has," wrote Lord Bryce,

> directly or implicitly, raised expectations and awakened
> impatience, misgivings as to the fitness to receive a
> gift may have to yield to the demand for it. . . . There
> are moments when it is safer to go forward than to
> stand still, wiser to confer institutions, even if they
> are liable to be misused than to foment discontent by
> withholding them.

Referring to this passage in 1923,[23] Hayden wondered if the
logic of events had brought the United States to such a moment
in the Philippines. He rejected, however, the suggestion that
the United States grant the Philippines immediate independence,
arguing that such an act would spell the loss of preferential
tariff rates for Philippine products in the American market,
a blow that would ruin the Philippine economy; that the expenses
of independence (financing a national defense force, for example)
would far outdistance the financial resources then available to
the Islands; and that immediate American withdrawal might only
be a prelude to internal turmoil. He concluded, therefore, that
immediate independence would jeopardize the permanence of the
political principles and material accomplishments of American
rule in the Philippines.

Hayden then addressed himself to the question of whether or
not to set a specific date for independence. He offered the
following plan of his own:

1. An immediate American guarantee of Philippine
   independence at a given date in the future.

2. Continued American control over Philippine foreign
   relations including the power to take out loans.

3. A gradually disappearing preferential tariff on
   Filipino exports to the United States.

4. American retention of certain naval bases in the
   Islands.

5. Continuation of the American right to intervene
   forcibly to preserve domestic order.[24]

How is one to explain this sudden departure from the colonial policy of Leonard Wood by one who so staunchly supported the Governor-General both before and after these articles appeared? In a way, Hayden answered this question himself. Having proffered his scheme in December, 1924, he indulged in a little thinking aloud. His suggestions, he allowed, were open to criticism on the grounds that Filipinos were not yet ready for such complete self-government. He also noted that such a plan would put the United States in a position of responsibility without commensurate authority. "America," however, was dealing "not with theories but with facts." An actual situation existed "which must be met and which cannot be met by an ideal course of action intended to produce ideal results." It was safer, therefore, "to move forward than to stand still."[25]

Although a supporter of Leonard Wood's conception of good colonial government, in 1923-24 Hayden recognized that no strong two-party system could develop so long as the independence issue united Filipinos against the United States.[26] He also recognized that a colonial policy which continued to leave uncertain the future of the Philippines would simply prolong the economic underdevelopment of the Islands. "It is a matter of cold, hard fact," he wrote, "that the Philippines is one of the most undeveloped countries in the world, in proportion to its population and resources."[27] Attributing this lack of development to the fact that capital is not attracted to uncertain and unstable situations, Hayden urged that the United States slough off its ambivalent colonial policy and adopt instead a posture of decision.

Convincing though this argument is, Hayden did not remain an exponent of early independence for long. When he had first come to the Philippines in the 1920's he had praised General Wood as both an efficient administrator and a great democrat. As long as these attributes did not conflict, Hayden remained a firm supporter of the Wood colonial policy. But when opposition mounted, he found the unpopularity of such a policy increasingly difficult to live with, and began as a consequence to consider various plans for ending American colonial tutelage. Nevertheless, his belief in both efficient and democratic government prevented him from actually pushing for an early American withdrawal. The plan which he suggested in 1923-24 represented not a decisive break with the Wood policy, but rather a growing disquietude with his own earlier and more simplistic point of view on the purposes and possibilities of American colonialism in the Philippines.

In the late 1920's and early 30's Hayden remained a proponent of strong American supervision in the Philippines. His support for such a policy, however, was not without serious reservations, for he continued to evidence in these years a growing awareness of the strength of the indigenous elite in the Philippine-American relationship.

President Calvin Coolidge in 1926 appointed a commission to investigate and report on the situation in the Philippines. Colonel Carmi A. Thompson headed the commission which left for Manila in June, and Joseph Hayden accompanied Thompson as an adviser, helping to write the report which was submitted to Congress by President Coolidge in December, 1926.

The Thompson Report commended General Wood "for his efficient conduct of affairs." It stated, however, that responsibility for the deadlock between the Governor-General and the Philippine legislature could be attributed to both parties, and was critical of "the military atmosphere" of Wood's administration, an atmosphere which Thompson felt inhibited cooperation between the Governor-General and Filipino leaders.[28] These rather mild criticisms were made over the opposition of Joseph Hayden. Writing to A. V. H. Hartendorp soon after returning with Thompson from the Philippines, Hayden said: "I don't think he does justice to General Wood, but you may believe that if I had not had a finger in the pie, that part of the document would have been very much worse than it is."[29]

Although he didn't persuade Thompson to "do justice" to Wood, Hayden did apparently play an important role in writing the Report. In his letter to Hartendorp, Hayden revealed that he had joined Thompson in Cleveland the day after the latter's return, and had "worked on the document almost continuously until . . . [Thompson] took it to Washington a week later."[30] Claiming "a considerable part in indoctrinating" Thompson, he contended in 1927 that certain sentences "in which I had stated what I think is our proper position more directly and unequivocally, were accepted by Thompson and embodied in his report as submitted to the President, but stricken out before the report was published."[31] Considering his support of Leonard Wood, it is probable that Hayden's sentences were not only less equivocal than the published report, but less conciliatory as well.

The Thompson Report interpreted America's primary task
as a colonial power in the Philippines to be the preparation of
Filipinos for "complete self-government," a task which it did
not believe had yet been achieved. Opposing those who demanded
immediate independence for the Islands, the Report asserted
that the Philippines was ill-prepared economically and politically
for independence, and that the gulf between upper and lower
classes there remained so wide that independence would only
result in the substitution of oligarchic for American rule. Not
until the position of the masses of the Filipino people had been
raised by education and economic improvement, would genuinely
popular government be possible.

But while immediate independence was adjudged to be
inadvisable, a continuation of the friction between General Wood
and Filipino legislators seemed hardly more desirable. The
Report thus recommended that steps be taken to re-establish
"cooperation" between the executive and legislative branches of
the Philippine government. [32] Spelled out more explicitly, this
proposal meant that the United States would retreat from Wood's
policy of active intervention in internal Philippine politics.

Being aware of the contradiction between the policy of
"cooperation" as proposed in the Thompson Report, and the
implementation of American standards of governmental efficiency
and responsiveness to the electorate, Hayden accepted the
cooperative approach only as a necessary evil. In July and
August, 1927, as Chairman of a Round Table on Philippine Affairs
at Williams College, he voiced a willingness to "sacrifice a
great deal" to obtain Philippine cooperation, for such cooperation
was "vital to our success in the Islands and to the attainment of
the ends to which both Americans and Filipinos are striving."
These "sacrifices" were not, however, to vitiate America's
fundamental purpose in governing the Philippines. They were
not to prevent the United States from helping the Filipino people
"develop into a self-governing, democratic nation capable of
maintaining an independent place among the other nations of the
world." [33]

By 1931, after he had spent a year in the Islands as a
Visiting Professor at the University of the Philippines, Hayden
had become reconciled to the necessity for cooperation between

American administrators and Filipino leaders. He admitted
that in any serious struggle between the Philippine elite and
the governor-general, "articulate public opinion in the Philippines
will be vociferously and almost unitedly against the American
'ruler'." During such a confrontation, the latter would be at a
considerable disadvantage, for "long-time presidential and
congressional support for any governor-general who seeks to
impose his will upon the Filipinos is not to be expected at the
present time." He concluded, therefore, that if any constructive work was to be accomplished at all, then the Governor-
General "must secure and retain the cooperation of the leaders
of the Filipino people. There is no other road to a successful
administration or even to a tolerable existence."[34]

By 1930-31 Hayden had also become reconciled to the
impossibility of imposing an American system of two-party
government on the Philippines. Commenting on the demise of
the Democrata Party, he predicted that the disappearance of
this real opposition group would mean "an almost complete
return to the personal politics which had previously characterized the activities of Philippine parties." Unlike in 1924-25,
however, Hayden in 1930 was resigned to the inevitability of
personal government in the Philippines. He wrote in the last
chapter of his edition of Worcester's Philippines Past and
Present that:

> The United States can give to the Islands, and they
> can accept, a form of government which rests upon
> American rather than Filipino experience and apti-
> tudes. The political parties that give that government
> life, however, are sure to be the expression of
> Filipino, rather than American political genius.
> They are the realities of political life in the
> Philippines, and they are bound to be organized
> and to function in harmony with the realities of
> Filipino character, modes of life, and methods of
> conducting human affairs. In all other relation-
> ships the Filipino is personal to an extent unknown
> in Anglo-Saxon countries. He is not otherwise,
> and will not soon become otherwise in the most
> vital of his political activities.[35]

Notwithstanding his admission of the need for cooperation,
Hayden always regretted the "price that must be paid by every

American official who expects to get along with the Filipinos."
In order to win the cooperation of Filipino leaders, he felt
Americans would have to compromise in matters where compromise would jeopardize "those principles and practices that
we believe to be fundamental to the existence of good government
in a democratic state." For example, when Filipino officials
were almost unanimous in attributing the Colorum uprising (which
rocked the town of Tayug, Pangasinan, on January 10, 1931) to
religious fanaticism, the American administrators proved
reluctant to contest this judgment. That the peasants involved
had in fact rebelled against "caciquism, agrarian oppression,
and constabulary abuses," seemed to Hayden self-evident. And
yet while the conditions responsible for the Tayug uprising
appeared obvious to him, their remedy remained elusive. Only
by challenging the power of the Philippine political and economic
elite could the colonial administration hope to uproot the underlying causes of the revolt. Aware that the United States was
unwilling to return to the confrontation of the Wood years, and
dubious of achieving significant reforms by way of the "cooperation"
policy, Hayden turned, therefore, once again to the alternative of
independence for the Philippines. Once again he pondered whether
the United States shouldn't leave the Islands rather than "remain
in a position where, after all, the best thing that its Governor-
General can do in a Tayug case is to allow it to be white-washed."[36]

Apparent throughout Hayden's search for a proper American
colonial policy in the Philippines is his compelling desire to
repair the Philippine political system in order to make it more
responsive to the Filipino people. At times, realizing the
difficulty of implementing reforms in the Islands, he would
throw up his arms in despair and aver that early independence
was, after all, the only alternative. For him, however, this
was always a policy of "scuttle," to be accepted only when all
hope for reform through American initiative was lost. More
often, his awareness of shortcomings in the political system led
him to tie independence to the achievement of greater social
and economic amelioration in the Philippines.

Hayden thus opposed both the Hare-Hawes-Cutting Bill and
the Tydings-McDuffie Act which granted the Philippines independence after a ten-year commonwealth period. In his attacks on
both these measures, he stressed the economic argument against
independence. Having made an economic dependency of the
Islands, the United States could not "with honor, or even with

decency and safety, withdraw from the Philippines without giving that country a considerable further period within which to develop economically under the protection of America."[37] But Hayden was opposed to these measures not only because they were unrealistic economically. The United States should, he urged in a plan which he sent to Michigan Senator Arthur Vandenberg, promise only to grant independence when certain "objective achievements in economic and social development are substantially attained."[38]

In keeping with his opposition to the policy of "scuttle," Hayden was critical of Frank Murphy's appointment as Governor-General in 1933. Predicting that "Murphy will allow them to have what they really want," he complained that "if public offices in the Philippines are to be used by American political parties for purely party political purposes, the sooner we leave the Islands the better."[39]

Hayden met Murphy at a dinner party given by Mrs. Fielding Yost (of the University of Michigan) in honor of the new Governor-General. The two men sat next to one another and talked Philippines right through the meal. As reported by Mrs. Yost, Murphy was very much impressed by the Professor, and confided after dinner that "I'm going to have him come out to the Philippines. I'm going to take it up with the President right away. He's the very man, the right age, he's the type of man."[40] Hayden, however, seems to have retained misgivings about Murphy. After talking with him a second time and giving him a copy of his article entitled "What Next for the Moro," Hayden commented that:

> Murphy is honest and warm hearted and he is going out to Manila with the most honest (and naive) intentions of serving his country. . . . His intellectual ability is not high and he knows absolutely nothing about the Philippines. Neither do any of the people who are going out with him from Detroit. The whole performance is fantastic.[41]

Hayden was soon to become a very important part of that "fantastic" performance. As a result of Murphy's recommendation he was appointed Vice-Governor of the Philippines on November 3, 1933.[42] After a short interview with President Roosevelt during which the President made passing mention of

his hope to visit the Philippines, Hayden departed once again for
the Islands. [43] This was to be his fourth visit to America's
colonial possession in Asia, but unlike the previous three, his
visit from 1933 to 1935 provided him the opportunity to exercise
an important influence on the Philippine policy of the United
States.

Between 1933 and 1935, Hayden and Frank Murphy evolved
a program in which they succeeded in instituting selected reforms
without antagonizing the Philippine elite. In the two years in which
they worked together in the Philippines, these men forged a policy
which was both reformist and cooperationist. They accomplished
this by concentrating not on revolutionizing the Philippines, a
policy which they realized to be hopeless, but on strengthening
Philippine national cohesion in the last years before independence.
In this effort, they concentrated first on providing ethnic minor-
ities with the opportunity to participate more fully in the nation-
building process, and secondly on making the national government
more responsive to the needs of its impoverished citizenry.

J. R. Hayden accepted his responsibilities as Vice-Governor
with enthusiasm, brimming with hopes of accomplishing significant
social and economic reforms. "The fascinating thing about this
country and this job," he wrote to Professor Jesse S. Reeves,
"is that it is still possible to accomplish things of importance, —
things that really affect the lives of the people and the destiny of
the land."[44] His hopes for instituting broad reforms suffered
a serious blow, however, when Congress passed the Tydings-
McDuffie Act in March, 1934. "In establishing the Commonwealth,"
he argued, "America has decided that the Filipino and not
American ideas and ideals shall rule in this country." He felt
that "Filipino and American ideas of what should be done for
the welfare of the country differ radically," and thus admitted
to a "feeling of frustration" when he contemplated how unlikely
it was that Filipinos would carry on from where he left off.[45]

Given this feeling for the disparity between Filipino and
American points of view, it is not surprising that Hayden grew
to admire Governor-General Murphy particularly for his ability
to get things done without making enemies. The professor-
turned-administrator had not been in Manila for even two months

when he admitted to having "gone Murphy."[46] After working
with the former mayor of Detroit for four months, he marvelled
at the "extraordinary degree" to which Murphy had won "the
confidence and respect of all elements in the Philippines."[47]
Still later he was to compare Murphy with his old favorite --
Leonard Wood -- noting that "Murphy was smart enough politically to make M. L. Q. [Manuel L. Quezon] do more things that
this gentleman did not want to do and prevent him from doing
more things that he did want to do than has any other American
Governor-General, and do it in such a way that Quezon could
not come into an open breach with him."[48]

Murphy made Hayden one of his "chief Advisors," and told
him to be cognizant of everything that was going on.[49] He
further invested his Vice-Governor with responsibility for determining policy on non-Christian problems in the Philippines.
Together with his official responsibilities as chief of the Department of Public Instruction (which subsumed the Bureau of
Education and the Bureau of Public Health), Hayden therefore
exercised considerable influence over the Moro policy of the
Murphy administration.

Murphy's program, dubbed "the New Deal for the Moros,"
encouraged the development of Sulu Province in order to afford
the Muslim people greater opportunity to participate in national
affairs. It consisted of two primary points of emphasis: it
stressed the de-Christianization of the administration in Sulu
Province, and it pushed for the establishment of modern institutions of justice and political authority over the traditional
institutions symbolized by the Sultan of Sulu.

The question of whether Christian Filipinos properly could
govern their Mohammedan countrymen had always bothered Hayden.
Writing in 1925, he predicted that were Christian Filipinos to
undertake such a task without American supervision, "an expensive and ruthless war, in which the Moros would be defeated
without being eliminated as a serious problem of government
would be quite possible."[50] That this prediction had a ring of
truth to it seemed evident during the administration of Theodore
Roosevelt, Jr., when a small-scale guerrilla war between the
Philippine Constabulary and Moros on the island of Jolo resulted
in the death of over 100 men. Murphy approved Hayden's
recommendation that non-Muslim officials be transferred out of
Sulu as rapidly as possible.[51] Such a policy did not, however,

meet with the approval of the Philippine Bureau of Non-Christian
Tribes. According to Hayden, only Governor-General Murphy's
prowess as a salesman prevented that Bureau from opposing the
program. [52]

The linchpin in the "New Deal for the Moros" was James R.
Fugate, whom Hayden recommended and supported without
reservation. [53] Fugate not only presided over the Muslimization
of the administration in Sulu but also directed the campaign
against the _Agama_ court structure of the Sulu Sultanate. Opposed
by both Christian Filipinos and the royal family of Sulu, Fugate
nevertheless succeeded in restoring order in the province. That
he was able to do so was due in part to his widespread popularity
in "Moroland," in part to the extensive program of public works
which he administered, and in part to his policy of appointing
Moro officers to Philippine Constabulary companies stationed
in Sulu. Hayden was ever aware of the importance of having a
man of great strength and dedication directing affairs in Sulu. He
took great pride in the fact that he had a part in Fugate's success,
and affirmed that of all his accomplishments he took "greatest
satisfaction in . . . the revolution that has occurred in the
situation in the province of Sulu."[54]

Hayden was also proud of his work in public health and social
welfare in the Philippines. He considered the accomplishments
made in this area his "most important and successful work."[55]
He admitted, however, that without the strong humanitarian
impulse of Frank Murphy such an extensive program could never
have been instituted. Counting Murphy among the "three great
leaders" in public health work in the Philippines, Hayden described how during his administration "the political leader and
the technical adviser" were encouraged to work "in perfect
collaboration" to advance the welfare of the Filipino people. [56]

The Murphy administration's public health and welfare program
embraced, according to Hayden, "all of the essential movements
to raise the standard of living of the poor in the Filipino community."[57] It did not, however, go far enough to alleviate the social
and economic ills of Philippine rural life. That more comprehensive measures were required became clear when some 60,000
peasants rose up in armed rebellion during the night of May 2, 1935.
The _Sakalista_ revolt, as it came to be known, lasted only until
May 3. In those two wild days, however, the _Sakdals_ compelled
Americans like Joseph Ralston Hayden to take one last searching

look at both their purpose as colonial administrators and their capacity for effecting significant reforms in the Philippines.

At the time of the Sakdalista uprising, Hayden was Acting Governor-General in the absence of Murphy. On the night of May 2, he and Mrs. Hayden were away on an inspection tour of Mountain Province.[58] They received news of the revolt in the dead of night somewhere north of the village of Banaue. Deciding to leave for Manila at once, Hayden mounted his horse, in company with the original party, in a driving rainstorm, and promptly disappeared over a cliff. Luckily for him the drop was not a long one, and he continued his hurried journey back to Manila where he began a lengthy investigation into the Sakdalista affair.[59]

The committee which investigated the causes of the uprising concluded that it was fundamentally "due to political factors of long standing." It blamed certain "radical leaders," who had denounced the "betrayal" of Quezon, Roxas, and Osmeña on the independence question, for fomenting a highly explosive situation among the "economically depressed classes." "Economic and social factors did not operate to bring about the uprising," the committee concluded, although "the poor economic and social status of the people [had] served to accentuate dissatisfaction with existing political conditions."[60]

Hayden did not openly disagree with the committee's report, but he regarded the Sakdalista uprising as a genuine "blow against caciquism [landlord exploitation] as well as for independence." Commenting that to the common peasant "caciquism is linked with the American domination," he pointed out that in Sakdal parlance Quezon, Osmeña, and Roxas were "traitors who wish to continue American rule in order that under the protection of American bayonets they and their class may exploit the masses of their own people." Once the Americans had been forced to withdraw, the argument continued, then the "have nots" could dispose of their own "tyrants." For Hayden, therefore, the probable cause of the uprisings of May 2-3, 1935, was "the abuse of power" by local landlords, officials, or usurers. Estimating that during forty years of American sovereignty caciquism had "been reduced in extent, softened in its methods, and morally discredited with a growing proportion of the people," he admitted that nonetheless, "it still exists."[61]

In view of the continued existence of _caciquism_ and the
failure of representative two-party democracy to develop in
the Philippines, what did Joseph Hayden propose to do? By
May, 1935, the Acting Governor-General proposed to do nothing
at all in the way of major reform of the Philippine social order.
After all, the United States had failed in better than thirty years
of colonial rule to uproot the fundamental causes which gave rise
to the _Sakdalista_ revolt. Now, with only six months left before
the inauguration of the Commonwealth, Hayden was prepared to
leave Filipino problems to Filipino solutions. [62]

Convinced that the limits to America's resolve in the
Philippines had been reached, Hayden left the Islands on
November 25, 1935, a defender of the ten-year commonwealth
plan of the Tydings-McDuffie Act. This time, however, his
support for independence did not simply express a desire to
"fish or cut bait." Rather he retained in the late 1930's and
early 40's a deep interest in and commitment to the welfare of
the emerging Philippine nation. His continued interest in the
Islands expressed itself first in his vigorous campaign against
the economic provisions of the Tydings-McDuffie Act, and
secondly in his decision to return to the Philippines again in
1944-45.

The Tydings-McDuffie Act provided for an export tax on
Philippine goods to begin in 1941 and to be raised by 5 percent
each year until 1946 when full tariffs would be imposed. [63] To
Hayden this provision of the act represented simply irresponsible
American isolationism. The United States, he repeated again
and again, "has an inescapable moral responsibility for this
Asiatic people." [64] He warned that the act, by strangling the
Philippine economy, might create a situation of chaos in the
Islands. And would it not be easy for the Japanese to gobble
up a chaotic and undefended Philippines? Thus an example of
irresponsible isolationism could in fact involve the United
States in the very sort of war in the Pacific that Congress had
thought to avoid in passing the independence act. For "our
investments, people, and sentimental interests in the Islands,"
Hayden maintained, "are so great that the Philippines in trouble
with internal revolution or invaded by another country would
constitute a very severe threat to American peace." [65]

With the outbreak of war in the Pacific, Hayden undertook an
exhaustive trip into the Pacific theater as a member of the Board

of Analysts of the Office for the Coordination of Information (later to become the OSS). Then, in 1943, he was appointed "Civil Adviser and Consultant on Philippine Affairs," and attached to the Philippine Regional Section of the Allied Intelligence Bureau, under General Douglas MacArthur's command. [66] In this capacity, Hayden set to work on problems such as how to deal with Philippine collaborators, how to re-establish the Philippine Commonwealth, how to restore the Philippine economy, and how to organize and train American Army civil affairs teams for work in the Philippines.

Hayden's efforts to plan for the establishment of Civil Affairs units to set up local governments in the Islands as areas were liberated met with resistance from MacArthur who argued that "an elaborate a priori plan and organization would melt in the fierce heat of battle." MacArthur also demurred when Hayden urged that provision be made for "a considerable" Philippine civil affairs staff. "If we send a big staff of outsiders in there to tell those people how to run their affairs, there'll be another '1898',"[67] said the general. It was not until September, 1944, that a tentative plan for Philippine Civil Affairs was circulated, and not until October that it was accepted. [68] Thus Hayden did not enjoy under MacArthur the influence on Philippine policy-making that he had experienced under Murphy. As the general told him shortly before the Leyte invasion, "You do not need to tell me a thing about the political situation, because I am spending practically all my time upon those problems." Relating this incident to the journalist Dale Pontius, Hayden commented that on Philippine affairs MacArthur seemed to think that he was "more competent than any other American, or than any other Filipino either."[69]

Hayden returned to the United States in May, 1945. At that time he was seriously contemplating an offer by Commonwealth President Sergio Osmeña to return to the Philippines still another time to become a presidential adviser. [70] It is probable that Hayden would have accepted this new opportunity to influence Philippine affairs. [71] He had only just returned home, however, when a cerebral hemorrhage ended his life suddenly and tragically on May 19, 1945. Said Frank Murphy of his departed colleague:

> Hayden brought to bear on delicate problems of state-
> craft an understanding of the Philippines, its people
> and institutions, that no other American possessed in
> the same degree. [72]

Every American who took part in the colonial experiment of
the United States in the Philippines had at one time or another to
decide how he would resolve the conflict inherent in America's
colonial ideals. Some chose to respect Filipino demands for
self-government organized in accord with Filipino customs and
attitudes. Others were motivated primarily by a desire to bring
efficient, honest, and/or democratic government to the Islands.
That all possessed a little or both of these ideals is evident from
the fact that American colonial rule in the Philippines was characterized more by compromise and cooperation than by conviction.

Joseph Ralston Hayden identified with those Americans who
sought to bring good government to the Philippines. Motivated
by a profound concern for the welfare of the Filipino people
together with a fundamental belief in the virtues of efficient and
democratic government, he always hoped to see the Philippine
political system become more responsive to the needs of its
citizenry. To be sure, there were occasions when he called in
dismay for an end to the uncertainty of American rule. For him,
however, independence was always a negative policy--a policy
of "scuttle."

In his search for a proper American colonial policy in the
Philippines, Hayden underwent a gradual change. When he first
arrived in the early 1920's, he supported Governor-General
Wood primarily because he believed that strong American leadership could serve both to challenge the old oligarchy and support
a genuine opposition party. Instead, Wood's policy tended to
shore up the oligarchs by uniting Filipinos beneath their nationalist banner. Out of the stalemate that followed, Hayden derived
a more realistic perception of what could and could not be accomplished by American colonialists in the Philippines. Although he
continued to be chary of praise for the Philippine political system,
he admitted that the cooperation of Filipino leaders was indispensible to the success of any American colonial administration. As
Vice-Governor in 1933-35 he asserted that "as long as we are here
with the authority that we now possess, we must do what we can to
maintain those standards that have been established under the
American flag."[73] He limited his reform efforts, however, to
measures that would not incur the wrath of the Philippine elite.
For he had come to realize that regardless of American initiatives

to bestow the "blessings of American democracy" on the Philippines, "a people held by force in a position of political subordination" achieves its own ends by twisting those initiatives "into the shape of native desires."[74]

APPENDIX

PUBLICATIONS OF JOSEPH RALSTON HAYDEN

I. BOOKS

The Philippines: A Study in National Development. New York:
The Macmillan Company, 1942.

The Senate and Treaties, 1789-1817: The Development of the
Treaty-Making Functions of the United States Senate during
their Formative Period. University of Michigan Publications.
Humanistic Papers, No. 4. New York: The Macmillan
Company, 1920.

Worcester, Dean C. The Philippines, Past and Present. New
Edition in One Volume with Biographical Sketch and Four
Additional Chapters by Ralston Hayden. New York: The
Macmillan Company, 1930.

II. ARTICLES

In American Historical Review: "The States' Rights Doctrine
and the Treaty-Making Power," XXII, No. 3 (April, 1917),
566-585.

In American Journal of International Law: "The Origin of the
United States Senate Committee on Foreign Relations,"
XI, No. 1 (Jan., 1917), 113-130.

In American Political Science Review: "Changes in British
Parliamentary Procedure," XIV, No. 3 (August, 1920),
471-477; "Higher Officials in the Philippine Civil Service,"
XXVII, No. 2 (April, 1933), 204-221; "The Institute of
Far Eastern Affairs," XXXII (Feb., 1938), 114-116;
"New European Constitutions," XVI, No. 2 (May, 1922),
211-227.

In Annals of the American Academy of Political and Social
Science: "The Philippines at the Threshold of Independence,"
CCXV (May, 1941), 100-106; "The United States and the
Philippines--A Survey of Some Political Aspects of Twenty-
Five Years of American Sovereignty," CXXI, No. 211
(Nov., 1925), 26-49.

In Atlantic Monthly: "The Netherlands Indies," CXXXIV, No. 3 (Sept., 1924), 401-411; "The Philippines: An Experiment in Democracy," CXXXVII, No. 3 (March, 1926), 403-417.

In The Christian Science Monitor, based upon research in Formosa: "Formosa Is Index to Japan's System," March 30, 1923; "Formosa Is Rigid Bureaucracy: Natives Dislike Japan's System," April 3, 1923; "Formosans See Sign of Liberty Under Baron Den's Government," April 9, 1923; "High Taxes Paid by Formosans Are Boon to Japan's Treasury," April 10, 1923; "Island of Formosa Gives Japan Gate to Northwestern Pacific," April 17, 1923; "The Hill People of Formosa Visit the Japanese in Taihoku," April 13, 1923; "Formosans Seek Self-Government," April 25, 1923.

Based upon research in the Philippines: "Legal Power Granted Filipinos Makes America's Position Weak," Aug. 7, 1923; "Philippines Held Badly Developed," Aug. 9, 1923; "American Political Strategy Seen in Filipinos' Conventions," Sept. 15, 1923; "Personalities, Not Platforms, Victors in Filipinos' Elections," Oct. 9, 1923; "Filipinos Connive to Make Freedom 1924 Issue in U.S.," Jan. 30, 1924; "Defeat of Bosses by Filipinos in '25 Freely Predicted," Jan. 31, 1924; "Philippines Lack Well Developed Political Lineup," Feb. 2, 1924; "Filipinos' Crusade for Independence Is Political Move," Feb. 5, 1924; "Gen. Wood Decried in Philippines for Asserting Rights," Feb. 6, 1924; "Filipino Politicos, Not Masses, Lose Reins Under Wood," Feb. 9, 1924; "Philippine Self-Government Waits Upon More and Better Education," Feb. 11, 1924; "Philippine Masses for Independence; Desire Not Urgent," Feb. 15, 1924; "The Philippine Language Problem," Feb. 18, 1924; "English in Second Place with Filipino," Feb. 25, 1924; "Filipinos Need Regime Resting on Consent of Governed," March 8, 1924; "The Future of the Philippines," March 10, 1924; "Thompson Visit to Philippines Pleases Native," Sept. 2, 1926; "Filipino Found Virtually Free in Provinces," Sept. 3, 1926; "Filipinos Need Pioneer's Urge Says Observer," Sept. 13, 1926; "Thompson Back with New Plan for Philippines," Nov. 20, 1926; "Thompson Returns with Call for End of Philippine Feud," Nov. 22, 1926; "Visayans Lead in Development of Philippines," Nov. 23, 1926; "Visayan

Natives Willing to Act with America," Nov. 23, 1926; "Lanao
Region of Mindanao Called a Camp," Dec. 1, 1926;
"Philippines Again Loom in Politics," Sept. 9, 1931;
"Governor-General's Message Plans Philippine Legislation,"
Sept. 10, 1931; "Governor Davis of Philippines Gets Results
Through Others," Sept. 11, 1931; "Co-operation in the
Philippines Found to Carry Its Penalties," Sept. 12, 1931;
"Economic Independence First Requisite for the Philippines,"
Sept. 14, 1931.

In Current History: "Nation-Building by India's First Parliament,"
XIX (Jan., 1924), 612-621; "Great Britain's Labor Strike,"
XXIV, 315-322; "British Imperial Conference Results,"
XXV, 562-569; "Lloyd George's Attempt to Revive British
Liberal Party," XXV, 879-882; "British Parliamentary
Program," XXVI, 109ff; "Newfoundland Gains 100,000
Square Miles," XXVI, 282f; "India in Turmoil," XXXII,
545-549.

In Foreign Affairs: "Japan's New Policy in Korea and Formosa,"
II, No. 3 (March, 1924), 474-487; "Malaya and the Philippines:
Colonial Contrast," V, No. 2 (Jan., 1927), 327-331; "What
Next for the Moro?" VI, No. 4 (July, 1928), 633-644; "China,
Japan and the Philippines," XI, No. 4 (July, 1933), 711-715;
"The Philippines in Transition," XIV, No. 4 (July, 1936),
639-653.

In Journal of the Michigan Schoolmasters' Club: "American
Policy in the Changing Orient," 1936, pp. 16-20.

In Magazine of History: "The Apostasy of Silas Deane," XVI,
No. 3 (March, 1913), 95-103.

In Michigan Alumni Quarterly Review: "The Changing Orient,"
XLII, No. 17 (March, 1936), 111-117.

In Philippine Social Science Review: "Is Democracy a Failure?"
III, No. 3 (May, 1931), 213-219.

In Philippine Teacher's Digest: "The Philippine Public Schools,"
III, No. 7 (Dec., 1934), 387-392.

In Round Table (London): "America and the Philippines," LVII
(Dec., 1924), 82-117.

In The Weekly Review (New York): "Two Plans for a National
Budget," II, No. 53 (May 15, 1919), 513-516; "Caveat

Negociator," I, No. 2 (July 26, 1919), 229-230; "The Rights
of the Senate," I, No. 28 (Nov. 22, 1919), 599-600; "The
Lesson of Haiti," III, No. 82 (Dec. 8, 1920), 551-552.

III. REPORTS, PAMPHLETS, ETC.

A History of the University Divisions Michigan Naval Militia.
    With R[oby] M[cKinley] Burley. Ann Arbor: Association
    of Former Members University Divisions, M.N.M., 1921.

Liang, Dapen. The Development of Philippine Political Parties.
    Hong Kong: South China Morning Post, 1939.
    Foreword by Joseph Ralston Hayden.

"Memorandum on American Experience with Problems of
    Population in the Philippines and Puerto Rico." United
    States Memorandum No. 4. International Studies Confer-
    ence, 10th Session, Paris, June 28-July 3, 1937.
    (Mimeographed. May, 1937.)

Michigan, State of. Commission on Reform and Modernization
    of Government. Report of a Preliminary Survey. Lansing,
    Michigan, December 20, 1938.
    Joseph R. Hayden, Chairman.

Pacific Politics. [Minneapolis]: University of Minnesota Press,
    1937. [The Day and Hour Series of the University of
    Minnesota, No. 16, March, 1937.]

"The Philippine Islands; Their Political Status." [Williamstown,
    Mass.]: Institute of Politics, Williams College. Seventh
    Session--1927. Round Table No. 2 [July 29-August 24, 1927.]
    (Typewritten.)
    Hayden presiding; includes speeches by Hayden and others.

"The Philippine Policy of the United States." New York: Institute
    of Pacific Relations, 1939. (Mimeographed for private
    circulation and as a part of the documentation of the
    Conference of the Institute of Pacific Relations, 1939.)

Topical Reading List on the Political and Constitutional History
    of the United States, for the Use of Students in History
    Fourteen and Fifteen, University of Michigan. Ann Arbor:
    G. Wahr, c. 1912. Revised edition, with Oie Worth
    Stephenson, c. 1918.

Notes

1. Joseph Ralston Hayden, <u>The Philippines: A Study in National Development</u> (New York, 1942), p. 444.

2. Hayden was born on September 24, 1887. For biographical data, see Joseph Ralston Hayden, Vertical File, Michigan Historical Collections; Edward W. Mill, "Joseph Ralston Hayden: Scholar in Government," <u>Michigan Alumnus: Quarterly Review</u>, LIV-20 (1948), 209-17; "Scholar-Administrator Dies," <u>The Michigan Alumnus</u>, LI-22 (1945), 413; James G. Wingo, "Dr. Joseph Ralston Hayden: A Tribute," The Philippine Hour, Manila, May 23, 1945 (a printed radio address).

3. This is the opinion of Mrs. Joseph Ralston Hayden, given in an interview with the author, Ann Arbor, April 10, 1969.

4. To Lieutenant Hayden was to go the distinction of having fired the last official shot of World War I, at 10:58 1/2 A.M. on November 11, 1918. A bronze plaque in the Smithsonian Institution records this deed.

5. Hayden, "The Lesson of Haiti," <u>The Weekly Review</u>, III-82 (1920), 551-52.

6. Hayden Papers (Michigan Historical Collections, The University of Michigan, Ann Arbor), Hayden to Brigadier-General Francis LeJ. Parker, Chief of the Bureau of Insular Affairs, July 8, 1933. (Hereinafter the Hayden Mss. will be referred to as HP.)

By the mid-1930's, Hayden had come to have a considerable respect for President Roosevelt and the New Deal. He voted for Roosevelt in 1936 and planned to vote for him again in 1940. Furthermore, he admitted that he had come to believe that "we should progress along the lines of social development that Roosevelt stands for." (HP, Hayden to Professor Thomas H. Reed, Republican Program Committee, Chicago, July 11, 1938.) As he noted in a letter to Dr. Esson

M. Gale, he had become convinced that "we are passing
through a period of profound change during which political
and social institutions will be brought into a nicer adjustment to the economic and industrial changes of the past
generation and more. There has been a lag between
economic progress and political and social progress in
this country that is going to be taken up." (HP, Hayden
to Dr. Esson M. Gale, Salt Revenue Administration,
Shanghai, China, no date.)

7. HP, Hayden, "What Does Wood Stand For? What Sort of
President Do the American People Want?" (Undated article.)

8. HP, Hayden to Mr. Worcester, Sept. 29, 1927.

9. HP, Hayden to Professor William H. Hobbs, Professor
Emeritus of Geology, University of Michigan, Jan. 29, 1935.

10. HP, Hayden to Governor Frank Mosher, Episcopal Bishop
for the Philippine Islands, and a good friend of the Haydens,
Dec. 26, 1936.

11. Hayden, "Filipino Politicos, Not Masses, Lose Reins under
Wood," Christian Science Monitor, Feb. 9, 1924. (Hereinafter
the Christian Science Monitor referred to as CSM.)

12. Hayden, "The Philippines: An Experiment in Democracy,"
Atlantic Monthly, CXXXVII - 3 (1926), 415. In 1924 Wood
had asked Hayden to write an article for the Atlantic
Monthly. Implicit in this suggestion was that Hayden should
respond to an article by Raymond L. Buell, entitled "What
About the Philippines?" Atlantic Monthly, CXXXIII-3 (1924).
When Hayden's article appeared, Wood wrote to thank him.
HP, Wood to Hayden, April 9 and April 13, 1924; and Wood
to Hayden, June 3, 1926.

13. Hayden, "Defeat of Bosses by Filipinos in '25 Freely
Predicted," CSM, Jan. 31, 1924.

14. Hayden, "American Political Strategy Seen in Filipinos'
Conventions," CSM, Sept. 15, 1923.

15. Hayden, "Philippines Lack Well Developed Political Lineup,"
CSM, Feb. 9, 1924.

220

16. A similar view of Wood is taken by Michael [P.] Onorato in several articles collected in A Brief Review of American Interest in Philippine Development and Other Essays (Berkeley, c. 1968).

17. Hayden, "General Wood Decried in Philippines for Asserting Rights," CSM, Feb. 6, 1924.

18. Hayden, "The United States and the Philippines--A Survey of Some Political Aspects of Twenty-five Years of American Sovereignty," The Annals of the American Academy of Political and Social Science, CXXI-211 (1925), 43.

19. Hayden, "Philippines Lack . . . ," CSM, Feb. 9, 1924.

20. Hayden, "The Philippines . . . ," Atlantic Monthly, CXXXVII-3 (1926), 407.

21. Among the alternatives which Hayden rejected was the Dutch policy of governing through the medium of indigenous customs and personalities. He considered such a policy "ostrich"-like, for the old traditional forces of unity in both the Dutch East Indies and the Philippines were, he believed, rapidly eroding to the point where they could no longer cope with the problems of modern society. Hayden, "The Netherlands Indies," Atlantic Monthly, CXXXIV-3 (1924), 408-11.

22. Hayden, "America and the Philippines," The Round Table (London), LVII (Dec., 1924), 115.

23. Hayden, "Philippines Held Badly Developed," CSM, Aug. 9, 1923.

24. Hayden offered this plan with minor alterations in the following articles: "Philippines Held Badly Developed," CSM, Aug. 9, 1923; "Filipinos Need Regime Resting on Consent of the Governed," CSM, Mar. 8, 1924; "America and the Philippines," The Round Table (London), LVII (Dec., 1924), 82-117. The particular scheme paraphrased above is taken from the Round Table article. In his first article, Hayden set 1929 as the date for independence. In his Mar. 8, 1924, formulation of the plan, however, he dropped any mention of a specific year for independence. Also, in his two articles in the Monitor he mentions twenty-five years as a good length of

time for accustoming the Philippines to relaxing tariff preferences. Finally, in the first two articles he adds still another specification--that the United States must approve the Philippine Constitution. He makes no mention of this stipulation in the Round Table article.

25. Hayden, "America and the Philippines," The Round Table, LVII (Dec., 1924), 117.

26. Ibid., 115.

27. Hayden, "Philippines Held Badly Developed," CSM, Aug. 9, 1923.

28. Carmi A. Thompson, "Conditions in the Philippine Islands," Report submitted to President Coolidge on December 4, 1926. A copy is supplied in Dean C. Worcester, The Philippines, Past and Present, revised edition by Joseph Ralston Hayden (New York, 1930), pp. 819-29.

29. HP, Hayden to A. V. H. Hartendorp, April 8, 1927.

30. Ibid.

31. HP, Hayden to Jackson Ralston, May 6, 1927.

32. Thompson Report, in Worcester, p. 822.

33. Hayden, "The Philippine Islands: Their Political Status" (Report of Round Table No. 2, Seventh Session, Institute of Politics, Williams College, [Williamstown, Mass., 1927]), First General Conference, July 30, 1927, pp. 9-10. (Typewritten.) The sacrifices which Hayden was prepared to make in 1927 seem to have been more in the realm of efficient administration than democratic institutions. For example, he chided Wood for complaining that the Insular government was only 75 percent efficient. See Ibid., Twelfth Meeting, August 2, 1927, p. 4. At this same twelfth meeting (pp. 1-6), Hayden seemed on the verge of reincarnating his old independence scheme. He told the pro-Harrison member of the group that he was "not so sure but that the best scheme to apply to the Philippines would be that which has worked so successfully in the relations of the United States and Cuba."

34. Hayden, "Davis Under Pressure in Philippines," CSM, Sept. 9, 1931.

35. Worcester, The Philippines, Past and Present, p. 783.

36. Hayden, "Co-operation in the Philippines Found to Carry its Penalties," CSM, Sept. 12, 1931.

37. Hayden, "Economic Independence First Requisite for the Philippines," CSM, Sept. 14, 1931. For a later statement of Hayden's opposition to the Hare-Hawes-Cutting Bill and "further legislation regarding Philippine independence" see HP, Office Memorandum of statement made by Hayden to General Cox, November 8, 1933.

38. Hayden outlined this plan without specifying the "objective achievements" that he desired in a letter to Vandenberg, HP, November 25, 1931. With respect to economic development, the plan proposed that the Philippines be given the power to initiate legislation concerning trade relations with the United States, and the power to lay export duties upon goods exported from the Islands. Hayden asserted that "the first demand of the situation is greatly to increase the taxable wealth of the Philippines, at the same time checking sugar and diversifying their other products. Without this increase, independence is unthinkable." The plan also provided for "further extension of autonomy under the Jones Law." Vandenberg did not adopt Hayden's suggestions, but he and Hayden both agreed that the United States should initiate at once a program to terminate gradually the economic dependence of the Islands. See also HP, Hayden to Vandenberg, October 16, 1931.

39. HP, Hayden to James R. Fugate, April 8, 1933.

40. Dr. Sidney Fine and Dr. Robert M. Warner, "An Interview with Mrs. Fielding Yost," October 28, 1963, Michigan Historical Collections, The University of Michigan, pp. 1-2.

41. HP, Hayden to Fugate, May 12, 1933.

42. Hayden was first asked if he would like to become Vice-Governor in July, 1933. (See HP, Brigadier General Francis LeJ. Parker, Chief of the Bureau of Insular Affairs, to Hayden, July 24, 1933.) Hayden inquired whether Murphy

had initiated the action. (HP, Hayden to Basil D. Edwards, War Department, Office of the Assistant Secretary, Sept. 27, 1933.) He was told that Murphy had recommended him, but that "nothing was said about whether he initiated the matter." (HP, Basil D. Edwards to Hayden, Sept. 29, 1933.)

43. See HP, notes made by Hayden on interview with F. D. R., November, 1933.

44. HP, Hayden to Professor Jesse S. Reeves, Political Science Department, University of Michigan, Feb. 9, 1934.

45. HP, Hayden to Reeves, June 14, 1934. See HP, Hayden to Professor Everett S. Brown, October 30, 1934, for Hayden reference to himself as a "reformer." In HP, Hayden to Wilfred B. Shaw, Director of Alumni Relations, the University of Michigan, June 30, 1934, Hayden predicts that in the Commonwealth period the government of the Islands "will express almost completely Spanish-Malayan and not Anglo-Saxon psychology."

46. HP, Hayden to Reeves, Feb. 9, 1934.

47. HP, Hayden to Hon. Junius E. Beal, May 15, 1934.

48. HP, Hayden to Nicholas Roosevelt, New York Herald Tribune editor, March 20, 1937. See also HP, Hayden's "off the record" remarks to the Ann Arbor Rotary Club on Feb. 25, 1936, in which he praises Murphy's tactic of putting the "cards on the table" with Quezon, Roxas, and Paredes early in his administration.

49. HP, Hayden to Reeves, Feb. 9, 1934.

50. Hayden, "The United States and the Philippines--A Survey of Some Political Aspects of Twenty-five Years of American Sovereignty," Annals of the American Academy of Political and Social Science, CXXI-211 (1925), 28-29.

51. HP, Hayden to James R. Fugate, April 11, 1934.

52. HP, Hayden to Reeves, Feb. 2, 1934.

53. Fugate had been Provincial Governor of Sulu before being
relieved of that position by Governor-General Roosevelt.
He was a man who tended to stimulate controversy, but
Hayden always gave him unwavering support. When Fugate
was murdered on December 15, 1938, at an Episcopal
mission station in Upi, Cotabato Province, Hayden was to
write: "He was a unique and great character, and I feel
that knowing him and working with him as I did is one of
the great experiences that I have had in life." HP, Hayden
to Fred Roth, May 4, 1939.

54. HP, Hayden to Colonel William C. Harllee, July 17, 1935.

55. Ibid. The advances made in public health during the Murphy
years included the expansion of the Insular Psychopathic
Hospital, the reorganization of the Philippine General
Hospital, the establishment of travelling health units in
Mountain Province and Sulu, the opening of Welfareville
for the care and education of feeble-minded children, and
the building of regional leprosaria. The social welfare
program was also impressive. Community health-social
centers were established in Manila and in other cities.
Slum clearance was planned for Tondo, Manila, and 250,000
pesos were appropriated for the construction of low-cost
homes for laborers. A National Emergency Relief Board,
which embraced all recognized private relief agencies, was
created. Settlement of unoccupied public lands in Mindanao
was promoted. And finally, Committees on Nutrition and
Rural Improvement were appointed. See Hayden, The
Philippines, pp. 650-67.

56. Hayden, The Philippines, pp. 648-49. Hayden also noted
that Major George C. Dunham, as Advisor to the Governor-
General on Public Health and Sanitation, also played an
indispensable part in the public health program. See HP,
Hayden to the Commanding General, Philippine Department,
U.S. Army, Manila, Nov. 12, 1935.

57. Hayden, The Philippines, p. 667.

58. Hayden had been advised on April 29 by Brigadier General
Basilio Valdez, Commander in Chief of the Philippine
Constabulary, that the Sakdalista Party would not likely

cause any trouble during his absence from Manila. HP, Hayden, "Preliminary Report on the Sakdalista Disturbance," May 7, 1935, p. 4.

59. As related by Mrs. Hayden in an interview with the author. In a letter to Mrs. Hayden written a week after his return to Manila, Hayden concluded that "not during the war or at any other time have I ever had a week of such heavy responsibility, so crowded with difficult and, in some cases, momentous decisions." HP, May 11, 1935.

60. HP, "Report of the Committee Appointed by the Acting Governor-General J. R. Hayden to Investigate the Uprisings of May 2 and 3, 1935," p. 6.

61. Hayden, The Philippines, pp. 398-400.

62. HP, Hayden notes on speech to the Ann Arbor Rotary Club, Feb. 25, 1936.

63. The Tydings-McDuffie Act provided for no reciprocal tariffs on American products entering the Philippines. Nor did it institute quotas on American goods as it did on certain Philippine products entering the United States.

64. Hayden, "The United States and the Philippine Commonwealth," An Address by Dr. Hayden presented at the Institute of Public Affairs, the University of Virginia, Charlottesville, Virginia, July 12, 1937. (A copy is in HP.) See also Hayden's article entitled "The Philippines in Transition," Foreign Affairs, XIV-4 (1936), 639-53.

65. Hayden, "America, Europe, and Asia," Alumni University Lectures, The University of Michigan, June 19-24, 1939, pp. 13-14. (A copy is in HP.) Outside of the Philippines, Hayden rejected any further American responsibility in Asia. In 1933 he asked if a "Monroe Doctrine [was] ethical in the Occident and criminal in the Orient." (HP, Hayden, Policy paper on Far East, March 31, 1933.) And in 1936 he admitted that "our strongest defensive position" would be to "fall back upon the Aleutian-Hawaiian-Samoan triangle." (HP, Hayden to Major General William C. Rivers, July 7, 1936.) He also claimed that "our obligation is to respect,

not to <u>protect</u> China's rights." (HP, Hayden, "America in Eastern Asia," Address given at Knox College, 1938.)

66. When G-1, GHQ was organized in 1944, Hayden's Philippine Civil Affairs office became a part of the Civil Affairs section of that organization. When, on September 28, 1944, the G-5 was organized, Hayden was transferred there. And when on November 27, 1944, the USAFFE was set up, he moved to USAFFE.

67. These quotes are taken from HP, Hayden's notes on an interview with MacArthur, August 4, 1944.

68. See HP, <u>Philippine Civil Affairs: Policy and Organization, a Preliminary Report</u>, Philippine Research and Information Section, USAFFE, April 16, 1945. Hayden and Joseph Rauh had put together a "Memorandum for General Fellers Concerning Civil Administration and Relief in the Philippines" on July 22, 1944. Not until October 9, 1944, however, was a similar plan made standing operating procedure.

69. Dale Pontius, "MacArthur and the Filipinos," Part II, <u>Asia and the Americas</u>, XLVI-11 (1946), 511.

70. MacArthur, in March, 1945, advised Hayden (over his earlier misgivings) to accept this position. See HP, Hayden notes on interviews with MacArthur, Nov. 24, 1944, and March, 1945.

71. HP, Hayden to Osmeña, April 4, 1945.

72. Edward W. Mill, "Joseph Ralston Hayden: Scholar in Government," <u>Michigan Alumnus: Quarterly Review</u>, LIV-20 (1948), 209-17.

73. HP, Hayden to Reeves, June 14, 1934.

74. Hayden, <u>The Philippines</u>, p. 34.

SELECT BIBLIOGRAPHY

Compiled by

Norman G. Owen and Michael Cullinane

Each of the authors was asked to supply a list of references which met two criteria--they were felt to be generally useful, and they were actually used (though not necessarily cited) in the writing of these papers. Those listed more than once were considered "General" works; those mentioned by only one author are listed separately under his name, in section III-B. The composite bibliography makes no pretense to be complete or even "balanced"; it is merely a collection of references we would recommend to those wishing to pursue these specific topics further. Some worthy books have been omitted simply because they did not bear directly on the subject matter of these papers; this even includes a few which are cited in the notes. For more comprehensive bibliographies, see:

Chicago, University of. Philippine Studies Program. Select Bibliography of the Philippines: Topically Arranged and Annotated. New Haven, 1956.
Program Directors, Fred Eggan and E[vett] B. Hester.
Published by Human Relations Area Files.

Houston, Charles O., Jr. Philippine Bibliography: I. An Annotated Preliminary Bibliography of Philippine Bibliographies (Since 1900). Manila, 1960.

————. Philippine Studies: The Poor Relation in American Scholarship. Manila, 1957.
Critical review of Chicago, Select Bibliography (above).

Library of Congress. List of Works Relating to the American Occupation of the Philippine Islands: 1898-1903, by Appleton Prentiss Clark Griffin. Washington, 1905.

Onorato, Michael P. Philippine Bibliography (1899-1946). Santa
     Barbara, Calif., 1968.
     Annotated; best single source on the American period, despite
     some major omissions (e.g., Elliott).

Saito, Shiro. The Philippines: A Review of Bibliographies.
     East-West Center Library, Occasional Paper No. 5.
     [Honolulu], 1966.

I. DOCUMENTS

No published calendar or catalogue is available for any of
these collections, but a brief description of their contents is
given in:

Powers, Thomas. Balita mula Maynila (News from Manila).
     Michigan Historical Collections, Bulletin No. 19;
     Center for South and Southeast Asian Studies, Special
     Publication No. 1. Ann Arbor, 1971.

Hayden Papers.(HP) Michigan Historical Collections, The
     University of Michigan.
     The correspondence of Professor Joseph Ralston Hayden
     (see Edgerton, "Joseph Ralston Hayden . . ."), along with
     reports, notes, budgets, and an extensive collection of
     clippings on the Philippines from both American and Philip-
     pine publications. Immensely valuable for events from the
     early 1920's through World War II; education and the Moro
     provinces are especially well represented. For this
     volume, Ronald Edgerton used the complete correspondence
     and miscellaneous notes; Joseph Hutchinson used reports
     and clippings pertaining to politics in the 1930's.

Quezon Papers. (QP) The National Library of the Republic of
     the Philippines; microfilm available at the Michigan
     Historical Collections, The University of Michigan.
     The letters, cablegrams, speeches, etc., of President
     Manuel Luis Quezon (see Hutchinson, "Quezon's Role . . . ").
     Documents are in English and/or Spanish; they cover his
     entire political career, although strongest on the 1930's.

Unlike many such collections, these papers do not appear
to have been extensively "edited" by someone wishing to
save Quezon's reputation from the truth. For this volume
Joseph Hutchinson used the correspondence, speeches,
etc., especially for the period 1929-34.

Worcester Papers. Michigan Historical Collections, The
    University of Michigan.
Worcester Philippine Collection. (WPC) Department of Rare
    Books and Special Collections, Harlan Hatcher Library,
    The University of Michigan.
Dean Conant Worcester, already one of America's few
qualified Filipinists before 1898, was named to the Philippine Commission in 1899 and remained a member of the
Commission, also holding such other posts as Secretary
of the Interior and Superintendent of Public Instruction,
until 1913. His papers and "collection" include compara-
tively little of his personal correspondence, but an incredible
array of official correspondence, notes, reports, documents,
clippings, and photographs, as well as an excellent collection
of published material on the nineteenth and early twentieth
century. The WPC is perhaps the finest single repository
in America outside of the National Archives of material
pertaining to the Taft Era in the Philippines.

Worcester was both very knowledgeable and very much aware
of his knowledge, the epitome of confident imperialism. He
mistrusted "ambitious" Filipino politicians and frequently
cautioned against too much accommodation with them. It is
evident that this mistrust often became dislike, a situation
which was apparently mutual. Presumably with the intention
of demonstrating the validity of his opinion, Worcester
gathered a considerable amount of material relating to misconduct and anomalies committed by Filipinos from the
highest levels of government down to the municipalities. His
"Documents and Papers" contain many reports of the Chief
of the Law Division, transcripts of court and other investi-
gative proceedings against officials, etc. This represents,
of course, just one facet of a man who was also intensely
interested in public health, the activities of the Anti-
Imperialists, slavery and peonage, protection of the "Non-
Christian" tribes, and the development of opportunities for

American investment--as well as the natural sciences for
which he was originally trained!

For this publication, Michael Cullinane and Frank Jenista
have both used reports pertaining to many Filipino officials
from the 21 volumes of "Documents and Papers, 1834-1915,"
WPC. (This title, by the way, is quite misleading, as an
estimated 98% of the documents date from the period after
1899.) Two typewritten volumes, apparently compiled by
Worcester, on "Bills of the Philippine Assembly . . ." provide material on the workings of the Philippine Legislature.
Several of the authors have also used many of the published
works available in the WPC, some of which are so indicated
in the rest of the bibliography, below. The Worcester
Papers, Michigan Historical Collections, were generally
of less relevance to the particular topics undertaken here,
although the long letter from Worcester to the Wood-Forbes
mission in 1921 was quite valuable.

II. OFFICIAL AND QUASI-OFFICIAL PUBLICATIONS

Several of the more important government documents--
instructions to commissions, proclamations, reports of missions,
etc.--have also been published in extenso in appendixes of
various of the general works cited in Section III-A below,
e.g., Forbes, Worcester, Hayden, etc.

PHILIPPINES/PHILIPPINE ISLANDS

["Bureau of Agriculture Golden Jubilee Committee."] A Half-
     Century of Philippine Agriculture: Written by the Men
     of the Bureau of Agriculture and its Successors . . .
     Manila, 1952.

[Bureau of Census and Statistics.] Yearbook of Philippine
     Statistics: 1940 ("issued by the Bureau under the
     Commonwealth of the Philippines.") Manila, 1941.

[Bureau of Internal Revenue.] . . . Annual Report[s] of the
     Collector of Internal Revenue. Manila, 1906-08,
     1912-14, 1916-21. (RCIR)

     Second and Third RCIR, 1906-07, John S. Hord, Collector.
     Fourth RCIR, 1908, Ellis Cromwell, Acting Collector.

Eighth and Ninth RCIR, 1912-1913, William T. Nolting,
   Collector.
Eleventh to Fourteenth RCIR, 1914-17, James J. Rafferty,
   Collector.
Fifteenth to Seventeenth RCIR, 1918-20, W. Trinidad,
   Collector.

Basic sources for fiscal policy; each report contains a
summary of collections and a short discussion of returns
from various taxes of the Insular Government and the City
of Manila. The format of the report varies from year
to year; the later reports are much more detailed, even
to giving the number of various licenses granted by province.

Census Office. Census of the Philippine Islands: Taken Under
   the Direction of the Philippine Legislature in the Year
   1918. 4 vols. in 6. Manila, 1920-21.
Commission of the Census. Census of the Philippines: 1939.
   5 vols. in 8. Manila, 1940-43.
   See Owen, "Philippine Economic Development . . . ,"
   Appendix I, "On Using the Philippine Census." For 1903
   census, see U.S., Bureau of the Census.

Independence Congress. Proceedings of the First Independence
   Congress: Held in the City of Manila, Philippine Islands,
   February 22-26, 1930. [Manila, 1930?]

Legislature. Philippine Assembly. Official Directory, Philippine
   Assembly, First Legislature. Manila, 1908. (Available
   in WPC)
   In Spanish. Short biographical sketches make this a useful
   index to the elite composition of the Assembly.

Legislature. Philippine Commission. Journal of the Philippine
   Commission. Vols. 1-6. Manila, 1908-13. (JPC)
   (Available in WPC)
   Although not as detailed as the Reports of the Commission
   (see U.S., War Dept., B.I.A.), the Journal often reveals
   far more of the reasoning behind Commission action,
   particularly in confrontation with the Assembly; see
   especially the sections entitled "Explanations of Votes"
   and "Reports of the Standing Committees."

232

Legislature. Philippine Commission. The Municipal Code
[Act No. 82] and the Provincial Government Act
[Act No. 83]. Manila, 1905.
As revised in the Reorganization Act of 1905.

Philippine Economic Association. Economic Problems of the
Philippines. Manila, 1934.

Technical Committee to the President. American-Philippine
Trade Relations. Summary of the Report of the
Technical Committee to the President of the Philippines.
Washington, 1944.

PHILIPPINES AND THE UNITED STATES

Joint Preparatory Committee on Philippine Affairs. Report of
May 20, 1938. 3 vols. in 4. Department of State,
Publication No. 1216, Conference Series 36. Washington,
1938.
Good source for detailed data on the problems, particularly
economic, involved in the transition to independence.
Includes hearings as well as conclusions of the committee.

UNITED STATES OF AMERICA

Bureau of the Census. Census of the Philippine Islands: Taken
under the Direction of the Philippine Commission in the
Year 1903. 4 vols. Washington, 1905.
See Owen, "Philippine Economic Development . . . ,"
Appendix I, "On Using the Philippine Census." For 1918
and 1939 censuses see Philippines, Census Office, and
Philippines, Commission of the Census.

Conditions in the Philippines, by Carmi A. Thompson. Sen.
Doc. No. 180, 69th Congress, 2d Sess. Washington,
1926.
Edgerton, "Joseph Ralston Hayden . . . ," discusses
Hayden's role in framing this report.

Congress. House of Representatives. Committee on Ways and
Means, Hearings.

Philippine Trade Act of 1945. House Repts. 4185,
    4676, and 5185. 79th Cong., 1st sess., 1945.
Philippine Trade Act of 1946. House Rept. 5856,
    79th Cong., 2d sess., 1946.
Both on (Bell) Trade Act eventually passed in April, 1946.

Congress. Senate. Committee on the Philippines, Hearings.
    Affairs in the Philippine Islands. Sen. Doc. No. 331,
    57th Cong., 1st Sess., 1902.
Three massive volumes of testimony on the first few years
of intervention; Taft alone testifies for over 400 pages.
Selected excerpts from these hearings have been edited by
Henry F. Graff and published as American Imperialism
and the Philippine Insurrection (Boston, 1969).

Congress. Senate. Committee on Territories and Insular
    Affairs, Hearings. 71st Cong., 2d sess., 1930.

Congress. Senate. Special Report of Wm. H. Taft, Secretary of
    War, to the President on the Philippines. [January 27,
    1908] Sen. Doc. No. 200, 60th Cong., 1st sess., 1908.
An illuminating retrospect of the early Taft Era by the man
most responsible for it. Ostensibly proud of American
achievements, Taft nevertheless warns that the obligation
of the United States is far from being fulfilled.

Department of Agriculture. Office of Foreign Agricultural
    Relations. Agricultural Geography of the Philippine
    Islands: A Graphic Summary, by Reginald G. Hains-
    worth and Raymond T. Moyer. Washington, 1945.
Excellent short (and "graphic") summary of the agro-
economic sections of the Census of . . . 1939.

Special Mission to the Philippines. Report of the Special
    [Wood-Forbes] Mission on Investigation to the Philippine
    Islands to the Secretary of War. Washington, 1921.

Tariff Commission. United States-Philippine Tariff and Trade
    Relations. Report No. 18, Second Series. Washington,
    1931.

War Department. Bureau of Insular Affairs. Philippine
    Commission, 1899-1900. Report of the [Schurman]

<u>Philippine Commission to the President</u>. 4 vols.
Washington, 1900-01. (<u>Schurman Report</u>)
War Department. Bureau of Insular Affairs. Philippine
Commission, 1900-16. <u>Report[s] of the Philippine
Commission to the Secretary of War</u> . . . Title varies.
Waohington, 1900-17. (<u>RPC</u>)
These are the indispensable sources for the Taft Era.
They contain records of major legislation, texts of
proclamations, transcripts of hearings, selected economic
statistics, Reports of the Executive Secretary and of
other departments, etc., as well as a wealth of information
(on Constabulary, Public Health, Education, etc.) totally
untapped in these papers. For the <u>Journal</u> of the Commission,
see Philippines, Legislature.

INTERNATIONAL INSTITUTE OF AGRICULTURE (Rome)

<u>International Yearbook of Agricultural Statistics</u>.
Provides prices, yields, acreage, etc. worldwide. The
1940 edition provides data from 1929 to 1938-39 for some
countries, but only to mid-1930's for the Philippines.

III. OTHER REFERENCES

A. GENERAL WORKS

Abueva, José, and Raul de Guzman, eds. <u>Foundations and
Dynamics of Philippine Government and Politics</u>.
Manila, 1969.
A standard textbook; articles of varying quality, but some
excellent ones (often reprinted from other publications) by
both editors, Corpuz, Hollnsteiner, Romani, Wurfel, Landé,
Frances Starner, Raul Manglapus, <u>et al</u>.

Agoncillo, Teodoro A. <u>Malolos: The Crisis of the Republic</u>.
Quezon City, 1960.
An impressively detailed study of the first Philippine
Republic. It is possible to question some of Agoncillo's
conclusions, but not the quality of his research.

—————, and Oscar M. Alfonso. History of the Filipino
  People. Revised edition. Quezon City, 1967.

Barrows, David P. A Decade of American Government in the
  Philippines: 1903-1913. Yonkers-on-Hudson, N.Y., 1914.
  Barrows was the Director of Education during much of this
  period; this short volume is sympathetic to American
  reformist efforts, but is not always in agreement with other
  colonial officials on many issues, especially with Forbes
  and his de-emphasis of politics.

Blount, James H[enderson]. The American Occupation of the
  Philippines: 1898-1912. New York, 1912.
  A hostile but well-documented account of early American
  conquest and rule by a former Judge in the Islands. Can
  be used as a corrective to Barrows, Forbes, Worcester,
  et al. Quezon helped finance Blount's anti-imperialist
  activities.

Corpuz, Onofre D. The Bureaucracy in the Philippines.
  Manila, 1957.
  Covers the Spanish tradition and post-Independence developments as well as the period of American rule; stresses
  continuity of bureaucratic behavior and values.

—————. The Philippines. Englewood Cliffs, N.J., 1966.

Eliott, Charles Burke. The Philippines to the End of the
  Military Régime. Indianapolis, 1916.
  —————. The Philippines to the End of the Commission
  Government: A Study in Tropical Democracy.
  Indianapolis, 1917.
  Of early American writers on the Philippines, ex-Commis-
  sioner Elliott displays the best grasp of the details of
  Spanish administration and of the significance of economics
  in colonialism.

Forbes, W[illiam] Cameron. The Philippine Islands. 2 vols.
  Boston and New York, 1928.
  Ex-Governor General Forbes (1909-13) presents the standard
  Commission view in great detail; long quotations from official
  documents in the text and appendixes make it a useful
  reference.

Friend, Theodore W. Between Two Empires: The Ordeal of
the Philippines, 1929-1946. New Haven, 1965.
The best account of the politics and diplomacy of the 1930's;
not always sympathetic to Quezon. Suggests prolonged U.S.
control kept Filipinos from having to run responsive,
responoible government.

——————. "American Interests and Philippine Independence,
1929-1933." PS, XI-4 (1963), 505-23.
——————. "Manuel Quezon: Charismatic Conservative."
Philippine Historical Review, I-1 (1965), 153-69.
——————. "Philippine Independence and the Mission for
Independence, 1929-1932." PS, XII-1 (1964), 63-82.
——————. "Philippine Independence and the Last Lame-Duck
Congress." PS, XII-2 (1964), 260-76.
——————. "The Philippine Sugar Industry and Politics of
Independence, 1929-1935." JAS, XXII-2 (1963), 179-92.
——————. "Veto and Repassage of the Hare-Hawes-Cutting Act:
A Catalogue of Motives." PS, XII-4 (1964), 666-80.
These short articles complement Between Two Empires,
especially on the interaction of economic and factional
interests surrounding the transition to the Commonwealth.

Golay, Frank H. The Philippines: Public Policy and National
Economic Development. Ithaca, N.Y., 1961.
Although the emphasis is on postwar developments, this
remains the best analytical study of the Philippine economy
in the first half of the twentieth century. Excellent for
both fiscal and tariff/trade policy.

——————, ed. The United States and the Philippines. The
American Assembly. Englewood Cliffs, N.J., 1966.
[Published in the Philippines, with short additional
articles, as Philippine-American Relations (Manila, 1966).]
Essays by distinguished scholars and diplomats on various
aspects of the relations between the two countries, most
focussing on the postwar period. Of particular relevance
to this volume is Salvador P. Lopez, "The Colonial
Relationship."

Grossholtz, Jean. Politics in the Philippines. Boston, 1964.

Grunder, Garel A., and William E. Livezey. The Philippines
and the United States. Norman, Okla., 1951.
Competent, but somewhat outdated; useful summary of
economic policy, etc.

Guthrie, George M., ed. Six Perspectives on the Philippines.
Manila, 1968.
Originally a set of lectures for Peace Corps trainees, these
essays are rapidly becoming "classics" in Philippine studies.
Of particular usefulness for this volume were Carl H. Landé,
"Party Politics in the Philippines"; Fred Eggan, "Philippine
Social Structure"; and Guthrie, "The Philippine Tempera-
ment."

Harrison, Francis B[urton]. The Cornerstone of Philippine
Independence: A Narrative of Seven Years. New York,
1922.
Essentially an explanation and attempted justification of
Harrison's term as Governor-General (1913-21); his
optimistic appraisal of Filipino potential for self-rule
stands in contrast to his Taft Era predecessors.

Hayden, Joseph Ralston. The Philippines: A Study in National
Development. New York, 1942.
Well-researched, well-written, unbiased, the best over-all
guide to four decades of American administration; Hayden
had a greater capacity for detailed but detached appraisal
than most colonial officials. The book is excellent on
administration, with surprisingly little on the Moro situation
(on which Hayden planned a book he never finished) and on
economics.

Hollnsteiner, Mary R. The Dynamics of Power in a Philippine
Municipality. Quezon City, 1963.
A contemporary examination of local society and government
which attempts to include earlier periods; a necessary
corrective to the formal models provided by official sources.

Houston, Charles O., Jr. "The Philippine Commonwealth,
1934-1946." UMJEAS, II-4 (1953), 29-38.

Jacoby, Erich H. Agrarian Unrest in Southeast Asia. New
York, 1949. Revised edition, New York, 1961.
More a description of the agrarian situation--tenantry,
etc. --than of actual unrest, which Jacoby assumes rises
naturally from the injustice he documents.

Jenkins, Shirley. American Economic Policy Toward the
Philippines. Stanford, Calif., 1954.
Focus on the immediate postwar period, but early chapters
provide in capsule form the essential economic events
under American rule.

Kalaw, Maximo M[anguiat]. The Development of Philippine
Politics (1872-1920): An Account of the Part Played by
Filipino Parties in the Political Development of the
Philippines. Manila, 1927.
Very detailed: more descriptive than analytical.

Kirk, Grayson L. Philippine Independence: Motives, Problems,
and Prospects. New York, 1936.
Sharp analysis of the independence issue of the 1930's with
particular emphasis on economic factors. The motives
were mixed, the problems great, the prospects none too
bright.

Landé, Carl H. Leaders, Factions, and Parties: The Structure
of Philippine Politics. [New Haven], 1965.
A modern classic on how Philippine politics really operate--
patron-client relationships, unstable factions, the pre-
eminence of personal ties over political issues, etc.

LeRoy, James A. The Americans in the Philippines. 2 vols.
Boston and New York, 1914.
The former secretary to Taft is more objective than most.
In this book he focuses on the Philippine-American War
years; diligent research combined with good on-the-scene
reportage.

Liang, Dapen. The Development of Philippine Political Parties.
Hong Kong, 1939. Revised edition published as
Philippine Parties and Politics, San Francisco, 1970.
Detailed guidebook through the intricacies of Filipino
political groupings (some hardly qualify as parties) from the
nineteenth century on; a handy reference.

Lynch, Frank, S.J., ed. Four Readings on Philippine Values.
Second revised edition. Quezon City, 1964.
Along with other writings by Father Lynch and his colleagues
at the Institute of Philippine Culture, fundamental in
explaining the Filipinos to themselves, to Americans, and
to the world. "Social acceptance," utang na loob, hiya,
among the more important concepts discussed.

Miller, Hugo H. Economic Conditions in the Philippines.
Boston, 1920.
A standard textbook in its time, it remains one of the more
useful studies of the economy in the first two decades of
American rule. Miller is non-polemical, aware of land/
tenant problems, and includes statistics not easily found
elsewhere.

Mintz, Sidney W., and Eric R. Wolf. "An Analysis of Ritual
Co-Parenthood (Compadrazgo)." Southwestern Journal
of Anthropology, VI-4 (1950), 341-69.
Pioneering study of a concept now widely incorporated in
many approaches to the Philippines.

Onorato, Michael [Paul]. A Brief Review of American Interest
in Philippine Development and Other Essays. Berkeley,
1968.
————. "Leonard Wood as Governor General: A Calendar
of Selected Correspondence." PS, XII (1964), 124-48,
296-314, 699-719; XIII-4 (1965), 822-49.
Onorato clearly stakes out his claim as the leading authority
on the administration of Governor Wood (1921-27). The
"Calendar" includes excerpts from letters by Barrows,
Harrison, Hayden, McCoy, Parker, Stimson, and Taft,
among others; it does not include anything from the Wood
Papers. The title article in A Brief Review is a good
short survey of the historiography of the whole American
period.

————. "The Philippines between 1929 and 1946." PS,
XIII-4 (1965), 859-65.
A provocative review article of Friend, Between Two
Empires; Onorato is more inclined to blame Filipino
leaders, rather than American administrators, for the
problems faced in the 1930's.

Pomeroy, William J. American Neo-Colonialism: Its Emergence in the Philippines and Asia. New York, 1970.
Sharply critical attack on American intervention by an ex-Huk; well-buttressed with testimony from Senate hearings, official reports, and early anti-imperialists.

Salamanca, Bonifacio S. The Filipino Reaction to American Rule: 1901-1913. [Hamden, Conn.], 1968.
Probably the most scholarly presentation of the revisionist approach to the Taft Era which sees collaboration between ilustrados and the Philippine Commission as the principal theme, with both American reformism and Filipino national-ist resistance reduced to subsidiary roles.

Steinberg, David Joel. Philippine Collaboration in World War II. Ann Arbor, 1967.
————, et al. In Search of Southeast Asia: A Modern History. New York, 1971.
Chapters 1 and 25, respectively, provide a brief but cogent articulation of the development of Filipino values (both social and national) in the context of American intervention.

Sturtevant, David R. "Guardia de Honor: Revitalization within the Revolution." Asian Studies (Quezon City), IV-2 (1966), 342-52. (Also published, along with an article on the Rizalistas, as Agrarian Unrest in the Philippines, [Athens, Ohio], 1969.)
————. "Philippine Social Structure and its Relation to Agrarian Unrest." Unpublished Ph.D. dissertation (History). Stanford, 1958.
————. "Sakdalism and Philippine Radicalism." JAS, XXI-2 (1962), 199-213.
Sturtevant is moving toward a radical reinterpretation of agrarian unrest in the Philippines; later articles challenge Jacoby's simple correlation of peasant revolts with economic conditions. A book on religious revolts, 1840-1940, is forthcoming and eagerly awaited.

Worcester, Dean C[onant]. The Philippines, Past and Present. 2 vols. New York, 1914.
————. The Philippines, Past and Present. New Edition in One Volume with Biographical Sketch and Four addition-al Chapters by [Joseph] Ralston Hayden. New York, 1930.

Of all the American officials of the Taft Era, Worcester
probably was the most outspoken in his mistrust of Filipino
politicians and the Harrison administration. But the book
is valuable, particularly in the revised edition where it is
tempered by Hayden's good biography of Worcester and
reasoned analysis of the period 1915-30; not all of the woes
hinted at by Worcester did come to pass.

Wurfel, David. "The Philippines." Government and Politics
of Southeast Asia. Edited by George McTurnan Kahin.
2d edition. Ithaca, N.Y., 1964.

B. WORKS LISTED BY INDIVIDUAL AUTHORS

CULLINANE:

Alfonso, Oscar M. "Expediency in Taft's Philippine Adminis-
tration." Philippine Journal of Public Administration,
XII-3 (1968), 246-55.
————. "Taft's Early Views on the Filipinos." Solidarity,
IV-6 (1969), 52-58.
————. "Taft's Views on 'The Philippines for Filipinos.'"
Asian Studies (Quezon City), VI-3 (1968), 237-47.
Three revealing articles on the private thoughts of Taft
as President of the Philippine Commission and Civil
Governor, 1900-03.

Corpuz, Onofre D. "The Cultural Foundations of Filipino
Politics." Philippine Journal of Public Administration,
IV-4 (1960), 297-310.
————. "Filipino Political Parties and Politics." PSSHR,
XXIII-2/4 (1958), 141-57.
Insights into Philippine politics by an astute observer of
political/bureaucratic behavior.

Cruz, Romeo. "The Filipino Collaboration with the Americans,
1899-1902." Comment (Manila), No. 10 (1960), 10-29.

Forbes, W. Cameron. "A Decade of American Rule in the
Philippines." Atlantic Monthly, CIII-2 (1909), 200-09.
Views expressed in the year Forbes became Governor-
General.

Jones, O. Garfield. "Teaching Citizenship to Filipinos by
  Local Self-Government." American Political Science
  Review, XVIII-2 (1924), 285-95.
  Former colonial official explains some of the problems and
  programs involved in the organization of local government;
  concludes with the usual colonial optimism based primarily
  on the passage of time.

José, F. Sionil. "America and the Filipino Revolution."
  Solidarity, IV-6 (1969), 1-2, 78.
  ————. "The American Response to the Philippine Revolution."
  Solidarity, VI-2 (1971), 2-8.
  ————. "The Betrayal of the Masses." Solidarity, I-4 (1966),
  1-10.
  ————. "The Ilustrado-American Collaboration." Solidarity,
  II-5 (1967), 1-2, 95-96.
  Provocative editorials which search for the roots of contem-
  porary Philippine problems in the colonial period, specifi-
  cally in the tacit bond between the Americans and the Filipino
  elite.

Lansang, Jose. "The Philippine-American Experiment: A
  Filipino View." PA, XXV-3 (1952), 226-34.

Laurel, Jose P. Local Government in the Philippine Islands.
  Manila, 1926.
  Structural development, rather than internal dynamics.

Romani, John H., and M. Ladd Thomas. A Survey of Local
  Governments in the Philippines. Manila, 1954.
  Focus on the postwar period, but with much information
  pertinent to the colonial era as well.

Spector, Robert. "W. Cameron Forbes in the Philippines:
  A Study in Proconsular Power." JSEAH, VII-2 (1966),
  74-92.
  Valuable study of one of the key officials of the Taft Era.

Taft, William H. "Political Parties in the Philippines."
  Annals of the American Academy of Political and
  Social Sciences, XX-2 (1906), 307-12.
  Taft's early public reaction to the development of Filipino
  political activity.

Yabes, Leopoldo. "The American Administration in the
Philippines." Solidarity, II-5 (1967), 16-26.
Sees education as the main American contribution to the
Philippines, and contends that American rule deterred the
development of true Philippine nationalism.

Zimmerman, Robert. "Philippine Clues to the Future of Local
Government in Southeast Asia." Journal of African
Administration, XII-1 (1960), 34-43.
Describes some of the forces responsible for centralization
of the government.

JENISTA:

LeRoy, James A. "The Philippine Assembly." The World
Today, XV-2 (1908), 847-52. (Clipping available in
WPC)
Robertson, James A. "The Extraordinary Session of the
Philippine Legislature, and the Work of the Philippine
Assembly." American Political Science Review, IV-4
(1910), 516-36.
————. "The Philippines Since the Inauguration of the
Philippine Assembly." American Historical Review,
XXII-4 (1917), 811-30.
Three good examples of contemporary political reportage,
describing both the composition and the workings of the
Assembly in its first decade.

Tuohy, Anthony. Album Histórico de la Primera Asamblea
Filipina. Manila, 1908. (Available in WPC)
Like the Official Directory, provides short biographical
sketches of the Assembly representatives which reveal
their elite backgrounds.

OWEN:

Abelarde, Pedro E. American Tariff Policy towards the
Philippines: 1898-1946. Morningside Heights, N.Y.,
1947.
Competent summary of legislation and some of the motives
behind it; useful reference source.

Allen, James S. "Agrarian Tendencies in the Philippines."
    PA, XI-1 (1938), 52-65.

Apostol, José P. "The American-Philippine Tariff." PSSR,
    III (1930-31), 42-47, 190-97, 254-63; IV-2 (1932), 142-51.
    Emphasizes Filipino opposition to mutual free trade.

Castro, Amado. "Philippine-American Tariff and Trade
    Relations, 1898-1954." Philippine Economic Journal,
    IV-1 (1965), 29-56.
    Straight chronicle of legislation, less detailed than Abelarde.

Corpuz, Onofre D. "Notes on Philippine Economic History."
    Economics and Development. Edited by G. P. Sicat.
    Quezon City, 1965.
    Useful for nineteenth century background.

Dawson, Owen L. "Philippine Agriculture, A Problem of
    Adjustment . . ." Foreign Agriculture, IV-7 (1940),
    383-456.

Farley, Miriam S. "Philippine Independence and Agricultural
    Readjustment." FES, V-8 (1936), 71-77.

————. "Sugar--A Commodity in Chaos." FES, IV-22
    (1935), 172-78.

Golay, Frank H. "Economic Consequences of the Philippine
    Trade Act." PA, XXVIII-1 (1955), 53-70.
    A model analysis of tariff/trade relations, looks at the
    economic impact of the Bell Trade Act of 1946 as well as
    the motives behind it.

Hartendorp, A. V. H. History of Industry and Trade in the
    Philippines. Vol. I. Manila, 1958.
    More comprehensive than analytical.

Hooley, Richard, and Vernon W. Ruttan. "The Philippines."
    Agricultural Development in Asia. Edited by R. T. Shand.
    Berkeley and Los Angeles, 1969.
    Attempts more mathematical analysis than most such
    surveys; questionable reliance on certain census statistics.

Houston, Charles O., Jr. "Other Philippine Crops and Industries: 1934-1950." UMJEAS, IV-1 (1955), 15-39.
————. "The Philippine Abaca Industry: 1934-1950." UMJEAS, III-4 (1954), 408-15; III-3 (1954), 267-86.
————. "The Philippine Coconut Industry: 1934-1950." UMJEAS, III-2 (1954), 153-81.
————. "The Philippine Sugar Industry: 1934-1950." UMJEAS, III-4 (1954), 370-407.
————. "Rice in the Philippine Economy: 1934-1950." UMJEAS, III-1 (1954), 13-82.
Well-researched, very detailed account of the agrarian economy 1934-50; too many facts for easy reading.

Huke, Robert E. Shadows on the Land: An Economic Geography of the Philippines. Manila, 1963.
Basic geography text, industry-by-industry approach, covers colonial developments as background to current situation.

Kurihara, Kenneth K. Labor in the Philippine Economy, Stanford, 1945.

Lachica, Eduardo. "Sugar and Trusts." Solidarity, VI-5 (1971), 32-41.
Close analysis of motives for U.S. sugar policy in Taft Era.

Larkin, John Alan. "The Evolution of Pampangan Society: A Case Study in Social and Economic Change in the Rural Philippines." Unpublished Ph.D. dissertation (History), NYU, 1966.
Important pioneering work in local socio-economic history; shows how local leaders learn to adapt to changing circumstances or cease to lead. Covers Spanish period, essentially. Larkin is currently doing further research on sugar and rice in Pampanga and Negros, covering the late 19th and early 20th century.

Lasker, Bruno F. Filipino Immigration to the Continental United States and Hawaii. Chicago, 1931.
Chapters by Frederic V. and Elizabeth Brown Field on "Philippine Inter-Island Migration" and "Social and Economic Background of Filipino Emigrants" are particularly useful.

Legarda, Benito F[ernandez], Jr. "Foreign Trade, Economic
Change, and Entrepreneurship in the Nineteenth-
Century Philippines." Unpublished Ph.D. dissertation
(Economics), Harvard, 1955.
Still the best study on the commercialization of the economy
in the late Spanish period, describes developments often
ignored by historians of the twentieth century.

—————. "The Philippine Economy Under Spanish Rule."
Solidarity, II-10 (1967), 1-21.
Excellent short summary of the pre-1898 background.

Low, Stephen. "The Effect of Colonial Rule on Population
Distribution in the Philippines: 1898-1941."
Unpublished Ph.D. dissertation, Fletcher School
of Law and Diplomacy, 1956.
Argues that U.S. did very little to correct existing
population imbalance, particularly between highlands
and lowlands; government services attracted more
migrants to already densely-populated areas.

McHale, Thomas Riley. "An Econoecological Approach to
Economic Development in the Philippines."
Unpublished Ph.D. dissertation (Political Economy
and Government), Harvard, 1959.
Mostly theoretical/methodological; emphasis twentieth
century, especially postwar. Rejects standard macro-
economic theory in favor of more socio-political approach.

—————. "The Philippines in Transition." JAS, XX-3 (1961),
331-41.

—————. "Sugar in the Seventies." Solidarity, VI-5 (1971),
6-17.
Five pages of history of Philippine sugar industry; McHale
is currently working on a book on that subject.

Odell, Lawrence H. "New Government Banks Created in the
Philippines." FES, VIII-18 (1939), 214-15.

Pelzer, Karl J. Pioneer Settlement in the Asiatic Tropics:
Studies in Land Utilization and Agricultural Colonization
in Southeastern Asia. New York, 1948.
Two chapters on the Philippines are the best single source
on all aspects of the pre-war land situation--tenantry, titles,
reform, resettlement, etc.

Porter, Catherine. "Philippine Industries Today and Tomorrow."
FES, VII-13 (1938), 143-49.

————. "Philippine Rice Control Showing Results." FES,
VII-5 (1938), 53-55.

————. "Steps Towards Economic Planning in the Philippines."
FES, VII-7 (1938), 73-79.

Resnick, Stephen A. "The Decline of Rural Industry Under
Export Expansion: A Comparison among Burma,
Philippines, and Thailand, 1870-1938." Journal of
Economic History, XXX-1 (1970), 51-73.
Tantalizing glimpse of the type of analysis possible but
largely untried; Resnick's forthcoming "Economic
Development of the Philippines" should be valuable.

Reyes, José S. Legislative History of America's Economic
Policy Toward the Philippines. New York, 1923.
Just what the title implies; workmanlike, useful, covers
fiscal-monetary, merchant shipping policies as well as
tariffs.

Rice, Lloyd P. "Philippine Copra and Coconut Oil in the
American Market." FES, IV-20 (1935), 151-61.

Roland, JoAnn. "Philippine-American Abaca Trade: 1818-1913."
Unpublished M.A. thesis, Ateneo de Manila, 1969.

Schul, Norman W. "Hacienda Magnitude and Philippine Sugar
Cane Production." Asian Studies (Quezon City), V-2
(1967), 258-73.
————. "A Philippine Sugar Cane Plantation: Land Tenure
and Sugar Cane Production." Economic Geography,
XLV-2 (1967), 157-69.
Study of Negros in the 1960's, but analysis relevant to earlier period.

248

Starner, Frances Lucille. "The Agrarian Impact on Philippine
Politics." Unpublished Ph.D. dissertation (Political
Science), Stanford, 1958.
Emphasis on postwar period, but some data on 1930's.

Stine, Leo C. "The Economic Policies of the Commonwealth
Government of the Philippine Islands." UMJEAS,
X-1 (1966), 1-136.

Takahashi, Akira. Land and Peasants in Central Luzon: Socio-
Economic Structure of a Bulacan Village. Tokyo, 1969.
Excellent local study, 1960's, but with implications for the
agrarian situation throughout the century.

Taussig, F[rank] W[illiam]. The Tariff History of the United
States. Eighth revised edition, c. 1931. New York, 1964.

VanderMeer, Canute. "Corn on the Island of Cebu." Unpublished
Ph.D. dissertation (Geography), Michigan, 1962.
————. "Population Patterns on the Island of Cebu, The
Philippines: 1500-1900." Annals of the Association of
American Geographers, LVII-2 (1967), 315-38.
Easily the best historian among Philippine geographers,
VanderMeer shows here what can be done in exploring the
interaction of human and "physical" factors over time,
discussing changes in population distribution, food consump-
tion, the whole ecology of Cebu.

————, and Bernard C. Agaloos. "Twentieth Century
Settlement of Mindanao." Papers of the Michigan
Academy of Science, Arts, and Letters, XLVII (1962),
537-48.

Wernstedt, Frederick L. "Agricultural Regionalism on Negros
Island, Philippines." Unpublished Ph.D. dissertation
(Geography), UCLA, 1953.
Rice, sugar, corn, and coconuts; history of Spanish period
weak.

————. The Role and Importance of Philippine Interisland
Shipping and Trade. Ithaca, N.Y., 1957.

————, and Paul D. Simkins. "Migrations and the Settlement of Mindanao." JAS, XXV (1965), 83-103.
  Excellent analysis, uses Census data well, puts government-
  sponsored resettlement in proper (i.e., minor) perspective.

————, and Joseph E. Spencer. The Philippine Island
  World: A Physical, Cultural, and Regional Geography.
  Berkeley and Los Angeles, 1967.
  Comprehensive, good region-by-region presentation;
  covers American period developments as background
  to current situation.

LUTON:

Baran, Paul A. The Political Economy of Growth. New York,
  1957.
  Probably the best Marxist critique of economic development
  theorists. The two chapters titled "Towards a Morphology
  of Backwardness" offer particularly stimulating suggestions
  for the study of colonial and post-colonial economics.

Hord, John S. "Internal Taxation in the Philippines." Johns
  Hopkins University Studies in Historical and Political
  Science, XXV-1 (1907), 7-45.
  Hord was centrally involved in drafting the Internal Revenue
  Law of 1904. While his summation of the Spanish internal
  revenue system is somewhat stereotyped, he offers a
  concise summary of the provisions of the Internal Revenue
  Law of 1904 and a tantalizing view of the method by which
  the law was drafted.

Ireland, Alleyne. The Far Eastern Tropics: Studies in the
  Administration of Tropical Dependencies. New York
  and Boston, 1905.
  A "comparative" approach to the study of the Philippines,
  discussing various British and French colonies with a
  view to determining the most efficient way to colonize
  the Philippines. This book offers insights into the weakness
  of American policy, as well as into the mind of an early
  twentieth century imperialist.

250

Kolko, Gabriel. The Triumph of Conservatism: A
Reinterpretation of American History, 1900-1916.
Chicago, 1967.

Leuchtenburg, William E. "Progressivism and Imperialism:
The Progressive Movement and American Foreign
Policy, 1898-1916." Mississippi Valley Historical
Review, XXXIX-3 (1952), 483-504.

Malcolm, George Arthur. The Government of the Philippine
Islands: Its Development and Fundamentals. Rochester,
N.Y., 1916.

Murphey, Rhoads. "Traditionalism and Colonialism: Changing
Urban Roles in Asia." JAS, XXIX-1 (1969), 67-84.
Basic to an introduction to the political geography of Southeast Asia. Murphey discusses the role of the city as a
dual one: it serves as the beachhead of foreign penetration
and as the focal point for the development of a new
nationalism.

Pitt, Harold M. The Facts as to the Philippines: Compiled for
the Enlightenment of the American People. Manila,
[1914]. (Available in WPC)
Speech by the President of the Manila Merchants Association,
a fine example of colonialist rhetoric.

Wolf, Eric R. Peasants. Englewood Cliffs, N.J., 1966.
The basic primer on anthropological approaches to the
study of peasantry, written in a deceptively simple style.
Covers both economic and social aspects of peasant life
and contains a thorough but select bibliography.

HUTCHINSON:

Caballero, Isabelo, and M. de Garcia Concepcion. Quezon:
The Story of a Nation and Its Foremost Statesman.
Manila, 1935.
A standard biography, somewhat critical but neither totally
reliable nor truly analytical; to be used with caution.

Campbell, Angus, et al. The American Voter. New York, 1964.

Callego, Manuel. The Price of Philippine Independence. Manila, 1939.

Hawes, Harry B. Philippine Uncertainty. New York, 1932. Undistinguished book by the second "H" of the "H-H-C" Bill.

Historical Bulletin (Manila), VI-3 (1962). Special Quezon Issue. Articles by Gabriel Fabella, Felix Gabriel, José-Burgos Padlan, and Carlos Quirino are most useful.

Kalaw, Maximo M[anguiat]. Introduction to Philippine Social Sciences. Manila, 1933.

Osias, Camilo. The Filipino Way of Life. Boston, 1940. A good articulation of Philippine values from a politician's perspective rather than a sociologist's.

Pacis, Vincente. Philippine Government and Politics. Quezon City, 1962.

Quezon, Manuel L[uis]. The Good Fight. New York, 1946. This autobiography is more useful than most, not so much for factual detail as for how Quezon chose to present himself. Basic to any study of Quezon, but must be used in conjunction with more critical sources.

——————. "Our Peaceful Struggle for Independence." PSSR, V-1 (1933), 71-86.

——————. Quezon in His Speeches. Edited by Pedro de la Llana, et al. Manila, [1937].

Quirino, Carlos. Quezon: Man of Destiny. Manila, 1935. Like Caballero and Concepcion, a standard biography, neither completely adulatory nor adequately analytical.

Rōyama Masamichi and Takeuchi Tatsuji. The Philippine Polity: A Japanese View. Edited by Theodore Friend. [New Haven, 1967.] Originally written in 1943 for the benefit of the Japanese administration, this not only provides a different perspective on the Philippines, but is a first-rate political analysis in its own right.

Zaide, Gregorio F., and Sonia M. Zaide. Government and
Politics of the Republic of the Philippines. Quezon
City, 1969.

EDGERTON:

[See Appendix to Edgerton, "Joseph Ralston Hayden . . ."
for a listing of Hayden's works.]

Mill, Edward W. "Joseph Ralston Hayden: Scholar in
Government." Michigan Alumnus: Quarterly
Review, LIV-20 (1948), 209-17.

Pontius, Dale. "MacArthur and the Filipinos: II." Asia and
the Americas, XLVI-11 (1946), 509-12.

"Scholar-Administrator Dies." Michigan Alumnus, LI-22
(1945), 413.

Wingo, James G. "Dr. Joseph Ralston Hayden: A Tribute."
The Philippine Hour, Manila, May 23, 1945. Printed
radio address.

Printed and bound by CPI Group (UK) Ltd, Croydon, CR0 4YY

13/04/2025